COUNSELING
FOR EMPOWERMENT

Ellen Hawley McWhirter, Ph.D.

AMERICAN
COUNSELING
ASSOCIATION

Counseling for Empowerment

10 9 8 7 6 5 4 3 2 1

American Counseling Association
5999 Stevenson Avenue
Alexandria, VA 22304

Director of Communications
Jennifer L. Sacks

Acquisitions and Development Editor
Carolyn Baker

Production/Design Manager
Michael Comlish

Copyeditor
Jean Bernard

Cover design by Martha Woolsey

Library of Congress Cataloging-in-Publication Data

McWhirter, Ellen Hawley.
    Counseling for empowerment / Ellen Hawley McWhirter.
        p. cm.
    Includes bibliographical references and index.
    ISBN 1-55620-135-4
    1. Counseling. 2. Minorities—Counseling of. 3. Handicapped—Counseling of. 4. Socially handicapped—Counseling of. 5. Marginality, Social—Psychological aspects.
I. Title.
BF637.C6M3878   1994
361.3'23—dc20   94-3945
                                                                      CIP

To those who hunger for justice
thirst for change
dare to hope
hope to transform
And especially to those
who dare not hope:

May we together find a way

TABLE OF CONTENTS

PART II: EMPOWERING SKILLS AND INTERVENTIONS

PART III: APPLICATIONS OF
COUNSELING FOR EMPOWERMENT

FOREWORD

Counseling for Empowerment provides the reader with a broad understanding of the concept of empowerment and offers practical suggestions for counselors, psychologists, and other mental health professionals who wish to facilitate the empowerment of their clients. Ellen Hawley McWhirter explores the nature of empowerment from feminist, multicultural, community psychology, social work, educational, and nursing perspectives. Building on this conceptual foundation, McWhirter eloquently addresses the significant and provocative notion that counseling can be a source of client empowerment or a mechanism of oppression. Counselors must understand not only the inherent paradox and process of empowerment, but also the personal change and commitment required if counseling is to be effective and empowering. She emphasizes that professionals must evaluate their own beliefs, values, attitudes, and behaviors as they relate to the counseling process, as well as become aware of power dynamics influencing the lives of clients.

The intrapersonal and interpersonal skills outlined in Part II of this book enable the reader to move from the conceptual to the concrete. All too often texts are written without relating theory to practice, but McWhirter beautifully bridges this gap by including specific suggestions for counselors and their clients and by incorporating detailed case examples throughout the text. She provides myriad interventions that will improve not only the counselor's skill level, but also the counselor's ability to use these skills in the service of client empowerment.

Chapters Five through Twelve of *Counseling for Empowerment* form the core of this text. These eight chapters introduce the reader to diverse groups within our society who, because of ethnic minority status, sexual orientation, disease, disability, life circumstances, age, or perceived appearance, present critical issues for which counseling for empowerment is highly relevant. The format consistency of these chapters adds to the reader's comprehension of the complex barriers and power dynamics experienced by members of these groups and allows for comparison and integration of concepts relevant within and among these groups. Pay particular attention to how McWhirter applies the counselor skills described in Part II to working specifically with persons from the diverse groups described in these chapters.

The inclusion of the "non-beautiful" in Chapter Twelve is an added bonus. Physical appearance is an area of great concern to many clients. Too often this subject is dealt with in the popular literature and ignored in the professional literature; its placement in this text is both appropriate and very much needed.

Counseling for Empowerment provides readers with information on the "cutting edge" of counseling. It is straightforward, comprehensive, and concise. Mental health professionals will find this book an excellent resource for enhancing skills and restructuring the implementation of these skills to facilitate client empowerment. All readers will gain insight into their own values and approaches to working with clients. *Counseling for Empowerment* will leave readers with a feeling of personal and professional challenge, with skills and insights to serve their clients more effectively and appropriately, and with renewed hope for the future.

—Douglas R. Gross
David Capuzzi

PREFACE

Is counseling an act of oppression? It can be. Does counseling help people accommodate to relationships and life circumstances that are unhealthy and disabling? Yes, sometimes it does. Are we—counselors, social workers, psychologists, nurses, ministers, and other helping professionals—a part of the problems confronted by those who seek our help? Perhaps. But we don't have to be.

Counseling for empowerment is a complex and multifaceted process that requires, for some, a radical departure from the traditional conceptualization of the helper's role. Empowerment goes far beyond helping people "adjust to" or "feel better about" their lives. The process of empowerment demands that professional helpers and their clients take an active, collaborative approach to identifying problems and goals. Counseling for empowerment also requires that the counseling relationship become a vehicle for fostering a critical awareness of the power dynamics influencing the client's life context. It involves working with clients to develop a repertoire of skills that enable more effective self-direction; to develop a sense of collective history, common identity, or community with others; and to help clients to support the empowerment of others. Helping professionals have an important role to play in the process of societal transformation, a responsibility to help create a society in which social justice and equal opportunity are realities rather than platitudes.

The purpose of this book is twofold. First, I hope that *Counseling for Empowerment* will promote a clear understanding of the nature of empowerment in the general context of helping relationships, and in particular, in the context of counseling. Second, I believe that this book will serve as a source of specific information and practical suggestions for counselors, psychologists, social workers, and other helping professionals who wish to incorporate an empowerment perspective into their work. Drawing from counseling, social work, nursing, rehabilitation, and other professional literature, as well as popular magazines, novels, and personal perspectives, *Counseling for Empowerment* links theoretical notions of empowerment with practical techniques applied to specific populations and issues.

This book is divided into four parts. Part I, consisting of two chapters, addresses the nature of empowerment and the nature of counseling. The definition of empowerment offered in Chapter One is derived from social work, community psychology, educational, feminist, nursing, and multicultural counseling literature. Understanding the nature of empowerment within these contexts lays a critical foundation for understanding empowerment as a framework for counseling. In the second chapter, counseling is analyzed from two perspectives: counseling as a mechanism of oppression, and counseling as a source of empowerment. This discussion is followed by an in-depth analysis of how various counselor characteristics support or detract from empowerment in counseling.

In Part II, a sample of intrapersonal and interpersonal skills are presented from the empowerment perspective. The intrapersonal skills include building self-esteem, fighting irrational beliefs, increasing self-efficacy, imagery training, decision making, and creative self-expression. Setting boundaries, assertiveness, leadership training, communication, and public speaking are the interpersonal skills discussed in Chapter Four. Case examples of skill applications are provided in these chapters and throughout Part III.

Part III consists of applications of counseling for empowerment in work with specific populations. These include the following: people of color (Chapter Five); gay, lesbian, and bisexual people (Chapter Six); people with HIV disease (Chapter Seven); people with disabilities (Chapter Eight); survivors of violence (Chapter Nine); older adults (Chapter Ten); adolescents (Chapter Eleven), and the "non-beautiful" (Chapter Twelve). Although each chapter focuses on a particular group, it is assumed that members of the group are *not* all Euro American, able-bodied, heterosexual, and middle class. Each chapter in Part III includes the following: (a) an introduction to the topic; (b) characteristics of the group discussed; (c) a personal statement from an individual who *lives* the issues discussed in the chapter; (d) barriers to empowerment often confronted by members of this group; and (e) suggestions for empowerment.

The personal statements in each chapter are first-person accounts of individual experiences; these statements give voice to the reality of one person's life. The statements are not intended to reflect *all* people's experiences, nor were the people specifically chosen with the intention of capturing all aspects of an issue. They are the unique and human voices of those with whom we are privileged to work; indeed, they are our own voices. The section on barriers to empowerment addresses social, political, economic, and other factors that contribute to the marginalization or powerlessness of members of this group in U.S.

society. This section provides information helpful to the exploration of power dynamics and the development of critical consciousness. Suggestions for empowerment are also provided in each of the chapters in Part III. These suggestions include information counselors should know, information that may be helpful to clients, discussion of power dynamics in the context of intervention strategies, suggestions and examples of group participation and community involvement, and an application of one of the sample intrapersonal or interpersonal skills via a case example. Each case example is based on an actual client, although information has been altered to preserve confidentiality. Resources such as professional literature, self-help books, organizations, and artistic writings are provided throughout.

Part IV consists of a final chapter addressing the following: (a) implications of empowerment for the practice of counseling; (b) programmatic implications for the training of counselors; and (c) empowerment of counselors and other mental health professionals. Ultimately, the empowerment process must be integrated into our daily lives, our work and leisure activities, and our professional and personal relationships.

Finally, each chapter begins with an original poem or song verse. These poems and songs reflect part of a personal attempt to integrate and honor the multitude of experiences, emotions, and triumphs that I have been privileged to share with others over the past ten years.

Counselors and other helping professionals committed to the work of empowerment will be found in settings ranging from inner city mental health agencies to university counseling centers. For helping professionals in all work settings, a commitment to empowerment means a willingness to leave our offices, to investigate resources, and to continually educate and re-educate ourselves; most of all, it means that we must commit to the process of social transformation. While helping professionals cannot be activists for every issue or march for every cause, we can devote energy to one issue or to a set of issues. Even as we support the emerging and existing voices of our clients, we can add our own voices to the call for social change, and add our own hands to the work of transformation.

ACKNOWLEDGMENTS

This book is the culmination of the commitment and efforts of many people. I am very grateful to ACA Press for the invitation to write this book; it has been a privilege and a challenge from beginning to end. Carolyn Baker, of ACA, saw this project through to completion, and was a terrific source of encouragement and a wonderful editor. Many thanks also to Elaine Pirone, the initial editor of the book.

Gail Hackett and Courtland Lee shared their expertise through thoughtful, thorough, and constructive reviews. Benedict McWhirter, Jeff McWhirter, George Howard, Karen O'Brien, and Christine Cibula also took the time to provide thorough critiques of the book. Each of these reviewers added immensely to the final manuscript. Thanks are also due to my poet-sister, Mary Hawley, who provided valuable feedback on each of the poems within. In addition to his editing contributions, Jeff McWhirter has been my primary model of the personal integrity and social commitment so fundamental to the counselor's role. My family and my colleagues have been wonderfully supportive of this project and a source of constant encouragement.

The authors of the essays and personal statements shared their lives and experiences in very meaningful and personal ways. Thank you, Peggy McClane Plumlee, Jessie Garcia, Sue Morrow, Joseph Conrad, Rodney Shuey, Fritz Bally, Scott DiStefano, Cynthia Mylum, Alicia Sexton, Meg, D. Parker, and my father, Patrick Hawley, for your courage and generosity. Cynthia Mylum's personal statement is especially meaningful; shortly after writing it, she died from complications related to diabetes. Special thanks to her parents, who supported Cynthia's wish to share her journey with others in this way.

Finally, Benedict McWhirter, and our daughter Anna Cecilia, have accompanied me through every step of this manuscript. Ben energetically participated in endless discussions of the content and organization of the book, and patiently reviewed and edited draft after draft of each chapter, adding his wisdom, insight, and expertise. His dedication to this project also included keeping our lives and our home running smoothly while I typed; his excitement and interest literally kept me going. Anna contributed by being her spirited, smiling self. She renewed my energy every time she catapulted her two-year-old frame into my arms at the end of a long day. Ben and Anna are truly coproducers of this book.

ABOUT THE AUTHOR

Ellen Hawley McWhirter received a B.A. from the University of Notre Dame, and has a master's degree in counseling and a Ph.D. in counseling psychology from Arizona State University. She is an assistant professor in the Counseling Psychology Program at the University of Nebraska-Lincoln. In addition to her experience working as an agency counselor, she has been a Head Start teacher; a home educator for Spanish-speaking families with developmentally delayed infants; a participant in the Program in Global Community, Cuernavaca, Mexico; and an instructor for a university study skills and survival course. Ellen was the recipient of a fellowship from the American Association of University Women that supported her dissertation research on the career development of Mexican-American adolescent girls. Her current research focuses on the career development of women and people of color and on empowerment issues related to youth at-risk. She has published numerous articles and book chapters in the field of counseling, and recently coauthored with her family *At-Risk Youth: A Comprehensive Response*. Ellen and her husband Benedict have a three-year-old daughter, Anna.

PART I

EMPOWERMENT AND COUNSELING

Part I of *Counseling for Empowerment* is devoted to exploration of the respective natures of empowerment and counseling, and sets the stage for all that is to follow. The term "empowerment" has been adopted by a variety of human service disciplines to signify a number of slightly different processes. Uses of the term are reviewed in Chapter One, followed by a comprehensive definition of empowerment for counseling. Although the fundamental characteristic of increasing control over the direction of one's life is integral to the definition proposed here, empowerment is also characterized by several other essential components. We do not *do* empowerment *to* others or bestow it *upon* them; empowerment happens with others, within a context, and we shape that context as do those with whom we work.

In Chapter Two, the nature of counseling is analyzed critically with respect to its potential to oppress or to empower clients. Critical self-analysis is described as an essential and ongoing task of the counselor. Counseling for empowerment requires that counselors and other mental health professionals commit to exploring how racism, heterosexism, and other biases influence our work with clients. Only through critical self-examination, and a willingness to ask for and receive feedback from our colleagues and our clients, can we hope to become aware of and reduce our personal biases. In addition to biases, other counselor characteristics such as reasons for entering the profession, counselor view of human nature, values, and assumptions regarding the balance of power in the counseling relationship are described in terms of oppression and empowerment.

Chapter One

THE NATURE OF EMPOWERMENT

---

i was water filling spaces
connecting structures accommodating
all shapes sizes and textures
i poured in without resistance left without comment
i did not question my nature i knew my place
later sometimes i froze stuck inside or unable to
accommodate the new shape
but i always melted back into fluid
then i turned into peanut butter
it just seemed to happen that i was
sticky and chunky requiring some pressure
before conformity and leaving pieces behind
sometimes nothing could coax me against a surface
no knife or spoon could round the corner to push me
finally i became wood living wood i
lost some flexibility but i
connect earth to sky dance
with many partners branch
and bud shade and sway
to inner voices

E.H.M.

INTRODUCTION

The first definition of "power" in *Webster's New Collegiate Dictionary* (1980) is "possession of control, authority, or influence over others" (p. 895). Power is always defined and understood in relation to others, be they individuals, organizations, or nations. Rollo May (1972) posits that there are five types of power, differentiated by the nature of the relationship: exploitative, manipulative, competitive, nutritive, and integrative. Exploitative power and manipulative power are clearly destructive in nature. Competitive power may be constructive or destructive, depending on the consequences of wielding this power. As positive and proactive as the final two types of power sound, nutritive power—or power for others, and integrative power—or power with others, also may be destructive. They are potentially destructive because regardless of intention, any form of help giving that places the receiver in a passive role, that supplants his or her existing capabilities, or that postpones the acquisition of necessary skills is, ultimately, disempowering.

Because of the potential for power to be destructive, its use in counseling, including attempts to "empower" clients as part of the counseling process, can be a tricky venture indeed. Perhaps the most fundamental and critical point is this: Our efforts to help others through counseling cannot be judged solely on our intent, our efficiency, even on the grateful thanks offered by a departing client. In fact, contrary to what we may wish to believe, our very best efforts to "help" may undermine the capabilities and resources of those with whom we work. Our attempts to wield power (education, knowledge, resources) for and with clients have an alarmingly subtle potential to be destructive. Therefore, the counselor who wishes to empower clients must understand thoroughly how various aspects of the counseling process can influence clients.

The term "empowerment" has been used with increasing frequency across social science and health literature in social work, community psychology, education, nursing, women's studies, and, more recently, in counseling (McWhirter, 1991). Empowerment seems to be understood vaguely as "power-with-and-for-others," but there is little consensus on precise definitions. Writers in the helping professions often have cited empowerment as a goal or a result of their intervention, but have failed to define it in the context of their work.

One result of the popularization and broad use of this term is that empowerment means "all things to all people"; empowerment is a theory, a framework, a plan of action, a goal, an ideology, an intervention, a process, and more. Empowerment has become another buzzword that implies good work. Indeed, popular use of this term overgeneralizes and underestimates the meaning and implications of empowerment. Therefore, this first chapter is devoted to exploring the use of empowerment across several perspectives: social work, community psychology, education, women's studies, and multicultural counseling. The articulation of empowerment in these contexts establishes a solid basis for the definition of empowerment in counseling and illustrates the radical and paradoxical nature of empowerment. Further, the definition of empowerment in the context of counseling and its application to various populations perhaps will dispel any notion of empowerment as simply a vague, popular trend in counseling.

DEFINITIONS OF EMPOWERMENT

Social Work Perspectives

In the social work literature, empowerment has been defined as a process that simultaneously affects the individual and the community. Pinderhughes (1983) describes client empowerment as the major goal of social work intervention. She proposes that for social workers to empower their clients effectively, they must understand power dynamics as they operate at societal, cultural, familial, and individual levels. Pinderhughes defines power as "the capacity to influence the forces which affect one's life space for one's own benefit" (p. 332). She describes empowerment as the development of "the ability and capacity to cope constructively with the forces that undermine and hinder coping, the achievement of some reasonable control over [one's] destiny" (p. 334).

Based on her extensive work with the African-American community, Solomon (1976) defines empowerment as

> the process whereby persons who belong to a stigmatized social category throughout their lives can be assisted to develop and increase skills in the exercise of interpersonal influence and the performance of valued social roles. (p. 6)

Valued social roles include those of parent, partner, employee, and community leader. The powerless are plagued by dependency and severely limited self-determination. Powerlessness is the end result of living with systematic disadvantages and limitations to individual and community growth (Solomon, 1976).

Empowerment, according to Solomon (1976, 1987) and Pinderhughes (1983), involves recognition of the way power operates within society and how individuals and communities are affected by the way power is used. This aspect of empowerment illustrates the view that problems are rooted in the system and not in those who are marginalized by the system, and is clearly inconsistent with the "blaming the victim" construct. This perspective is particularly important in light of the fact that not only does society as a whole tend to blame victims, but the members of marginalized groups also tend to blame themselves. This perspective also recognizes the existing resources and fundamental abilities of those who are marginalized.

Gutiérrez (1988) emphasizes cognitive components in her definition of empowerment. She defines empowerment as

> a means for addressing the problems of powerless populations and for mediating the role powerlessness plays in creating and perpetuating social problems...a psychological transformation which requires the development of a new self concept.... A combination of feelings of shared identity and shared fate with a group of like others, with the belief that actions toward change will be effective comprise the core of psychological empowerment. (p.2)

According to Gutiérrez, three mutually reinforcing cognitive components of the empowered sense of self are: (a) *group identification* ("understanding areas of common experience and concern...feelings of shared fate"); (b) *stratum consciousness* ("realistic appraisal of the status and power of groups in society"); and (c) *self- and collective efficacy* ("beliefs that one is capable as an individual or member of a group, of making desired changes in one's life") (p. 2). Thus, having the skills to create change is not enough; people also must believe that they are capable of *using* such skills effectively.

In an experimental study designed to investigate aspects of empowerment among Hispanics, Gutiérrez (1990) found that participants in a consciousness-raising group achieved higher scores on ethnic consciousness, were more likely to attribute the problems of Hispanics to social structural factors (as opposed to individual deficits), and were more likely to suggest collective solutions to the problems of individual Hispanics. Participants in all three groups expressed interest in joining Hispanic organizations and in participating in events that benefited the Hispanic community.

Community Psychology Perspectives

Rappaport (1981, 1987) has written extensively about the role of empowerment in community psychology. He defines empowerment as a mechanism by which people and groups gain mastery over their affairs. According to Rappaport (1987), empowerment involves a psychological sense of personal control and a concern with actual social influence and political power. It includes individual self-determination and community participation. Similar to definitions from the social work literature, the community psychology perspective of empowerment involves engaging the existing competencies of the individual or group, with deficits in coping viewed not as individual deficits, but as a failure on the part of the system to maximize the potential of its members (Rappaport,

1981). Rappaport (1987) also contends that the empowerment construct involves individual, organizational, political, sociological, economic, and spiritual facets. Legal rights, reform in education and health care, and other issues of social justice are all incorporated into the community psychology perspective of empowerment.

Kieffer (1984) describes the empowerment process as resulting, ultimately, in the development of *participatory competence*. Participatory competence refers to a set of commitments and capabilities related to playing a conscious, active role in the construction of an individual's environment, including participation in community social change efforts (Kieffer, 1984). Research by community psychologists has identified an association between empowerment and participation in community organizations (Zimmerman & Rappaport, 1988), and Zimmerman (1991) found that participation in community organizations has a direct and positive effect on psychological empowerment.

The common definitional characteristics of empowerment highlighted in the community psychology perspective include the multidimensional nature of empowerment and an emphasis on community participation. Empowerment is viewed as far more than an individual phenomenon, with wider effects occurring at social and community levels.

Educational Perspectives

Coll (1986) has argued that while education may appear on the surface to be inherently empowering, it is not necessarily so. In fact, she writes:

> Much of what passes for education in institutions of learning keeps students in passive roles; the professor is dominant in the relationship by virtue of role, knowledge and the power to judge the student's work. Even though we profess to aim at empowerment, the process often rewards students for compliance, acceptance and obedience. (p. 420)

Truly empowering students through education includes preparing students to challenge their educators, an uncomfortable risk at best.

Paulo Freire (1971) describes two forms of educating—the traditional banking model and the problem-posing model. In the former, the teacher serves as the source of knowledge, filling passive students with "truth," making deposit after deposit until students are full. The teacher is an authoritarian figure, retaining the power to judge the student's work. In the problem-posing model, teacher and students critically reflect on problems together. Rather than providing a prior definition of the problem and its solutions, the teacher voices his or her thought processes as they occur and students do the same. The teacher becomes a "student among students" (p. 62), so that, "[T]hrough dialogue, the teacher-of-the-students and the students-of-the-teacher cease to exist and a new term emerges: teacher-student with students-teachers" (Freire, 1971, p. 67). Such a process empowers students by developing their critical thinking skills, increasing their ability to articulate their thought processes with confidence, and enhancing their knowledge base. The process demands vulnerability on the part of teachers, who must give up what may be to them a more comfortable status in the classroom.

Cummins (1986) argues that the adoption of an empowerment framework in education would diminish significantly the continuing and pervasive problem of academic failure among ethnic minority students. Citing examples from literature on the academic progress of minority students worldwide, Cummins argues that power and status relations between minority and majority groups, locally and nationally, are an influential mediator of school performance. In other words, the role minority groups play in society is reflected in the role minority students play in the schools. He proposes that interventions that include changing teacher/student and school/minority community relationships will enable schools to *transform* society by empowering minority students rather than *reflect* society by disabling them.

According to Cummins (1986), four school characteristics influence the extent to which minority students are empowered vs. disabled: (a) participation of minority communities in their children's educational process; (b) incorporation of minority students' language and culture into the school program; (c) promotion of intrinsic motivation on the part of students to use language actively and generate their own knowledge; and (d) advocacy for minority students by professionals involved in assessment (Cummins, 1986, p. 21). Cummins stresses that student empowerment requires changes that offset the negative effects of majority/minority societal group relations. Academic and group identity factors must be addressed to empower students; neglecting either will result in the continuing school failure of ethnic minority students.

The complexity of applying empowerment to the concrete reality of a particular school is illustrated in the work of Gruber and Trickett (1987). They describe the results of efforts to empower parents and students of an alternative public high school through equal representation on the council governing the school. The school was established with a commitment to egalitarianism and empowerment. The goal of empowerment failed, Gruber and Trickett contend, for two fundamental reasons. First, council members (students, parents, and teachers) were on very unequal footing with respect to knowledge of school organization and functioning; teachers clearly had more knowledge and experience. Second, the school's fundamental ideology of egalitarianism fostered a set of dynamics that made these initial inequalities impossible to overcome. Gruber and Trickett (1987) point out, "there is a fundamental paradox in the idea of people empowering others because the very institutional structure that puts one group in a position to empower also works to undermine the act of empowerment" (p. 353). The paradoxical nature of empowerment evident in this example will surface again and again as we explore the nature of empowerment in counseling.

The educational perspectives on empowerment contribute several important points. First, while increasing knowledge in itself is potentially empowering, the process of obtaining knowledge—the educational process—must be analyzed carefully to determine whether it is empowering. We cannot assume that education—or counseling—is an inherently empowering process. Second, to the extent that the process of education—or counseling—reflects the power structure of the larger society, it may disenfranchise further those who are already marginalized. Thus, empowerment may require altering traditional status roles. Finally, the process of empowerment involves a fundamental paradox. In a nutshell, the implied dependency of the powerless on the powerful for their empowerment can seriously undermine the very process of empowerment! The feminist perspectives discussed below touch upon this issue.

Feminist Perspectives

The concept of power has played a central role in feminist theory. Beginning with the earliest writings on feminist theory, power has been associated with the domination of women by men. Identifying the nature, extent, and effect of this domination has been important in the task of societal transformation (Wartenberg, 1988). More recently, a second aspect of power has emerged among feminists to whom Wartenberg (1988) refers as the "feminist theorists of power." In his words, "this second face of power is the transformative use of power, an agent's use of power to empower another agent, to bring her to a more developed manner of existing" (Wartenberg, 1988, p. 302). Thus, the goal or purpose of transformative power is to empower others.

The concept of empowerment has been incorporated into feminist models of therapy, education, and organization. According to Hawxhurst and Morrow (1984), empowerment is defined as the process of gaining control over one's life and supporting others' control over their lives. They point out that empowerment includes:

> (1) an analysis of power; (2) an understanding of female socialization and sex-role stereotyping; (3) the attainment of power at personal, interpersonal, and social levels; (4) advocacy for ourselves and others. (p. 35)

Smith and Siegal's (1985) outline of the stages of feminist therapy incorporates several of these characteristics. These stages include identification of the sociopolitical and interpersonal forces affecting women's development; understanding how these forces influence the client's exercise of power; and facilitating the development of new, self-determining behaviors.

Similar to the interpersonal, community, and educational perspectives of empowerment, feminist writers describe empowerment as more than an individual's increased interpersonal power. Recognition of the political, economic, and social influences on women as individuals and as a group is essential to the empowerment process. Attempting to influence change in each of these areas is also central. In addition, the use of newfound strengths and understanding toward the empowerment of similar others is considered an intrinsic component of empowerment.

Nursing Perspectives

Contrary to traditional models of health in which the patient is viewed as passive and reactive, recent nursing literature has articulated a new and proactive perspective. Given that mental health professionals consistently work with people with HIV and many other chronic or disabling medical conditions, views of empowerment from the nursing literature are of particular value. Gibson's (1991) review yielded the following definition of empowerment in the context of nursing:

> a social process of recognizing, promoting and enhancing people's abilities to meet their own needs, solve their own problems and mobilize the necessary resources in order to feel in control of their own lives...a process of helping people to assert control over the factors which affect their health. (p. 359)

This radical shift from traditional nursing practice would require that nurses be aware of existing social, political, economic, and demographic conditions, political activities, the structural and functional relationships within the health care system, and the barriers that create conflict between the individual and the health care system (Gibson, 1991). This perspective embraces a transformation of the role of patient from passive recipient of care to active participant in achieving and maintaining health.

Multicultural Counseling Perspectives

Although not always labeled as such, the work of practitioners and researchers in the area of multicultural counseling has embraced an empowerment perspective from its beginnings. Working with people of color in the counseling setting necessitates confronting the context in which people of color live and the context in which counseling takes place. Lee (1991a) writes:

A pervasive theme in much of the multicultural counseling literature is that environmental adaptation and psychological well-being have generally been problematic for people of color due to the social forces of racism and oppression that have negatively affected their academic, career, and personal development. People from ethnic groups of color, by and large, have experienced considerable frustration in their person-environment transactions with American society. (p. 229)

The context Lee describes is not addressed directly in traditional counseling approaches, which were developed by White middle-class theorists for a White, middle-class population (Atkinson, Morten, & Sue, 1979). Traditional counseling theory and practice evolved out of the values and norms of White culture (Katz, 1985; Sue & Sue, 1991). This establishes a context for counseling that, by its very nature, is at risk of alienating, blaming, or disabling clients of color.

Sue (1981) reviews how people of color have been characterized in the counseling literature throughout the history of counseling. He describes four chronological stages in terms of models: the pathological model, the genetic deficiency model, the culturally deficient model, and the culturally different model. Implicit in each of these stages is the assumption that Euro-American culture is the standard against which all else is compared. This perspective is not only unrealistic and biased, it is damaging to all those who do not ascribe to the values and norms of Euro-American culture. Katz (1985) argues that to make the counseling profession more responsive to the needs of multicultural populations, we must abandon the notion that counseling is a morally, politically, and ethnically neutral activity. Further, she emphasizes the need for self-examination, to make implicit cultural values and norms explicit and to become conscious of Euro American cultural identity.

By directly confronting the culture-bound nature of counseling, multicultural counseling theorists have integrated the analysis of power dynamics into the discipline of counseling. By addressing the systematic consequences of being a person of color and drawing this into the counseling process, multicultural counselors have begun the empowerment process. Thus, before the term empowerment was "discovered" and popularized, multicultural counselors were engaged in the empowerment process (Lee, 1991a).

A DEFINITION OF EMPOWERMENT IN COUNSELING

The preceding discussion illustrates a fairly high degree of similarity across existing definitions and perspectives of empowerment. It also reveals the lack of a commonly held and precise understanding of empowerment and its implications for the practice of counseling. Clearly, the recent upsurge of references to empowerment in the counseling literature has not served to clarify its meaning.

Empowerment refers to a comprehensive process affecting the individual in relation to others, to the community, and to society. This distinguishes empowerment from concepts such as autonomy and efficacy in that the focus extends beyond the individual. While increased autonomy is certainly one aspect of empowerment, such a term is not broad enough to capture the interpersonal, group, and community aspects of empowerment. Self- and group efficacy refer to an individual's or group's belief in his, her, or its ability to accomplish specific tasks or behaviors. Efficacy is a cognitive appraisal of performance capabilities while empowerment is a global process involving behavioral and cognitive components. The ability to say "no," interview for a job, or organize a neighborhood committee undoubtedly contributes to empowerment; increased efficacy in and of itself, however, does not constitute empowerment. The following definition, slightly modified from an earlier version (McWhirter, 1991), should serve to clarify these distinctions:

Empowerment is the process by which people, organizations, or groups who are powerless or marginalized (a) become aware of the power dynamics at work in their life context, (b) develop the skills and capacity for gaining some reasonable control over their lives, (c) which they exercise, (d) without infringing on the rights of others, and (e) which coincides with actively supporting the empowerment of others in their community.

"Powerless" refers to being unable to direct the course of one's life due to societal conditions, power dynamics, lack of skills, and/or lack of belief that one can change one's life. "Marginalized" refers to those who are excluded from positions of power socially, politically, economically, or otherwise. "Become aware of the power dynamics" refers to increasing awareness of multiple systems such as interpersonal relationships, family dynamics, school systems, local political dynamics, societal norms, and the capitalist economic system. Within each system, the analysis of power dynamics may focus on a wide variety of phenomena, including prejudice, discrimination, gender role stereotyping, family roles, peer pressure, cultural values, and patterns of communication. The emphasis on power dynamics implies that problems are inherent in the system rather than in its "victims" (the powerless), while solutions to problems may be effected by action on the part of "victims" as well as through systemic change. Finally, "community" refers to the group or groups with whom individuals come to identify as they attempt to gain control over the quality and direction of their lives. An individual's community could be Mexican Americans, residents of the neighborhood, members of an AIDS support group, members of the deaf community, and innumerable others.

In addition, to use "empowerment" in counseling implies that (a) the control gained in counseling has an impact on the client's life context at personal, interpersonal, and societal levels; (b) that the client eventually participates in some form of community involvement (such as joining a support group, campaigning for a political leader, joining a neighborhood block watch, or sharing creative writing with interested others); and (c) the traditional power differential maintained in therapy is altered in the direction of increased equality between counselor and client.

The multitude and variety of power relationships in society are such that how empowerment takes place will vary across individuals and across time. The scope and nature of the empowerment process also will depend on the context within which empowerment occurs. Each experience will have characteristics unique to the roles of the people and the situations involved, for what empowers some members of an ethnic or nonethnic minority group, for example, may be inappropriate and disempowering for other members of the same group. It is also important to recognize that the empowerment process represents a continuum rather than a dichotomy. Likewise, there are no specific beginning and end states of empowerment.

Empowerment may be represented in the transformation of a traumatized, newly paraplegic young woman into an active member and role model in an organization that promotes awareness of wheelchair accessibility issues. However, the increasing awareness of power dynamics, the emergence of group identity, the development of skills that enhance her sense of control and autonomy, and community participation that supports the empowerment of others, will not necessarily coincide in the short term. At any point in this young woman's journey, for example, one might deny that empowerment is occurring because of the absence of an essential component. One way to resolve this dilemma may be to consider processes or experiences that enhance any of these components to be "empowering," but to consider a person, group, or community "empowered" only when each component of the definition is evident or has been achieved. Once empowered, a person, group, or community can become *more* empowered, giving recognition to the progressive and continuous nature of empowerment.

In her discussion of power, Hagberg (1984) describes six stages that incorporate the nutritive and integrative types of power proposed by May (1972). Stage One is powerlessness, followed by Stage Two, power by association with powerful people. In Stage Three power is attained by symbols such as titles or degrees. Stage Four is power by reflection, or power through the mentoring of others. Stage Five consists of power by purpose, power through the conscious and consistent empowerment of others. Finally, Stage Six, is power by gestalt. This last stage is characterized by integrative power or power with others. People in this stage concurrently empower the marginalized and the powerful, essentially enabling the powerful to examine critically the ramifications of their actions and policies on others. A person's development through these stages of power has no inherently corruptive or destructive element, and Hagberg's framework offers a new way of thinking about the process of empowerment. Ideally, our work with clients will come to reflect Hagberg's fifth and sixth stages.

CONCLUSION

As references to the term "empowerment" increase across the mental health fields, it has become important to define exactly what this concept means. Defining empowerment, however, like empowerment itself, is more likely to be a process than a once-and-for-all accomplishment. The definition offered here should be considered a working definition, one that will be modified and adapted as counseling professionals explore its implications more fully.

The perspectives of empowerment reviewed in this chapter provide a basis for defining empowerment in the context of counseling. Drawing from these sources, empowerment emerges as a concept distinct from autonomy, efficacy, or general personal growth. The concept of empowerment encompasses skill development, awareness of the power dynamics affecting one's life context, development of a sense of group identity, social and community participation, and support of the empowerment of others. In addition, the definition of empowerment that has been proposed in this chapter implies an expanded role for the traditional counselor. It requires that counselors develop awareness of the social, political, and economic barriers to growth and autonomy experienced by clients who are marginalized. It requires altering our traditional authoritative role as expert. In addition, empowering clients in the context of counseling means that we need to develop an awareness of existing community organizations, support groups, neighborhood action committees, and other channels of collective effort, so that we can inform our clients of opportunities for involvement. Finally, it means that as mental health professionals we must use our individual and collective resources to challenge the systems and structures that oppress. Some may claim that this role is overly political. To encourage community involvement, for example, may imply taking a stand on issues critical to the struggle of marginalized groups. Yet it is a role that I would argue is long overdue for counselors, because to remain passive is to accept a status quo that continues to marginalize and oppress many members of our society.

Having defined empowerment in the context of counseling, we are ready to explore the ramifications of counseling for empowerment in some detail. In the next chapter, the counseling process and specific counselor attitudes and behaviors will be examined in relation to how they may undermine or foster empowerment.

Chapter Two

THE NATURE OF COUNSELING

---

middle of the road was a long best seller
kept some of us fed and sleeping at night
but never did the middle move a muscle that mattered
only pointed fingers at the left and the right

From "Tightrope," E.H.M.

INTRODUCTION

In Chapter One, empowerment was defined in the context of counseling. Without question, the counseling process has vast potential to facilitate empowerment among a wide variety of people. Indeed, Chapters Three through Thirteen are intended to illustrate this point exactly. Nevertheless, this chapter will consider arguments that counseling is by its very nature an oppressive process. Steinbock (1988) and others (Beit-Hallahmi, 1974; Grauman, 1970) have argued that counseling often promotes adjustment to a state of neediness and decreases the incentive of people to confront injustice in their lives and pursue societal transformation. Such criticism deserves our attention; we know, for example, that counseling sometimes provides just enough relief to distressed individuals that they prolong involvement in activities, relationships, or behaviors that ultimately may be self-destructive. We know that clients often become quite dependent on their counselors. We also know that restricted time availability, inadequate staffing, and budget constraints often limit counselors to frustrating, "Band-Aid" interventions. Thus, we must consider carefully how the counseling process may affect negatively those with whom we work.

In conjunction with examining the potentially destructive role of counseling, we will consider the paradoxical nature of counseling for empowerment. Counselors wishing to empower others must confront at some level their status as educated—and therefore "privileged"—members of society. To empower others, we must give up aspects of our own power, such as control and immunity from criticism. This has personal and societal implications, including the need to examine critically the very society in which we live, as well as to examine ourselves continuously and vigorously. Thus, a framework for this essential process concludes this chapter. Five areas are explored: choosing this profession, view of human nature, conceptualization of the problem, values and biases, and the power balance in therapy.

COUNSELING: OPPRESSIVE OR EMPOWERING?

Steinbock (1988) offers a critical examination of the institution of helping in Western society, and we will consider his critique in some detail. Steinbock refers to "helping" as therapeutic interaction, and includes the range of therapies (e.g., cognitive, behavioral, feminist) associated with counseling and psychotherapy. He argues that helping, regardless of intent, serves as a very subtle method of oppression. Helping presupposes that the help-seeker is lacking, needy, and helpless; thus help-seekers must reinforce their own neediness or victimization in the act of getting help. Further, helping facilitates dependency, if not on the individual helper (counselor), then on the institution of helping (counseling) itself. In addition, in the helping paradigm, the exercise of power is restricted to the power to cope, the power to deal with a problem. The focus on "coping" and "dealing with" problems, Steinbock contends, leads to individualistic problem solving and precludes options that would facilitate societal transformation, such as political activism.

Steinbock illustrates some of the larger sociopolitical implications of the helping paradigm through the example of a battered women's shelter. The helping paradigm presupposes that the women in the shelter are needy; residents define themselves in terms of neediness and learn to cope with those needs. He writes:

> Such a practice fails to recognize that the fundamental insight into one's situation is not that of oppression, anger, vulnerability or neediness, but rather, the recognition of one's own power.... It is this fundamental insight—which spurs one to leave or fight an oppressive situation—which must be cultivated, not the ontologically secondary and dependent insight of domination. (p. 35)

When people focus on their individual neediness rather than on their individual and collective power, they are less likely to challenge the structures that oppress, limit, and stifle their full potential. Steinbock argues that women "helped" in a shelter are not likely to collectively challenge patriarchy or misogyny by, for example, confronting the media's portrayal of women as helpless sexual objects. Steinbock's bottom line is that helping, or counseling, enables sociopolitical phenomenon (such as sexism, discrimination, the feminization of poverty, and inadequate AIDS prevention programming) to continue unchecked by helping individuals only to "cope" with these problems.

Steinbock identifies the "homogenization of power" as a second troubling aspect of the helping paradigm. He describes this phenomenon as a response to the inherent paradox of the powerful helping the powerless; homogeneity of power refers to creating a situation in which all participants are equal and share, noncompetitively, their viewpoints, suggestions, feelings, etc. (For example, recall the attempt at one alternative school, described in Chapter One, to empower everyone involved by giving administrators, teachers, parents, and students "equal" representation and power in the governing body.) In this context, argues Steinbock, power is "domesticated": no one person's views take precedence over another's; debate, contestation, and refutation of another's views are replaced with acceptance in the name of respect. In such a situation, no one is right or wrong, no one need be threatened or offended, and *no one needs to change*. As such, the homogeneity of power does not elevate all participants to an equal power status; it eliminates the possibility of exercising power and consequently prevents transformation of the situation or problem at hand. The duty to accept everyone's point of view results in a paralysis of sorts, reinforcing the powerlessness of the participants and serving to maintain the status quo. The status quo, with its victims and beneficiaries, continues uninterrupted. The homogeneity of power, Steinbock contends, merely disguises how power is used to maintain the current situation.

Although Steinbock addresses helping in general, his critique has implications for counseling. First, the existence of the counseling profession implies, at least overtly, that a significant proportion of the population cannot manage its own mental health. Furthermore, the way we label and conceptualize the general client population and individual clients affects their empowerment. For example, consider the differential impact on a client who is being viewed as a resource, an expert on his or her life experiences, and who is presumed to have many skills and competencies, versus a client who is being viewed as dysfunctional and needy. This basic presumption of ongoing neediness and dependency is ultimately disabling. Second, Steinbock's critique challenges us to consider the long-range implications of our traditional focus on intra- and interpersonal solutions to problems. Such a focus places the onus for change on the client, which *can*, unfortunately, become a form of blaming the victim. In addition, an intra- or interpersonal focus may reduce or eliminate the possibility that the client will join with similar others and challenge the structures that limit his or her full human potential. While individual clients certainly have the right to learn to "cope with" their problems and so on, it is easy to see how counseling as a whole, and across all such clients, becomes a champion of the status quo. We must focus not simply on *what* distresses clients but on *how* their environment creates and maintains that distress and what might be done about it.

A third implication of Steinbock's argument is that the counselor/client power differential must be acknowledged; ignoring this difference does not eliminate it. Further, acting as if the client is a resource and collaborator while retaining the belief that, ultimately, "*I* know best" is destructive and dishonest. If changing the balance of power in therapy takes the form of "homogenization of power," then the power balance has not changed at all, and we are merely placating ourselves and our client at our client's expense.

To summarize Steinbock's critique, counseling is an act of oppression when entering into a counseling relationship requires clients to embrace a view of themselves as needy and helpless rather than resourceful and powerful; when the "help" rendered enables the client to "cope with" rather than confront and change situations of oppression or injustice; and when a facade of shared power obfuscates the real power differential between counselor and client. Whenever counseling serves to maintain the status quo at the expense of the client's self-determination or dignity, counseling is oppressive.

The idea that counseling may be oppressive, and that we, by extension, may be oppressors, is alarming to say the least. Before applying this idea to the personal level through critical self-examination, let us consider another fundamental problem at hand: the basic paradox inherent in efforts to empower others.

THE PARADOX OF COUNSELING FOR EMPOWERMENT

According to Gruber and Trickett (1987), "there is a fundamental paradox in the idea of people empowering others because the very institutional structure that puts one group in a position to empower also works to undermine the act of empowerment" (p. 353). Our own power is rooted in a system that depends on powerless others to maintain itself

(Nikelly, 1988). Pinderhughes (1983) draws from Bowen's social projection concept to illustrate the paradox of empowerment. Social projection is the process whereby one group, the benefactors in a society, perceive and treat another group, the victims, as inferior or incompetent. The poor, for example, are often "explained" by such statements as, "They're lazy," "My father made it from nothing, they could too if they tried hard enough," "All they want is someone to take care of them without lifting a finger." The cause of poverty is attributed to what the poor are or are not doing, and the benefactors need not feel responsible (Ryan, 1971).

Counselors, social workers, and other mental health professionals become a part of the societal projection process. As benefactors, we reflect this process when we are overly sympathetic with clients, when we pity or protect them, and when we treat our clients as helpless victims. We also reflect the projection when we respond with exclusively individual solutions; such solutions suggest, "If *you* were only more competent, less inferior, you wouldn't be a victim anymore." Individual solutions also ignore the fundamental issues of racism, sexism, homophobia, and ageism that so frequently form the backbone of victimization. If race, gender, sexual orientation, and age were easily changeable, would we encourage clients to "deal with" their victimization through surgery rather than by challenging the existence of these "isms"?

Those of us who are formally educated, or middle class, or Euro American, or heterosexual, or able-bodied must confront the fact that we are benefactors in a system that victimizes groups of people and individuals, and must be able to risk losing our status as benefactors if we are to empower others. What exactly does it mean to risk that status? To what extent can White, or male, or middle-class counselors actually give up power without falling into Steinbock's homogeneity of power? Certainly it does not mean that counselors with benefactor characteristics must live in a constant state of guilt and apology (although a temporary phase of guilt is built into most models of White racial identity development). In addition, it does not mean that we deny our training, experience, and expertise so as to be "equal" with our clients. It *does* mean that we acknowledge and confront systemic injustices, even when those injustices are to our benefit. And it does mean that we internalize a notion of expertise that acknowledges our ignorance, biases, and other personal and professional limitations, as well as the expertise, resources, and strengths of each of our clients. Additional implications are addressed throughout the remainder of this text.

As indicated in the proposed definition, the empowerment process demands far more than simple skill development. The chapters in this text devoted to skill development are only tools for empowerment when enacted in conjunction with other vital components. In the following section, a guide for critical self-examination is described. Such self-examination, practiced continually, helps ensure that counseling is an act of empowerment rather than a source of oppression.

SELF AS TOOL: CRITICAL SELF-EXAMINATION

Freire (1971) argues that members of the elite class who renounce their role as oppressors and want to join in the effort to transform society (that is, many of us who want to help improve the lot of our clients) are *always* suspect:

> Our converts, on the other hand, truly desire to transform the unjust order; but because of their background they believe that they must be executors of the transformation. They talk about the people, but they do not trust them; and trusting the people is the indispensable precondition for revolutionary change.... Those who authentically commit themselves to the people must re-examine themselves constantly.... The convert who approaches the people but feels alarm at each step they take, each doubt they express, and each suggestion they offer, and attempts to impose his [or her] "status," remains nostalgic toward his [or her] origins. (pp. 46–47)

We must be constantly on guard, constantly involved in the process of self-examination to identify when the counseling process has become one that merely reflects the client's experience of powerlessness. Those of us who are White, or male, or middle to upper class, or heterosexual, or temporarily able-bodied, or young, or free of HIV disease are to some degree "converts" when we choose to work as counselors with persons who are marginalized by virtue of their being in one of these categories. Critical self-examination is a lifelong professional commitment that counselors must be prepared to make in conjunction with the goal of empowerment. Sue and Sue (1990) note that many counselor training programs fail to provide the opportunity for rigorous self-exploration of motives and biases. None of us is invulnerable to the pressures of a society that respects and encourages the use of status and power to meet objectives. None of us is invulnerable to the insistence of a client that we play the role of expert or magician. And, certainly, none of us is invulnerable to the "nostalgia toward her origins" to which Freire refers above. Several points of departure for critical self-examination are presented below.

Choosing This Profession

Why do we choose to become counselors? In answer to this question, we might say, "I like helping people"; "I seemed to have a knack for listening and problem solving"; "I wanted to make a difference in people's lives"; or "It makes me feel good to help others." These responses are fairly typical. One would not expect to hear, "Because I want to help maintain the social system equilibrium that benefits me and keeps many others in a position of powerlessness." Yet, Pinderhughes (1983) argues that human service workers continually must ask to what extent they are indeed contributing to that equilibrium. Further, she contends that helping professionals are vulnerable to exploiting the helping encounter for their own benefit to compensate for powerlessness elsewhere in their lives (p. 337).

We must be starkly honest with ourselves: If we have chosen this profession because it "feels good" to "help" others, the client's potential for empowerment is in grave danger, because the goal of "feeling good" will conflict unavoidably with client empowerment. When the client "prevents" the counselor from "feeling good" by, for example, staying depressed or returning to the abuser, what happens to the counseling relationship? The client who needs to express anger, frustration, or helplessness may get the subtle message that such expression would hurt, disappoint, or anger the counselor.

When counselors suspect that a client is protecting them, they must examine how their own behavior encourages or facilitates this protection. When we are invested in feeling good, when we blame our clients for not "getting better" and ignore the role of our own expectations and methodologies, and when our clients see fit to protect us from their feelings, expectations, or behaviors, the counseling relationship oppresses rather than empowers.

View of Human Nature

The counselor's view of human nature has implications for client empowerment. Specifically, belief in the inherent goodness or neutrality of human nature is more empowering than viewing human nature as inherently negative. If people are inherently prone to selfishness and other evils, we can hardly hold humans accountable for situations of injustice and oppression. Furthermore, adherence to a deterministic view of human nature, in effect, limits the amount of control that clients can expect to achieve over their lives (Howard, 1985; Lichtenberg, 1985). Even though counselors may not espouse a deterministic or negative view of human nature, those suffering from "burnout" may convey a general cynicism about human nature to the client (Spicuzza & DeVoe, 1982) that is also potentially disempowering. Freire (1971) addresses this issue in his discussion of the importance of faith as a prerequisite to authentic encounters between people. Faith in the power of human beings to create and recreate, to become more fully human, and to transform their lives, is essential—without this faith our encounters with others become "a farce which inevitably degenerates into paternalistic manipulation" (Freire, 1971, p. 79).

Without faith in our clients' power, we may fall into rescuing, protecting, and ultimately disabling them (Hawxhurst & Morrow, 1984). Counselors will be most empowering when they believe in their clients' ability to make constructive changes in their lives and in the lives of others. Awareness of the extent to which we believe human beings *can* transform society is an important area to explore. Counselor knowledge of how local groups are actively involved in such transformation processes is a concrete and important form of testimony to a positive view of human nature.

Conceptualization of the Problem

The counselor's conceptualization of the problem is critical in determining the potential empowerment of the client. To ignore the political, social, and economic context within which the client operates and survives is to risk identifying the source of problems as the client, even when these external variables clearly play at least a contributing role in client problems. In many cases, clients themselves firmly believe that they "caused" their problems. Freire (1971) writes:

> The oppressed are regarded as the pathology of the healthy society, which must therefore adjust these "incompetent and lazy" folk to its own patterns by changing their mentality. These marginals need to be "integrated," "incorporated" into the healthy society that they have "forsaken." (p. 61)

All too often our approaches to problem conceptualization reinforce the notion that difficulties are the client's fault. Beit-Hallahmi (1974) suggested 20 years ago that clients seeing psychologists often wonder, "Is it me or is it the world that has the problem?" He contends, "with few exceptions, psychologists tell them that there is something wrong with them and nothing wrong with the world. We usually ignore the possibility of structural social problems, which in turn cause some of the discomfort in our clients" (p. 125).

The empowering counselor must be prepared to help clients realistically appraise the impact of relevant influences in their lives such as socialization, discrimination, and economic stratification. Further, it is critical to distinguish between responsibility for problems and for taking action to solve problems. To leave the client believing that what the system "did" only the system can or should "undo" would be very disempowering. If the problem is rooted in inadequate educational opportunities or cutbacks in social programs, for example, the client can develop a critical awareness of these systemic factors while exploring alternative behaviors and opportunities for making change, such as participation in grass roots community organizations. In other words, growing awareness of power dynamics must be accompanied by the development of concrete alternatives, or the counseling experience will leave clients feeling even less in control of their lives.

Finally, defining the problem should be a collaborative activity. It is important to validate the subjective experience of the client. Just as the feminist therapist may help a female client to see "that she is not crazy" (Gilbert, 1980, p. 248), so too the empowering counselor helps clients to conceptualize their behavior as a means of coping with their reality. In other words, clients should be viewed *not* as "sick" people in the system, but as people attempting to cope as best they can within a "sick" system.

To illustrate the potential difference in empowering versus disempowering problem conceptualization, imagine the case of a young Hispanic mother who expresses hopelessness and anger at the school for assigning her child to a special education classroom. She believes that her child needs additional language training, not special education. She reports a verbal confrontation with her child's teacher that resulted in her removal from the school grounds. The counselor may view the mother as the problem and focus on helping her to work through denial and accept her child's placement. Alternatively, the counselor and client may explore together how the assessment system, the school structure, and racism are integral parts of the problem. In this case the counselor might affirm the mother's experience and assist her in locating the resources she needs to effect a culturally appropriate evaluation of her child, and at the same time help her to develop more productive ways of expressing her anger at the system. The second approach would be empowering to the client.

Values and Biases

We all have values and biases and we are all influenced by them. Our families, our cultural heritages, our communities, our educational experiences, and our socioeconomic status are among the influences that shape and reshape these values and biases. To say, "I am not influenced by my values in the counseling relationship; I put them aside and focus on the other person," is to deceive oneself. When values and biases are thought to be "under control" or "no longer an issue," they are least likely to be controlled and most likely to be an issue. In the words of Beit-Hallahmi (1974), "It is exactly what we take for granted that most clearly reflects our biases" (p. 124). As counselors we are often embarrassed by the biases and prejudices that confront us in our professional and personal lives. We think we should have grown beyond such thoughts, reactions, or beliefs (Sue & Sue, 1990). It is unfortunate that the vast majority of us have not, and more unfortunate that our embarrassment often keeps us from naming and facing our biases up front.

In addition to examining our overt, personal values, we also must examine the values embedded within the counseling profession. Values are woven so subtly into educational experiences that they are often unnoticed. Traditional counseling theories are based on Euro-American, middle-class, male behavior. As such, the health and development of people of color, members of the lower socioeconomic classes, and girls and women traditionally have been evaluated in contrast to inappropriate standards. Although value-free or value-neutral counseling has been seen as an ideal, the value-laden foundation of our counseling models makes such an endeavor impossible (Sue, 1981). Even the common use of descriptors such as "non-White" conveys the subtle message that Euro Americans are the standard; everyone else is "not *that*." As Katz (1985) argues, "As counseling professionals, we have for too long beguiled ourselves into thinking that the practice of counseling and the data base that underlies the profession are morally, politically, and ethically neutral" (p. 615). Consistent with feminist therapists, Corey and Corey (1991) argue that counselors should not only be aware of their values but should be honest and direct about their values with clients as well. They make a clear distinction between *exposing* and *imposing* counselor values, and acknowledge the harmfulness of the latter.

Many Euro Americans view people of color as having cultures and cultural values while they themselves do not (see, for example, Katz & Ivey, 1977). Katz argues that this is because "White culture is omnipresent. It is so interwoven in the fabric of everyday living that Whites cannot step outside and see their beliefs, values, and behaviors as creating a distinct cultural group" (1985, p. 617). If we cannot make a distinction among our values, the values embedded in the profession, and the values embedded in the wider society in which counseling occurs, we are sure to encounter clients who "just don't want to change"; people who "aren't suited to counseling"; and groups who are "beyond being helped."

Helms (1984; 1990; 1993) proposed a model of White racial identity development to characterize White people's progression from lack of racial awareness to racial consciousness. Although described in the context of Euro Americans' relations with African Americans, the former's identity development may occur in relation to other people of color as well. The most recent version of the model (Helms, 1993) consists of six phases. The positive resolution of each phase leads to more effective cross-cultural relations and better personal adjustment, and the first three phases involve the abandonment of racism. The first phase, *contact*, is characterized by lack of knowledge about Blacks and lack of awareness of one's own Whiteness. The second phase, *disintegration*, is characterized by feelings of guilt and anxiety related to a growing awareness of the injustice experienced by Blacks. People in this phase feel conflicted because they also fear ostracism by other Whites for violating norms governing White-Black behavior. *Reintegration* is characterized by hostility toward Blacks and positive feelings toward Whites.

The final three phases involve the development of a positive White identity. During *pseudoindependence*, positive feelings about Whiteness continue, along with the development of curiosity about Blacks and an intellectualized acceptance of Blacks. *Immersion/emersion* is characterized by attempts to understand what it means to be White, while *autonomy*, the final phase, is characterized by appreciation and acceptance of racial differences and attempts to participate in cross-cultural experiences.

Helms's model provides a framework for Euro American counselors to explore their ethnic identity development. Katz's (1985) articulation of the common Euro American values that form the context in which counseling (and counselor training) largely occurs may also be a useful basis for counselor self-exploration. These values include rugged individualism, nuclear families, competition, independence, Christianity, and future orientation. Sue and Sue (1990) contrast the values and experiences of people of color with cultural and class-bound values typically embedded in counseling. Smith (1991) has proposed an initial theory of minority/majority identity development that incorporates the identity development of Euro Americans and people of color. The integration of these and other perspectives into counselor training curriculum will reduce the likelihood of imposing our values and worldviews on clients.

Finally, each counselor must identify and challenge his or her own biases such as racism, sexism, heterosexism, ageism, and able-bodied assumptions. To the extent that we are ignorant of how these biases influence our attitudes and behaviors, we perpetuate their oppressive influence on the lives of our clients. As biases are explored, brutal honesty may be difficult, because as mental health professionals we are likely to have struggled to "eradicate" these forms of oppression within ourselves. But such honesty is abolutely essential. Counselor biases are addressed again in Part III.

Power Balance in Therapy

No group has done more to articulate the nature and consequences of the power balance in counseling than the proponents of feminist therapy. The power differential between client and counselor in psychotherapy is a recognized source of incongruity for feminist therapists (Douglas, 1985; Gannon, 1982; Gilbert, 1980; Worell & Remer, 1992). Gannon (1982) attributes part of the impetus for developing a feminist therapy to the desire to equalize power in the therapeutic relationship. Consistent with Steinbock's analysis, Gannon notes that traditionally, the therapist is viewed as having all the power. Clients come for counseling because they do not know how to resolve conflicts themselves and need the counselor's "power" to do so. Gannon (1982) argues that one way this power imbalance is maintained is through perpetuation of the myth that therapists are free of personal problems. Minimal self-disclosure hides the humanity and fallibility of the therapist. In addition, many therapists are loath to say to their clients, "I don't know," and will instead give the impression that they *do* know but that the client will have to figure it out independently. Similarly, by presenting a set of questions to the client with an obvious but unknown (to the client) hypothesis in mind, the therapist encourages the client to trust passively in the counselor's own expertise.

Another way counselors maintain the power imbalance is through mystification of the therapeutic process (Gannon, 1982). Three common means of mystification include using psychological jargon, blaming the client for not getting better, and refusing to share knowledge with and educate the client. If the counseling process is "magic," the client has little hope of performing such magic by him or herself. The absence of educational information in counseling not only may foster dependency but also may perpetuate client feelings of being unable to cope with his or her own problems or issues.

Discarding the typical trappings of power, the comfortable pedestal of expertise, is but one aspect of equalizing the power differential in therapy. Clients also must be recognized as experts, as survivors of their circumstances with a wide variety of skills, capacities, experiences, and resources. Joint problem definition, collaborative goal setting, and validation of the client's experience in the world as valid and real further support the client's role as coexpert.

Recall Freire's (1971) distinction between banking education and problem-posing education. In the former, the teacher possesses all the knowledge—and thereby power—while the students are encouraged to be passive consumers of that knowledge. We must invite and encourage clients to challenge and enlarge our perspectives on a continual basis. If we do not view this as an integral component of the client's role in the counseling relationship, we will merely be paying lip service to diminishing the power differential, and this will be clear to our clients. Finally, the power differential in counseling is lessened by incorporating educational strategies and skill building that foster clients' ability to advocate for themselves and others.

Power Analysis

Empowerment requires that clients gain some degree of critical awareness of their life context. Consciousness raising, or facilitating critical awareness of power dynamics at various levels (societal, familial, interpersonal), has long been an important part of feminist therapy process (Hawxhurst & Morrow, 1984). Counselor and client might identify together, for example, how established patterns of family interaction have discouraged the client from practicing assertive behaviors (Thomas, 1985), or how existing stipulations for federal or state assistance have trapped the client into choosing between the indignity of welfare versus a job that pays less than the monthly bills. Understanding the differential influence of socialization on the performance of male/female gender roles (Worell & Remer, 1992) or ethnic majority/minority roles (Thomas, 1985; White & Sedlacek, 1987) also may provide important insight into directing efforts toward effective change. An individual who is aware of how passivity or low self-esteem is being reinforced by institutions and people might direct his or her efforts toward learning to manipulate the environment so that reinforcement for more desirable characteristics is available. For example, a woman with HIV disease might become critically aware of how the medical profession in general and her doctor in particular support a passive patient role. She might find another doctor or join a group for people with HIV to obtain support for her wish to be an active agent in managing her health.

In addition to analysis of the power dynamics, the client's awareness of how his or her own behavior interacts with these dynamics is essential. Counselors can facilitate clients' ability to analyze their own behavior in terms of long- and short-term consequences, adaptivity and maladaptivity, efficiency and inefficiency, relative to the client's ultimate goals rather than to an external standard of behavior. Power analysis, borrowing the words of Freire (1971), involves people developing "their power to perceive critically *the way they exist* in the world *with which* and *in which* they find themselves; they come to see the world not as a static reality, but as a reality in process, in transformation" (emphasis author's) (p. 71).

Community participation is a natural offspring of the client's growing awareness of power dynamics. An empowering counselor will supplement the client's growing awareness with information on community efforts toward changing elements of the system that the client experiences as problematic. These may be grass roots neighborhood efforts, self-help groups, or national organizations. Regardless of scope, they offer the client an external source of support, a means of empowering similar others, and an outlet for newfound knowledge and skills. Analysis of power dynamics, enhancing the clients' critical awareness of their context, and supporting community participation increase the likelihood that clients will participate in transformative action and challenge the status quo. As such, power analysis contributes to empowerment.

CONCLUSION

The counseling process is complex and dynamic. The overt and widely accepted goal of counseling—to help people—is not necessarily the outcome. When counseling enables people to better tolerate a situation that is unjust or abusive, when counseling allows enough release of frustration and tension that the desire to fight an inequality subsides, then counseling is oppressive. Counseling then serves to maintain the status quo and to enable the continued oppression of others.

How do we ensure that our work empowers clients rather than postponing or disabling their efforts to improve their lives? Critical self-examination is the cornerstone of such an endeavor. We must engage in a continual process of reviewing our motives, our values, our actions in light of empowerment. Our professional colleagues will be an invaluable resource in this effort.

The counseling process is most likely to be disempowering when the counselor holds a negative or deterministic view of human nature; there are wide discrepancies between counselor and client power; the client's subjective experience of reality or cultural values is ignored, contradicted, or downplayed; and the problem is defined by the counselor alone and without acknowledgment of the economic, political, and social context within which the client operates. A *non*empowering aspect likely to be shared by many counseling approaches is the lack of direct encouragement for community participation. An underlying belief in basic human potential and in clients' ability to cope with their life problems, collaborative definition of the problem and therapeutic goals, skill enhancement and development, recognition and analysis of systemic power dynamics, and an emphasis on group and community identity are all potentially empowering aspects of counseling. The skills presented in Part II are described in the context of counseling for empowerment.

PART II

EMPOWERING SKILLS AND INTERVENTIONS

The role of skill acquisition in the empowerment process is articulated in Kieffer's (1984) discussion of the development of participatory competence. As noted earlier, Kieffer (1984) describes empowerment as a developmental task culminating in a set of commitments and capabilities he refers to as "participatory competence." Specifically, he defines participatory competence as "the combination of attitudes, understandings, and abilities required to play a conscious and assertive role in the ongoing social construction of one's political environment" (p. 31). Further, participatory competence involves the development of a greater sense of self-competence, a more critical understanding of the surrounding environment, and the cultivation of individual and collective resources for social and political action (Kieffer, 1984). A description of this developmental process appears at the end of Part II.

Skills training is a common component of counseling. Assuming that the counselor has a large repertoire of useful skills, it may be easy to slip into a "banking model" of counseling (Freire, 1971) when the focus is on skill acquisition. In other words, the counselor may be more likely to fall into rigid teacher/expert roles that involve "depositing" skill information into a passive, receptive client. Many clients, and unfortunately some counselors, continue to conceptualize counseling in medical terms: the counselor diagnoses and prescribes, the client obediently swallows the pill. Such an approach is ultimately disempowering.

The process of skill development is most likely to be empowering when a) the counselor and client identify the client's strengths and resources and harness these in the service of developing other skills; b) the counselor and client identify skill-deficit areas relevant to the client's concerns; c) the counselor and client negotiate or otherwise arrive at a mutually agreed upon skill or set of skills that the client would like to learn; d) the counselor and client discuss the implications and potential consequences of acquiring these skills with respect to familial, cultural, social, and other relevant life arenas; e) the client plays an active role in developing these skills and provides ongoing input, suggestions, and feedback to the counselor about the process; and f) the counselor approaches the skill development process as a colearner.

The skills included in the following two chapters should be considered illustrative rather than exhaustive examples of skills that potentially contribute to client empowerment. In Chapter Three, five skill development areas involving intrapersonal processes have been selected for discussion: building self-esteem, fighting irrational beliefs, decision making, increasing self-efficacy, and facilitating creative self-expression. Chapter Four addresses skills that involve interactions with others; the skills included are assertiveness training, leadership skills, setting boundaries, interpersonal communication skills, and public speaking. Because there are many excellent sources of information in the counseling literature, each skill is described only briefly, with suggestions for integrating these skills into the process of counseling for empowerment. Counselors should assess the range, utility, and implementation of skills learned or enhanced during the counseling process as one means of evaluating the extent to which counseling was empowering.

Finally, Smith (1981) noted that counseling people of color should incorporate both survival and change mechanisms; her recommendation is extended here to all clients. Survival skills assist individuals to cope with the environment and control their own behavior in that context; change mechanisms are those that challenge the environment itself and act on it to bring about change. The skills described in the following two chapters sometimes emphasize internal skills (survival mechanisms) and sometimes emphasize internal skills and external dimensions of change (change mechanisms).

Chapter Three
INTRAPERSONAL SKILLS

I am the only one who can tell this story
only I can tell
Maybe you've got your clean and careful categories
but I was there without a sign from the almighty
so leave me be it's not your job it's my story

You got your signs and placards, petitions and clamors
for justice and you march the streets
But under that cold knife I was not marching
I was not sighing for a just land I only longed for
the far far future I am just one woman no
soldier no saint, and all I know is no black
and white proclamation will soothe the past
they may be your laws but it's my story

And I am the only one who can tell this story
Only I can tell
And it's I who live with the past
who knows the circumstance, the portion
of bitter to sweet
so don't try to use me as a case example, a demonstration
of right or wrong 'cause it's not your job it's my story

You say he could've been president
I say hell, he could've been a mutant
But either way you just can't say you'd have
looked twice at my boy
on your shortcut home to the fine life
You'd just drive on by thinking about your job
never knowing my story
my story

E.H.M.

INTRODUCTION

When clients develop or enhance their existing ability to change their cognitions and behaviors, they are often in a better position to effect change in their lives. The skills and interventions described below involve intrapersonal processes that have an impact on the client's interactions with others, their own behaviors, and their feelings about themselves. Each skill requires that clients change and, therefore, each holds the potential for being presented or perceived as client-blaming: "Your difficulties are rooted in your irrational thoughts"; "Your problems stem from the awful things you say to yourself." It is vitally important that counselors understand and address how the client's context contributes to the client's difficulties. When exploring irrational beliefs, for instance, counselors should help clients identify how their family and the larger social environment supported the development of these irrational beliefs. Otherwise clients may view themselves as irrational and as the source of their problems, both of which are fundamentally disabling.

BUILDING SELF-ESTEEM

Self-esteem is a widely studied phenomenon, the subject of countless popular self-help books, and a cornerstone of the practice of counseling. Low self-esteem is something of an epidemic; it has been associated with nearly every malaise known to humans, from alcoholism to xenophobia. Although low self-esteem may not be quite so potent, it is certainly true that the way we feel about ourselves is likely to influence many aspects of our thoughts, feelings, and behaviors.

Working with clients on issues of self-esteem can be empowering in several ways. First, people who feel good about themselves are more willing to be proactive, take risks, and try new behaviors. Second, exploring the sources of low self-esteem offers clients a way to identify the power dynamics at work in their lives. For example, a young woman may discover that her early experiences of criticism and ridicule about her weight are linked with her current susceptibility to mass media messages about what is physically acceptable and unacceptable. The more she understands how external forces influence her internal self-worth, the greater number of choices she has for responding to and diminishing the potency of these forces. Third, human identity is intimately linked with gender, ethnicity, physical appearance, abilities, and so on. The value that I place on my gender, ethnicity, appearance, and abilities will influence my self-esteem. Interventions that enhance self-esteem through fostering pride and knowledge of the history of one's community (e.g., women, African-American men, survivors of incest, and so on) bear directly on the "group identity" aspect of empowerment. Finally, understanding the dynamics of self-esteem enables people to support and enhance the self-esteem of others. People who freely give genuine praise, who recognize the strengths and talents of others, who provide constructive criticism, and who model nondefensive consideration of feedback, provide support for increasing the self-esteem of others around them. In so doing, they are supporting the empowerment of others, another important component of the empowerment process.

There are clear links between self-esteem and childhood experiences, particularly experiences with parents. Some writers describe the internal critic as an echo of messages we received from parents, peers, significant adults, and society while we grew up. McKay and Fanning (1987) suggest that five factors determine the strength of early low self-esteem: a) the degree to which issues of taste, personal needs, safety, or good judgment were mislabeled as moral imperatives (e.g., forgetting your book at school is *terribly* wrong; wanting to wear that outfit is *disgusting*); b) the degree to which parents fail to distinguish between behavior and identity (e.g., you are a *bad child* when you break the rules rather than a good child with bad behavior); c) the frequency of negative messages (e.g., how often the child hears, "you screwed up," "you didn't do it right," "why can't you do things well like your brother?"); d) the consistency of negative messages (e.g., the same behavior that was ignored yesterday is attacked today); and e) the frequency with which negative messages are tied to parental anger or withdrawal (e.g., direct or indirect messages such as, "you did something wrong so I'm not speaking to you," "you aren't worth my time right now," "you're so awful that I'm pretending you aren't here"). In many families, bringing up one's own achievements or making positive self-statements ("I'm really happy about how I did today") is considered boastful and inappropriate. Although often resisted initially, encouragement to make positive self-statements, or affirmations, can help clients create a more nurturing environment for themselves.

Walz and Bleuer's (in press; described in Walz, 1992) comprehensive model for building self-esteem offers one framework for intervention efforts. The model has three dimensions: personal initiatives, life arenas, and intervention strategies. *Personal initiatives* are behaviors contributing to increased self-esteem: appreciate your uniqueness; connect with others; be goal driven; strive to achieve; act courageously; respond with resilience; live your values; value your spirituality; and release your creativity. Within the dominant culture, achievement often is defined as having money and prestige, and to be "goal-driven" means pursuing the goals of money and prestige. Yet these personal initiatives need not be reflective of the dominant culture. "Goal-drivenness" can consist of striving to live in harmony with the environment; "appreciate your uniqueness" can mean appreciating the collective uniqueness of Navajo culture, for example, rather than simply an individual Navajo's personal qualities. Counselors should explore the personal meanings of the personal initiatives with every client rather than making assumptions about the client's values. *Life arenas* consist of education, work, friends, family, physical self, and possessions. Finally, *intervention strategies* consist of affective, behavioral, cognitive, and environmental approaches to increasing self-esteem.

Self-esteem interventions can be designed with this model in mind. Counselors can work with clients to assess self-esteem across relevant life arenas and can identify, within each arena, which personal initiatives or behaviors the client currently enacts and which the client would like to target. Then together they can determine an appropriate intervention approach. To illustrate, the counselor and client may decide to focus on the client's self-esteem in the arena of friends. They might assess personal initiatives in this arena by exploring questions such as, "Do I exercise my creativity with my friends?" "Have I chosen friends with similar values?" "Can I live my values within this group of friends?" "Do I appreciate the ways in which I am unique among my friends and have I chosen friends who appreciate my uniqueness?" A combination of intervention approaches may be selected for enhancing personal initiatives. Behaviorally, the client may work on conversational skills by asking more open-ended questions, by making and maintaining eye contact, and by refraining from interrupting. Cognitive approaches for the friend arena might include learning to identify negative self-talk and fighting irrational beliefs. These approaches may support the initiatives of "connect with others" (by improving relationship skills) and "be goal-driven" (by actively working to increase self-esteem).

Group models of self-esteem intervention can be especially powerful because of the availability of numerous sources of support and feedback. When such an intervention is organized for a particular group, exploration of the collective history of the group is often important. For example, a group for incest survivors might explore society's changing attitudes toward people who reveal a history of abuse; a support group for older adults might discuss the role of organizations such as the American Association of Retired People in advocating for the rights and needs of older members of society. Bowman (1992) describes a self-esteem group for African American high school males. The group met twice a month, once with a speaker (usually African Americans representing a wide range of occupations and life experiences) and once for an activity (ranging from interpersonal process activities to field trips providing contact with some aspect of the African American experience). Bowman reported considerable success with the group, including gains in self-esteem for the group participants.

FIGHTING IRRATIONAL BELIEFS

Ellis (1973) identifies 11 common irrational beliefs in his book, *Humanistic Psychotherapy*. He argues that irrational beliefs are at the core of all human discontent. Some of the irrational beliefs identified by Ellis include: It is a dire necessity to be loved or approved by virtually every significant person in my community; I should be thoroughly competent, adequate, and achieving in all possible respects if I am to consider myself worthwhile; certain people are bad, wicked, or villainous and should be severely blamed and punished; it is awful and catastrophic when things are not the way I would very much like them to be; human unhappiness is externally caused and I have little or no ability to control my sorrows and disturbances; my past history is an all-important determinant of my present behavior, and because something once strongly affected my life, it should indefinitely have a similar effect; there is invariably a right, precise, or perfect solution to human problems and it is quite catastrophic if I cannot find this perfect solution (pp. 152–153).

Keep in mind that these beliefs are considered irrational with respect to degree. For example, there *are* wicked people in the world. Some of the content of our television entertainment (murder, rape, torture) mirrors the actual life experiences of many of this nation's refugees, not to mention the daily violence experienced by many residents of our urban areas. It is not irrational to wish that perpetrators of violence and murder be placed behind bars for the remainder of their lives. This notion becomes irrational when people are so preoccupied with the wickedness and need to punish someone that they devote all of their energy to discussing, contemplating, or attempting to carry out this punishment. To illustrate how irrational beliefs might detract from the empowerment process and how a counselor might respond, consider the following example.

Charlene is a 52-year-old African American woman who has worked in a large office for 14 years. She performs secretarial duties for three managers, each of whom is under a different set of pressures and time lines. Until six months ago, two people were doing the work that Charlene alone is now responsible for, but the office has undergone significant downsizing as a result of the recession. Charlene seeks counseling through the employee assistance program, reporting that she no longer likes her job, dreads coming to work each day, and is becoming so preoccupied with these thoughts that her productivity is decreasing. As she and the counselor discuss her situation, they bring to light the following pieces of information: The managers for whom Charlene works have responded to the downsizing by becoming edgy, impatient, more demanding, and less friendly; the woman who shared Charlene's respon- sibilities before the layoff had become a good friend over the years; and Charlene is very pragmatic, seeing her job primarily as a means of supporting her children, yet she firmly believes that she should make the best of her workday by maintaining a positive attitude and by producing high-quality work. Finally, Charlene is unable to maintain the same quality of work—although it is still quite adequate—since her work load doubled. As a consequence, she feels out of control regarding her attitude, her job performance, and the future of her position.

Charlene and the counselor discover that the decrease in office small talk, smiling, and joking that had occurred is a major source of stress for Charlene. Not only did she feel energized by those informal exchanges, she also interpreted them as approval of herself as a person and as a worker. Because the decrease in friendliness coincided with her inability to commit the same amount of time and attention to her work projects, Charlene had made the internal assumption, "I'm not performing as I *should*, and now the managers don't *like* me as much as they used to, *and this is intolerable.*"

Returning to Ellis's list, it appears that Charlene's integration of the first two irrational beliefs was exacerbating an already difficult work situation. Part of Charlene's performance motivation is associated with being a Black woman working for three White managers; she has a vague but powerful sense that her work must reflect the abilities of *all* African American women, not just her own abilities. She also believes it is her responsibility to maintain a friendly and positive attitude in the work- place. This was not problematic until the downsizing occurred. Then her already high performance standards rose higher (to insure that she herself would not be laid off) and she was faced with a work load that she could not realistically tackle with the same thoroughness and precision. In addition, she was unable to singlehandedly keep the mood of the office positive and friendly. She was feeling like a complete failure. Not until this time of stress did her beliefs become problematic and interfere with her performance.

Ellis's "ABCDE" model outlines the steps in identifying and dealing with irrational beliefs. "A" refers to the activating event. For Charlene this might be a manager dropping a file on her desk, saying "Finish this before you go today; it *has* to get out right away," rushing back into his office without a smile, and slamming the door. "B" refers to the individual's belief about the event—for example, "He must be really angry with me; what didn't I get done on time? He's going to lay me off next. I can't work with people who dislike me!" "C" refers to the consequences or feelings arising from the beliefs about the event, such as anxiety, fear, or anger, and difficulty concentrating. "D" stands for disputing the irrational beliefs about the event. Charlene might dispute her thoughts as follows: "I'm working to the best of my ability; my performance is quite adequate"; "If I get laid off, I'll be in a really difficult situation, but it certainly won't be because I'm not doing my job"; "His mood has nothing to do with me personally; it's how *he* is choosing to deal with his anxiety"; "I don't *like* his recent unfriendliness, but I can protect myself from feeling hurt by it, and maybe even discuss this with him." "E" is the effect or new emotional consequence that results from disputing the belief; in Charlene's case, she may experience a reduction in anxiety, an increased sense of control over her attitude, and a more realistic set of work expectations for herself. Charlene and the counselor also might explore how irrational beliefs influence other aspects of Charlene's life. They may examine the *function* of specific irrational beliefs—for example, if it is essential that I be liked by all people, it is doubtful that I will raise critical issues, stir up controversy, or in any way challenge the status quo. An important component of Charlene's work with her counselor is to identify how racism and the local economic situation contribute to the current office situation and support her beliefs. In addition to showing Charlene how to dispute her beliefs internally, the counselor might help her request and plan an office meeting to discuss the increased tension and ways to diminish it. This aspect of the intervention supports the notion that the problem is systemic and not caused by Charlene, and also represents an active approach to the situation.

The partnership of self-observational skills with confronting irrational beliefs can be very valuable. Kopp (1989) proposes that self-observation skills are a potential source of client empowerment. Specifically, she states:

> self-observation during the assessment phase may be utilized by clients (1) as a source in information about a problem or situation, (2) to gain knowledge about the environmental context of a problem, (3) to increase self-awareness and stimulate insights, and (4) to increase involvement and control. (p. 279)

Clients can use self-observation techniques to identify the frequency and nature of their irrational belief statements and the circumstances more and less likely to produce irrational self-statements.

While fighting irrational beliefs provides clients with an inner resource for dealing with certain cognitive problems, counselors must recognize that Ellis's list of irrational beliefs is specific to the dominant culture. The belief that "it is a dire necessity for an adult to be loved or approved by virtually every significant person in his or her community" takes on a different cast with an individual from a community-oriented culture, for example. Cooperation and interdependence in a collective society are literally vital to survival; misapplication of Ellis's approach could lead to trivialization of the client's value system. Further, a review of Ellis's work quickly reveals an aggressive, direct, and highly verbal style that may be ineffective, inappropriate, and off-putting to clients. The highly directive nature of this approach is a potentially disempowering means to achieving the goal of greater internal control over moods and reactions. The counselor's role is that of expert, "namer of the irrational," while the client's role is initially that of naive learner of what is irrational. The experienced counselor will consider carefully the appropriateness of this technique and modify its implementation freely.

DECISION MAKING

Many models of decision making are described in the counseling literature. When clients indicate that attention to decision-making strategies may be of value, counselors must consider their own assumptions and biases regarding decision making. For example, does the counselor believe at heart that rational methods of decision making are superior to intuitive methods? Given the value placed on rationality in the dominant culture, such a bias would not be unusual. It is important to respect the role that omens, dreams, and inner voices play in some people's decision-making strategies. At the same time, components of rational decision-making models, such as information gathering, can be integrated with other intuitive strategies. The counselor should keep in mind that "you've got to go this alone" and "decide what's best for *you*, not everyone else" are slogans of the dominant culture. Following the counsel and approval of others is an entirely valid approach to decision making. Find out whose advice is valued by the client: parents; extended family members; ministers, priests, rabbis, or other spiritual leaders; political or community leaders; friends; spouses or partners; children; or mentors.

Often it is helpful to evaluate the client's current decision-making strategies. How satisfied is the client with previous decisions? What outcomes have been achieved using these strategies? What are the strengths and weaknesses of these strategies? How can the client's decision making be enhanced for better outcomes? It may be helpful to explore and validate the client's experience of the power to actually *make* decisions. Perceptions of powerlessness do not always coincide with a lack of power.

Power analysis has been described already as a vital component of empowerment. In the context of decision making, it will be quite important to explore how the client's decisions have been influenced by environmental and contextual factors. Specifically, how have family circumstances; family members; work issues; the community; and cultural, political, and economic factors influenced the client's decisions? Look for links between irrational beliefs and decision making. For example, Scott is in the process of deciding whether to "come out" to his family. He has not come out to his family yet because he fears he will be rejected. Without underestimating the risk and the emotional consequences of rejection by the family, a counselor could explore the influence of irrational beliefs in his decision. Specifically, they might consider together whether Scott continues to draw upon the emotional support of his family as he did in the past, whether he is strong enough to support himself if he is indeed rejected, and whether he feels bound to hide his sexual orientation from his family forever simply because he has done so in the past. A power analysis in this situation would involve identifying the influences on Scott's decisions. Once these are identified, Scott is in a better position to make an active choice to come out or to remain silent on this issue, rather than feeling forced to remain silent. He can assess concretely the likelihood and the nature of being rejected. Then he can say, "If I tell my parents that I'm gay, there's about a 50% chance that they would break off communication with me for at least six months. This would be quite painful, but not impossible to live with. They would probably reach out to me again eventually, although our relationship would never be the same. I would really miss our old relationship, and although losing it wouldn't kill me, I don't think I'm ready to give it up right now. So I won't tell my parents for now; in one year I'll re-evaluate this decision." The difference between this statement and his former, "I just can't tell them, it's impossible" is enormous, even though the actual decision is the same.

The example below illustrates the difficulty of working on decision making while being respectful of culture.

Guadalupe was the 33-year-old mother of seven children, ranging in age from three months to 14 years. She and her husband Gerardo were Mexican citizens, and had resided in the United States without legal status for five years. They were living in a rented one-bedroom house with dirt floors, barely surviving on Gerardo's yearly income of $4,000. Their 15-month-old daughter, Araceli, was born with spina bifida, a condition resulting in lower body paralysis. Guadalupe had recently heard that a child with spina bifida had been healed through prayer and was now walking. As a result, she decided to bring Araceli to the shrine of la Virgen de Guadalupe *in Mexico City, in hopes of a miracle. People had traveled to the shrine for over a century, asking that their prayers be answered by* la Virgen, *the patroness of Mexico. Guadalupe was convinced that the merciful* Virgen *would provide a cure for Araceli.*

The counselor/home educator was working with the family in their home to enhance Araceli's social, cognitive, and physical development. The dilemma was this: The family had no resources to support such a trip; Guadalupe was planning to walk to the border and hitch rides from there, just as she had originally come to the United States. She was planning to carry Araceli and her 3-month-old child, as well as their supplies. For the return trip, she hoped to get enough money from family members in Mexico to pay for a coyote *(a person hired to smuggle people across the border). She believed Araceli would be walking by then, so the trip back would be easier. The counselor saw her task as one of respecting and supporting Guadalupe's deep faith while encouraging her to consider the implications of such a trip. There were multiple problems. Gerardo had been picked up by immigration once and deported without a chance to let the family know what had happened; if this occurred while Guadalupe was gone, the rest of the children would be essentially alone. The sheer physical demands of walking to the border—a four-hour journey through the desert by car, with two heavy children and supplies—were incredible, to say nothing of the thousands of miles between the border and Mexico City. Guadalupe would be exposing herself and her children to very real physical danger.*

The counselor drew upon her knowledge of the history of la Virgen de Guadalupe *to convey understanding of and respect for Guadalupe's devotion. Rather than directly pointing out the difficulties of the trip, the counselor engaged Guadalupe in storytelling about her original trip to the United States with her husband, her brother, and three of her children, as well as stories of other people's personal experiences at the shrine. They contemplated together the compassion of* la Virgen, *and her deep love for the poor of Mexico. The counselor then explored how devotion to* la Virgen *was expressed by those living in the United States. Ultimately, Guadalupe concluded that her prayers would be heard by* la Virgen *wherever she was, and she began planning for a special appeal for her daughter from home. Thus, the common rational decision-making step, "consider the consequences of each potential alternative," was implemented in the form of storytelling. Guadalupe's faith was respected, and the well-being of her family was preserved.*

INCREASING SELF-EFFICACY EXPECTATIONS

Self-efficacy expectations are defined by Bandura (1977a; 1982) as beliefs about one's ability to perform a specific task or behavior successfully. If Tomas perceives himself to be an excellent driver, he has high self-efficacy for driving a car. Self-efficacy expectations are not necessarily accurate; that is, in spite of Tomas's high self-efficacy expectations, he actually may have a tendency to cut corners too closely, tailgate, and drive carelessly. Likewise, individuals sometimes have low self-efficacy for tasks they are quite capable of doing.

Self-efficacy expectations influence decisions about whether to attempt particular behaviors and how long to persist in those behaviors. If I have the impression that I am musically talented, I might be willing to try learning a new instrument; further, if my initial efforts yield poor results, I might continue working with this instrument until I have achieved satisfactory progress. In contrast, if I perceive myself to be bereft of musical ability, I am unlikely to attempt to play an instrument, but if I do, I will probably see initial difficulty as evidence of my lack of skills and give up early in the effort.

Clearly, self-efficacy expectations have implications for empowerment. The acquisition of new skills and the performance of new behaviors cannot happen unless a person is willing to try them. As suggested above, low self-efficacy for skills identified as important to an individual's empowerment process may prevent the person from taking the first step. For example, suppose Stephan has been asked to speak to a group of local businesspersons at their annual conference. As an active member of the gay community, he has been identified as an educational resource for this group. Stephan believes that many other people would have been better suited to this task; he dislikes public speaking and avoids doing so at all costs. His low self-efficacy for public speaking might keep him from accepting this opportunity; he may, however, have the potential to be an excellent public spokesperson. This same example can be used to illustrate the difference between self-efficacy expectations and *outcome expectations*. *Outcome expectations* are beliefs about the consequences of a certain behavior. Stephan may believe that such a speech would result in the achievement of a greater degree of acceptance and respect for gay and lesbian employees; he may believe that it would have no effect whatsoever, or that it would heighten homophobia among the small business owners. Thus, outcome expectations also influence decisions about whether to attempt a behavior and how long to persist in that behavior.

Self-efficacy expectations are based on four primary sources of information: a) performance attainments; b) vicarious experiences; c) verbal persuasion; and d) physiological state (Bandura, 1982). Performance attainments refer to the direct experience of personal success at a given task. Reaching the top of the cliff, receiving an acceptance letter from a literary magazine, and fixing a broken radio are performance attainments that might raise self-efficacy for cliff climbing, poetry publishing, and radio repair, respectively. Performance attainments are the most powerful source of information for self-efficacy expectations. Individuals also base self-efficacy expectations on vicarious experiences. Watching others perform a behavior or complete a task often convinces us that we could—or could not possibly—do the same. Verbal persuasion, or the feedback received by other people, serves as another basis for self-efficacy expectations. An individual may be told frequently, for example, that she would be a good community organizer because of her people skills, enthusiasm, and dedication to community issues. Even if she has never served in this capacity, this feedback could influence her perceptions of her ability to do so. Finally, an individual's physiological state may contribute to self-efficacy expectations. A concerned father might not go to the principal on his child's behalf if he interprets his pounding heart, sweating palms, and other signs of anxiety as evidence of his inability to talk to people in positions of authority.

When low self-efficacy expectations hinder an individual's empowerment process, performance attainments, vicarious experiences, verbal persuasion, and physiological states can be used to increase self-efficacy. If Lilia doesn't see herself as ready to move from student-teacher to teacher, her self-efficacy for running her own classroom might be enhanced through the following: observations of experienced and first-year teachers; review of her student-teacher evaluations; discussion of the teaching skills required for success and how she performed these skills as a student-teacher and in other relevant arenas; soliciting feedback (encouragement) from her fellow student-teachers, her teachers, and her students; and relaxation/imagery training. When past performance attainments are not applicable to the target behavior, counselor and client can set up a series of "experiments" in which aspects of the behavior are tried out and evaluated.

IMAGERY TRAINING

The use of imagery in counseling is not uncommon. Imagery training has been used with a wide range of problems. For example, Wynd (1990) used guided imagery as an intervention with smokers. Specifically, adult smokers were taught guided power imagery—drawing on an image of themselves acting powerful and confident in the past—or relaxation imagery—drawing on peaceful and pleasant scenes. After training, participants in the guided power imagery conditions felt more powerful and in control of their lives than participants in the relaxation imagery or the control conditions, and participants in both imagery groups were smoking significantly fewer cigarettes than control group members. I have used imagery successfully in the treatment of depression, fear related to being a hostage in an armed robbery, recurrent nightmares, and recovery from childhood sexual abuse. Imagery training—that is, teaching clients how to use imagery to achieve various goals—provides clients with a lifelong tool and a very potent resource.

One advantage of imagery training is that it is not simply effective with highly verbal and educated clients; nor is it bound by the cultural constraints of some other techniques. Because clients provide the information used in the imagery work, it is less likely to violate cultural norms. Imagery work can be structured or unstructured, and is ideally suited for clients who have a tendency to "talk in pictures," clients who naturally use metaphors and analogies to communicate their ideas and experiences. Among the most potent are imagery experiences that link people with their inner resources, their inner wisdom and strength. It also can be used to link people with a spiritual mentor, an important historical figure, or some other external source of power.

Consider an example. A 21-year-old African American woman initiated counseling to deal with her depression. Marla was extremely frustrated with student apathy on her college campus, and was feeling very far from home and disconnected. During the third session, the counselor led her through a semistructured imagery exercise. Beginning with progressive muscle relaxation (alternately tensing and relaxing the body's main muscle groups from toes to forehead, releasing tension and leading to a relaxed state) (Wolpe, 1958), the counselor then "led" Marla into an encounter with one of Marla's heroes, Harriet Tubman. On bringing the women together, the counselor simply suggested that the two of them would have a conversation. After several minutes, Marla sighed and grinned. The counselor slowly drew her back into a state of normal alertness. Marla described her encounter with excitement:

> I sat down next to her because I wanted her to hold me and maybe even rub my head. Instead, she told me to "Quit your sorry-assed whining." She held my hand and I felt this tremendous energy and impatience and power. She told me I had a lot of work to do, and it wouldn't be easy, but she would be there for me. I can still feel the grip of her hand.

The counselor could not have directed such a powerful encounter, and would not have predicted that Marla would react so positively to being "scolded." Semistructured exercises give clients the control to create a positive experience for themselves. Marla was encouraged to repeat this imagery exercise outside of counseling sessions at least once a week.

Imagery training facilitates empowerment because the client is in control of what happens and can initiate this strategy at will. Imagery training can be effective regardless of a person's "stage" in counseling, and the degree of structure is easily modified for consistency with the client's needs. For example, a very structured approach was used with one client after she had been held hostage in a robbery (McWhirter & Linzer, in press). After progressive muscle relaxation, the client was slowly brought into an encounter with the assailant, who had worn a mask throughout the actual event. The client practiced deep breathing and used a physical gesture to signal when her fears were becoming overwhelming. The client was "given" the strength to overpower the assailant if needed. Ultimately, at the counselor's suggestion, the client lifted the mask from the assailant's head, revealing the face of a frightened, spoiled little boy who wanted to impose his own way. Again at the counselor's suggestion, the client lifted this boy into the air, allowing his feet to dangle helplessly, and then heaved him over a cliff. The structured nature of this exercise provided direction and ideas for the client. The client used this same exercise with her own modifications when she felt overwhelmed with fear resulting from the incident.

Clients who experience difficulty returning from imagery exercises may need extensive work to anchor themselves in the present before conducting these exercises on their own. For example, the counselor might establish an imagery pattern of the client tying a safety rope around his or her waist, and using this rope to guide the way back as needed. When the client has experienced smooth returns in the presence of the counselor, experiments with imagery outside the session might be undertaken. Imagery work may be inappropriate in some cases however; the counselor must assess carefully the client's ability to benefit from imagery work prior to initiating such activity.

CREATIVE SELF-EXPRESSION

Much of what we struggle with and celebrate as human beings is intangible and difficult to articulate. There is a certain isolation inherent in experiencing an event, a process, or a lifetime, because we can never fully share its depth, richness, and intensity. To choreograph a dance that captures some aspect of a personal experience is to bridge that isolation, to link the world of feelings with the world of visible action.

The isolation attached to negative experiences is all the more potent because it compounds the negativity of the experience. People often turn the negativity of an experience inward. Sometimes capturing a painful experience with words, paint, or movement has the effect of diminishing this potency. It transfers power to the creator, as the creator acts on the experience and transforms it in some tangible way. The person is no longer victim to the feeling or the memory but a participant in the drama of the event with the power to change it. *Naming the devil* refers to identifying the source of one's troubles. To voice anger through a poem means that I am giving shape to that anger, clarifying what it is, legitimizing its existence, and opening up the possibility that others might understand and share this anger through reading the poem. Each of these elements has the potential to heal. The creative arts provide a vast array of tools with which to name, and exorcise, the "devil."

The use of art for therapeutic purposes is practiced formally by art therapists, and a growing number of counselors and psychologists are exploring this modality (Mahoney, 1991; Vernon, 1991). Art can facilitate the discovery of one's voice, the exploration of power dynamics, and the search for and celebration of group identity. Creative self-expression can be a proclamation of who *I* am or who *we* are. *Who I am* may be represented by where I have been, where I am going, where I am now; how I feel or felt; how I view the world; where I feel safe; what I do; what I have experienced; what I have to offer; my source of power; and my hopes. *Who we are* may refer to me and my children, spouse, partner, family, or extended family; members of my ethnic group; my social class; we who were children during the Great Depression; we who are political refugees; or my neighborhood. The activities of creative self-expression may involve song, musical instruments, poetry, journal writing, dance, movement, painting, drawing, weaving, work with clay or fabric or wood, storytelling, dramatic interpretation, or playwriting. And creative self-expression may help to establish any of the following: I *exist*; I exist as a physical, spiritual, emotional entity in the world; my feelings exist and are legitimate; my experiences are a part of me; I have rights; I have a great deal to say; I am powerful; I am valuable; I am insightful; we have a common history; we are a beautiful people; we are a rich resource; we are survivors of oppression; we are strong; we are human beings; we have dignity; we have a voice.

In addition to writing or expressing one's own thoughts, the creative works of others may be used in the empowerment process. One of the primary benefits of reading literature is to recognize that one is not alone—that others have faced and surmounted similar difficulties. Autobiographies such as Maya Angelou's *I Know Why the Caged Bird Sings* offer powerful testament to the struggles and pain of life as well as the possibility of overcoming tremendous barriers. Hobus (1992) provides an excellent description of the use of literature such as poetry, stories, and journals in the empowerment of people with chronic illnesses. In the following paragraphs, Peggy shares how one form of creative expression facilitated her personal journey of self-discovery.

> My mother used to stand in the kitchen and iron and dream, the radio taking precedence over my four-year-old chatter. I don't remember

talking to her, but I do remember not talking because she was listening to the radio. She tells me about a time when I used to recite entire commercials, and I still know the words to country-western songs from 40 years ago. I love those old songs, too. I feel comfortable with them. It must have been a happy time for me.

But somehow in my short life I had learned that my own thoughts and ideas were of little worth, whereas those of others, even coming from me, were important enough for listening.

My sister was two and a half when this noisy, mother-demanding little intruder came along, so I wasn't very popular with her. And she was not shy about showing me how she felt. She had a frown of disapproval which had a powerful effect on me, and which I still see on her face, even though it probably hasn't been there for years.

By the time I was five I knew I was "less than" other people.

The kids in the neighborhood and at school used to tease me and I would cry. I never recognized that my misery had to do with choices I was making, even though my mother used to tell me to "ignore them." How could I ignore three or four people in my face distorting my name into ugly phrases and making fun of my looks, my clothing?

At some point between the ages of six and 10 I began to protect myself from the world by building strong, thick walls around my fragile little self, and with each layer of brick, I moved further inside. By the time I was 18, when I graduated from high school and went away to college, I was safe. And hopelessly imprisoned.

I had a few friends, growing up in my small hometown, so I really had never had to make any. Also I had my family. When I got to college, not only did I not have or know how to make any friends, but I was too timid and self-centered to attempt communication with instructors or advisors or anyone. I was sure they would scorn me as not worth their time. These people reinforced my low self-worth with their busy-ness and matter-of-fact attitudes, and with the grades I received. I knew this was my fault because I was not very bright and didn't put much effort into anything. I knew a lot about fault. And it was mostly mine.

My sister was a senior at the same college, and excelling at everything she attempted. To avoid continuing an 18-year tradition of living in her shadow, I went even further into myself. I refused to pledge her sorority or to have much to do with her friends, even thought I desperately needed friends. I was sure they were just being nice because Pat was my sister.

Thus I spent the worst two years of my life.

Then I quit school and worked for two years, while living at home. During this time I grew not at all and felt only slightly better about me.

Finally I gathered all of my strength (I now call it "power") and moved myself 1,500 miles to a new state and a new life and, miraculously, let someone into my world.

Until then—all of the many years of those walls—I wanted people in my life, but I always managed to shut them out—keep them away with the knowledge that they weren't really interested in me and that I wasn't worth it anyway.

But Jerry got in and we settled into 20 years of marriage and children and college and me becoming a teacher. And not growing up. We had each other. I had him and the children, Chris first, then three years later, Celeste, and they became my esteem. Other-esteem. Better than no esteem at all, right?

I didn't realize until the last year of my marriage that I still had no opinions. I had built up layers of other people's from reading and listening, but no confidence to venture into any of my own. I had *lived* inside of myself most of my life, but had never *looked* inside.

Then one day in 1986 at my very first 12-step meeting I needed an opinion. I had to respond and I didn't know terms and phrases in this new territory, so I couldn't fake it. I also didn't know anyone whose words I could borrow for the occasion. I realized I had to look inside and find my own. I also realized at that moment that I was terrified of looking inside and finding no one there.

But there was someone there. I was there. I was pretty deeply buried, and shaky at best, when the exhumation began, and I still had very little awareness of me. Yet, I poked and prodded until there was a stirring inside of me, a baby flame. I alternately nurtured and starved, and often ignored it, but my spirit seemed to grow in power in spite of my neglect.

It was that tiny knowledge of me that saved me a year later when my husband and I separated, and I truly hit bottom.

And somewhere around this point I began to write.

I wrote on the backs of envelopes and in the remnants of old college spiral notebooks. I wrote in a kind of prose and a kind of poetry. I wrote the anger and the pain:

> As I heal
> some pieces of US
> heal inside
> and remain
> forever
> a part of me.
> Some
> heal outside
> and are lost.

I wrote first at my husband, then later ventured into a wide range of hurts and wants. I bought a journal. (It took many months to convince myself that I was worth the $10.)

I took a class called "Writing and Being" at the university. I began to write me, and as I wrote I discovered me. I wrote about my relationships. About Mom and Dad and my sisters and growing up. I wrote about the torment and the unhappiness. I wrote about, and remembered, the good times and the closeness and the love.

I published every week in that class, and read aloud. I listened to other people who were in similar places, and to people who were in vastly different places, and I grew. The awareness of the chasmic void in my life has created a need to fill it, and writing has given me the tools to do that.

Writing has helped find in me the power that I buried with my "little girl" behind those high walls all those years ago. It's helped me to see more expansively both into myself and as I look outward. It is giving me back my soul.

From finger painting to dancing, journal writing to weaving, creative self-expression is a tremendous source of self-validation in which all people can participate: artistic "ability" is neither a prerequisite nor a guaranteed asset. The production of creative works is not intended to please anyone but the creator.

CONCLUSION

Building self-esteem, fighting irrational beliefs, enhancing decision-making skills, imagery training, and creative self-expression are intrapersonal skills that can facilitate the empowerment process in counseling. As each of these skills involves changes in behavior, counselors may wish to stress that a focus on personal change does not imply that clients are solely responsible for difficulties they are experiencing. The development of these skills is amenable to individual and group modalities. In Part III specific applications of these skills are described.

Chapter Four
INTERPERSONAL SKILLS

---

i used to cower in corners at that look,
that oughta-smack-you edge, that gesture
i used to wear curtains and umbrellas and
skitter away from mice
but now i name the devil
cross streets sleeveless
dance in my livingroom

i used to cry weightless tears at that stare,
that you-trash-don't-have-the-deposit yawn
i used to pray for mercy and luck and
kind faces, low rent, no mice
but now we name the devil
we pray for strength alone
my tears are bricks
we collect and pile
into houses

E.H.M.

INTRODUCTION

Setting boundaries, assertiveness, leadership skills, communication skills, and public speaking are interpersonal skills that can contribute to the process of empowerment. Specifically, learning and exercising these skills can facilitate an individual's efforts toward greater self-direction, an increased sense of competency and mastery, and greater effectiveness in communicating, relating to, and working with others. A description of each of these skills is provided in this chapter.

SETTING BOUNDARIES

The ability to set boundaries often is described as an essential ingredient in intimate relationships and a valuable skill in all interpersonal relationships. In *The Dance of Intimacy*, Lerner (1989) suggests that intimacy means we can "be who we are in a relationship, and allow others to do the same" (p. 3). Further, she describes the goal of enhancing intimacy in relationships as "to have relationships with both men and women that do not operate at the expense of the self, and to have a self that does not operate at the expense of the other" (p. 4). It is important to note the underlying Euro American values embedded in the concepts of setting boundaries and in Lerner's definition of intimacy. There is a clear element of individualism in these concepts that may conflict with a sense of self that is drawn primarily from the family or the community. Nevertheless, some degree of boundary setting between self and others is probably always necessary for "psychological health" across all cultures; the nature and extent of culturally appropriate boundary setting, however, will vary greatly. Author Amy Tan beautifully and realistically illustrates the complexity of boundary setting within relationships between Chinese mothers and their Chinese-American daughters in *The Joy Luck Club* and *The Kitchen God's Wife*. For example:

> Every night after dinner, my mother and I would sit at the Formica kitchen table. She would present new tests, taking her examples from stories of amazing children she had read in *Ripley's Believe It or Not*, or *Good Housekeeping, Reader's Digest*, and a dozen other magazines she kept in a pile in our bathroom....
>
> And after seeing my mother's disappointed face once again, something inside of me began to die. I hated the tests, the raised hopes and failed expectations. Before going to bed that night, I looked in the mirror above the bathroom sink and when I saw only my face staring back—and that it would always be this ordinary face—I began to cry. Such a sad, ugly girl! I made high-pitched noises like a crazed animal, trying to scratch out the face in the mirror.
>
> And then I saw what seemed to be the prodigy side of me—because I had never seen that face before. I looked at my reflection, blinking so I could see more clearly. The girl staring back at me was angry, powerful. This girl and I were the same. I had new thoughts, willful thoughts, or rather thoughts filled with lots of won'ts. I won't let her change me, I promised myself. I won't be what I'm not.
>
> So now on nights when my mother presented her tests, I performed listlessly, my head propped on one arm. I pretended to be bored. And I was. I got so bored I started counting the bellows of the foghorns out on the bay while my mother drilled me in other areas. The sound was comforting and reminded me of the cow jumping over the moon. And the next day, I played a game with myself, seeing if my mother would give up on me

before eight bellows. After a while I usually counted only one, maybe two bellows at most. At last she was beginning to give up hope. (Tan, 1989, pp. 143–144)

In a society based on community values rather than individualism, some forms of boundary setting might be obsolete; the distinction between self and others might be "protected" by cultural norms in such a way as to render efforts to preserve this distinction crude and unnecessary. But boundary setting also applies to setting boundaries between the family and the dominant culture. In the United States, the influence of the dominant culture is pervasive and often destructive of other cultural values and practices. Counselors may find boundary-setting skills to be a valuable component of counseling across a variety of situations.

At an interpersonal level, setting boundaries enables people to define themselves as unique and worthy of respect, and helps to prevent the powerless position implied in such common statements as, "You *made* me feel that way" (someone else controls the speaker's feelings); "Well I guess if I have to, I'll go ahead and cover for you again, but I don't like it" (someone else controls the speaker's actions); and "You're always doing that to me!" (the speaker is a helpless victim of the other's actions). On a larger level, setting boundaries can serve as a vehicle for fostering respect and helping to mobilize community responses to some violation of boundaries. For example, residents of a neighborhood might organize a march to let the community know that they "have had enough," and are taking an active approach to reducing the crime rate in their area. The following recommendations are drawn from Beattie (1989) and elaborated with examples. Consider each recommendation as applicable to interpersonal relationships and societal issues.

1. Boundaries or limits should be set clearly, without anger, rationalizing, or apologizing. For example, "I don't want you going into my room when I'm not around; if you can't respect my request, I'm going to find another housemate, because this isn't acceptable to me."
2. Setting a boundary and simultaneously taking care of another person's feelings are mutually exclusive acts. For example, if Roger asks his wife for 20 minutes of alone time after work each day, no matter how carefully he asks, he must risk hurting her feelings; he cannot *prevent* her from feeling rejected.
3. It is important to set boundaries even when feelings of shame, rejection, or fear result; people use people they can use, and respect people they can't use. Everyone benefits from healthy limits. For example, Jackson suspects that the overly personal

questions of his live-in attendant are related to the attendant's confusing Jackson's need for intimate physical care with emotional neediness. Although the attendant is initially "cold" after Jackson stops answering her questions, she becomes more respectful of his privacy and eventually returns to a more professional degree of warmth.

4. Anger, rage, complaining, and whining are clues to boundaries being violated; so are feelings of being threatened, "suffocated," or victimized by someone. For example, Angela now recognizes that whenever she has the urge to really SCREAM at her children, she is usually also feeling overwhelmed by their demands on her.

5. Expect boundaries to be tested and be ready to reinforce them. For example, once John understands that "children are *programmed* to test rules," he stops interpreting his son's rebellion as a sign of bad parenting decisions. His increasing calm and refusal to back down in the face of boundary testing results in fewer challenges to the family rules.

6. When setting boundaries affects a family or other social system, people may react with anger. For example, when Gloria decides to spend the holiday with members of her Asian American community instead of with members of her lesbian community, her lesbian friends become upset with her, arguing that she shouldn't go, since she isn't "out" there and that she is "more White than Asian."

7. Members of a support system can provide feedback about boundary-setting efforts and can be a source of encouragement. For example, although Trini's mother doesn't approve of her gang membership, they work out a system in which Trini's mother provides support and assistance in setting limits with her "sisters" regarding school attendance.

8. Boundary setting also includes identifying what one likes, what feels good, and what brings pleasure. For example, Dave remarks in wonder, "It never *occurred* to me that I might have a different opinion from my father; once I figured out that it was OK to have new ideas, and even to voice them, I started to take a renewed interest in the business and my old enthusiasm eventually came back."

We can facilitate our clients' efforts to set boundaries by helping them identify when and how their boundaries are being violated, clarifying the relative importance of various boundaries, and discovering ways to establish and maintain healthy and satisfying boundaries. Sharing personally helpful strategies, role-playing situations in which the client sets boundaries, and discussing the possible consequences in advance are likely to be helpful. One thing is certain: As soon as we begin to define "healthy, satisfying boundaries" *for* instead of *with* our clients, we become a part of the problem.

ASSERTIVENESS TRAINING

Just as empowerment is the buzzword of the '90s, assertiveness training achieved common household status in the 1970s, and has been with us ever since. Assertiveness training is founded on the idea that all individuals have certain interpersonal rights, including to be treated with respect, to have and express feelings and opinions, to be listened to and taken seriously, to say no without guilt, to ask for information from professionals, to make mistakes, and to choose not to be assertive. Numerous popular self-help books on assertiveness are available, including the still timely *The New Assertive Woman* by Bloom, Coburn, and Pearlman (1975).

Important aspects of assertiveness training generally include learning to understand the differences among assertiveness, nonassertiveness, and aggressiveness; becoming aware of human rights and how they apply to interpersonal situations; developing sensitivity to the rights and feelings of others; becoming aware of how one's own behavior might contribute to dissatisfaction with relationships; recognizing that one can learn *and* unlearn behavior; taking responsibility for one's behavior; and learning to express thoughts and feelings in honest and direct ways. Components of assertiveness training usually include expressing positive and negative feelings; the ability to initiate, continue, and terminate general conversations; and setting boundaries.

Although primarily developed by Euro Americans, the objectives of assertiveness training are not necessarily Eurocentric. For example, Victor, a Chinese American office supervisor, finds it difficult to extricate himself from uninteresting and time-consuming conversations at work. He perceives his coworkers to be wasting time—his as well as their own—yet he has a strong desire to be sensitive to the personal issues they discuss. He feels extra pressure because his next performance review is coming up, and he has been criticized in the past both for being too impersonal and for not completing work fast enough. Victor's growing frustration might be addressed via assertiveness training. Specifically, he might be assisted in developing a variety of statements that express concern but clearly end his participation in the conversation and free him to return to his work. These statements might include various forms of indirect and direct encouragement to his coworkers to resume working as well. Victor contributes to the development of these statements and experiments to identify those that he is most comfortable employing. The situational specificity of assertive behavior is acknowledged—that is, the counselor recognizes that generalization of these skills to Victor's relationship with his parents, for example, may be unlikely, unwarranted, and/or inappropriate. Sue and Sue (1991) describe guidelines for conducting an assertiveness training group with Chinese American participants. Among other issues, they note the importance of addressing the contributions of both culture and racism to nonassertive behavior. Briefly, they suggest that participants explore how nonassertive behaviors are consistent with traditional Chinese cultural values such as filial piety, and how subtle and overt messages from the dominant culture reinforce nonassertive behaviors among people of color. Such a discussion incorporates critical awareness of power dynamics and also helps participants clarify valued aspects of Chinese and Western cultures.

Although assertiveness skills may be useful to members of a variety of ethnic groups, counselors must tailor training in accord with each client's culture. Direct eye contact is a nonverbal behavior promoted in much of the assertiveness literature. However, direct eye contact is considered disrespectful and intrusive among many Native American tribes. This does not mean that counselors working with Native Americans should presume that this component of training is inappropriate. Rather, the issue of eye contact may serve to stimulate discussion between counselor and client of this and other cross-cultural behavioral differences. A client may well find that direct eye contact and strong vocal intonation are very helpful in specific situations, such as in conversations with medical staff. It is absolutely critical that counselors recognize their own biases when working with clients on assertiveness training. The message that direct eye contact is a *superior* rather than a *possibly useful* alternative will reach the client, be it ever so subtle. The overt statement of values used by many feminist therapists may be useful here. For example, a Euro American counselor may say, "Because of my cultural background, looking directly at people seems comfortable and natural to me, and I sometimes find myself thinking it's actually better for everybody. That's a weakness of mine, and I'll try not to impose this bias on you."

Enns (1993) notes that feminists have criticized assertiveness training because it implies that the behaviors associated with men and male success are the standard to which people should adhere to be healthy. Further, when clients are encouraged to change or develop new skills, attention potentially is turned away from the fundamental need for societal transformation. Enns recommends that assertiveness training be accompanied by consciousness-raising (including a critique of the assumptions of assertiveness training) and self-esteem-building techniques. These recommendations are consistent with the notion advanced here: empowerment involves critical analysis of power dynamics, community participation, and action in addition to simple skills development.

LEADERSHIP TRAINING

If one is to draw conclusions from traditional textbooks, leadership in the United States has historically been the privilege of Euro American males. Only in recent years has headway been made in formally recognizing the effective and productive leadership of women and people of color. Furthermore, similar to power (as discussed in Chapter One), leadership is understood most popularly as an authoritarian, hierarchical relationship between one who dictates (along a continuum from "humanely" to "inhumanely") and those who follow. Such a conceptualization of leadership logically excludes women and people of color, who have not had the social or political power *to* dictate.

Astin (1989) describes leadership as a creative process, suggesting that "leadership manifests itself when there is a goal or action intended to bring about change in an organization, an institution, the social system; a change that would improve people's lives" (p. 4). She further describes the leader as "someone who by virtue of her position or opportunity empowers others to collective action toward accomplishing [a common] goal or vision" (p. 9). Her perspective is consistent with feminist perspectives of leadership: Leaders are people who share power with others rather than wield power over others. This nonhierarchical view of leadership is at odds with much of the dominant culture, as well as with the norms of many ethnic minority cultural groups. For example, the previously noted Confucian value of filial piety, embraced by many Korean and Chinese Americans, emphasizes the importance of distinctly hierarchical relationships for the maintenance of harmony. The father, leader of the family, is expected to be authoritative and strict (Lee & Cynn, 1991); "sharing the power" could be seen as a failure to fulfill familial obligations.

Astin (1989) noted four key behaviors involved in empowering leadership: a) meeting people on their own turf and listening; b) hiring strong people, allowing them to point out mistakes, and being nondefensive; c) providing feedback, credit, and visibility to coworkers; and d) consulting frequently and using consensus (p. 14). Modeling, role-playing, and providing constructive feedback will help clients develop specific skills. For example, counselors can model leadership skills such as reflective listening ("So you're not just frustrated with the situation; it also sounds like you're afraid I won't respond to those frustrations"); being nondefensive in both tone and words ("How else would you like to see me respond to these issues?"); providing feedback ("I think you stated your position very well; the way you described your perceptions helped me to see the situation in a different light"); and providing genuine compliments ("You've really got a knack for putting people at ease; I appreciate that quality in you"). It is very important to identify these as leadership skills, since people often view leadership as an innate trait rather than a learnable skill. In addition, people often don't think of themselves as capable of leadership because they cannot imagine "ordering people around." Exposure to nonhierarchical leadership styles may be enlightening for people who have experienced only negative or hierarchical leadership styles.

Leadership skills can be developed in individual sessions, but group settings can be an even more powerful context for experimenting with and receiving feedback on leadership skills. Opportunities for leadership training are often available to high school and college students. Stiles (1986) developed a successful two-day leadership training program for adolescent girls on the high school student council. The program included communication skills such as active listening; leadership concepts; decision-making methods; group-building activities; discussion of femininity, leadership, and women leaders; and goal setting. Fertman and Long (1990) noted that leadership programs often are targeted at students who already occupy positions of leadership. They developed a program for eighth- and ninth-grade students not currently in positions of leadership or perceived as leaders by parents and teachers. Their assumption was that all students can learn to be effective leaders. The program included a five-day summer program, followed by year-round booster sessions. Participants were trained in leadership awareness, communication, decision making, stress management, and assertiveness. Opportunities to practice skills and to develop and implement personal leadership plans were provided. The results of the program indicated significant gains in leadership knowledge and attitudes (Fertman & Long, 1990).

Programs targeted at fostering leadership skills among adolescents are ideal because they serve a preventive purpose and set the stage for future involvement in leadership roles (McWhirter, et al., 1993). The tendency for females to become less confident, ambitious, and assertive during these years (AAUW, 1991; Brown & Gilligan, 1992; Erickson, 1978) makes leadership skills training optimal for adolescent girls in particular. School counselors are in a good position to oversee programs of this nature. For nonstudents, opportunities for leadership training may be less readily available. Community mental health centers, senior centers, parent organizations, and self-help groups are all potential sources of group leadership training.

COMMUNICATION SKILLS

Complete and Single Messages

Complete and single messages consist of three components: (1) identification of one's perception of the situation; (2) sharing what one is feeling; and (3) stating what one wants. These are sometimes referred to as the "perception-feeling-want" triad, but can also be conveyed as "eyes, guts, and hands;" some type of label is helpful when individuals are attempting to integrate the components into a specific (and perhaps emotionally charged) situation. Similarly, the components can be embedded into a short story-lesson, such as the one that follows.

The young man went to his father. "Father, I am very angry!" His father nodded in respectful acknowledgement of his son's anger, and then went about his work. The young man was left alone with his anger. He approached his father again later, this time trembling with anger. "Father," he repeated, "I am very angry and you don't even care!!" Again his father nodded in acknowledgment of his son's anger, pausing for a moment to convey that he had also heard his son's perception. Then he returned to his work. The son only grew more angry. His hands trembled and his face turned bright red. He wanted to scream and shout his anger to the heavens. "Father!" he called with great intensity. His father turned from his work and faced his son expectantly. "Father, I was angry, and now I am more angry than ever because you don't even want to hear me. Listen to me! Please hear what I have to say!" The father put aside his work, and motioned his son to sit beside him. Now that his son had voiced a whole thought, instead of simply making a proclamation, the talking could begin.

Incomplete messages—those with only one or two of the three components—may result in unnecessary conflict or escalate existing tensions. Sharing a perception alone ("I think you do that on purpose, just to bother me!") can be very inflammatory, launching an exchange of labels. Sharing feelings and perceptions, without ever specifying what one wants, can leave the other person in a corner ("I get so frustrated when you bring up my past and use it against me like this! We both know I can't change what happened and I think you're just being nasty when you bring it up."). Making a request ("I want you to stop bringing my past into our arguments") is certainly no guarantee of achieving an agreement. But it provides the other person with room to respond beyond confirming or challenging the first person's perceptions. Further, it provides a means of resolution of the disagreement, at least tempo-rarily. This is important when the two people have to move on to other tasks together, such as getting children ready for bed, planning a community event, or joining coworkers for a meeting.

Conflict Resolution

There is perhaps no other single communication skill more useful than the ability to tolerate and resolve conflict in a just manner. Fighting styles vary across and within the range of North American ethnic groups. For some, outward indications of conflict and anger are taboo publicly and privately; for others, arguments and raised voices are as commonplace as comments on the weather. The "appropriate" expression of anger is defined by cultural and familial influences or norms. Sometimes the simple recognition and validation of the variety of legitimate fighting styles is an enormous eye opener to a client who believes there is only one "right" way to manage disagreements.

Attempts to resolve conflict are more likely to be productive when the people involved can *tolerate* conflict—that is, when people view conflict (in general) as a necessary and inevitable part of being human rather than an awful and paralyzing occurrence. While specific conflicts may indeed be very unpleasant, it is because of the content or form of the conflict and not simply because of the fact that a conflict is occurring. People who experience difficulty tolerating conflict may react by shut-ting down, avoiding, or attacking, none of which is likely to contribute to conflict resolution.

Conflict resolution is also more likely to be productive when there is a minimum of blaming and labeling, when complete and single messages are used by the involved parties, when those involved act in a respectful manner toward each other, and when those involved are tolerant of each others' personal styles. With respect to the last point, it is important, for example, that a person comfortable with intense, heated discussions be tolerant of another person's more reserved and measured response to conflict. Consider the following example.

Andrea was referred for counseling by her doctor, who suggested that her headaches might be alleviated through relaxation training. As the counselor worked with Andrea on using relaxation and imagery techniques, they discussed her work and family situations. Staff meetings at Andrea's place of work gradually emerged as a source of great anxiety. She frequently was asked to represent her boss's viewpoints at meetings when her boss was unavailable; her boss said that this was "good training" and would help advance Andrea's position at the office. However, Andrea's boss frequently had controversial viewpoints. Andrea felt that some of these viewpoints were inappropriate and was embarrassed to express them; at the same time, she felt obligated to do as her boss requested, especially since her boss ostensibly was trying to help her. To make the situation even more difficult, two older male coworkers frequently interrupted Andrea when she began to speak, and dismissed her absent boss's opinions as trivial. Andrea began to dread staff meetings, encounters with the two male coworkers, and interactions with her own boss. She felt trapped between powerful people, pressured to convey their negative statements, and blamed herself for not knowing how to resolve the situation. Her headaches began shortly after her second "solo" staff meeting.

The counselor asked Andrea to share how conflict was resolved within her own family. Together they also began to analyze the power dynamics going on at Andrea's workplace, and clarified her role in the conflict. Next, they identified a variety of steps Andrea could take to remove or protect herself from what was essentially a conflict between other people. Because the counselor had clearly defined Andrea's role in counseling as that of collaborator, Andrea offered a critique of each potential step that they generated with a fair degree of comfort. They agreed to the following plan: (a) explore the relationship between Andrea's ethnicity (three of four grandparents were born in Germany) and her family norms around conflict as well as discuss alternative styles of family conflict; (b) use a series of relaxation and imagery exercises that involved Andrea observing heated discussions without becoming upset; (c) construct a series of questions for her boss that tapped into her boss's mentoring role and brought the conflict and discomfort out into the open (thus providing her boss with an opportunity to reconsider Andrea's role of speaking for her); (d) prepare and rehearse extensively a phrase to use when Andrea was interrupted by her male coworkers ("Excuse me, I haven't finished my point"); and (e) explore other options in the event that Andrea's boss responded poorly to her request for assistance.

This intervention served to expand Andrea's awareness of conflict styles, highlighted the power dynamics in her workplace that created stress and a sense of powerlessness, clarified Andrea's options with respect to proactive responses, and taught her skills that could be used in other contexts.

Meta-Communication

Meta-communication, that is, talking about communication, is something counselors model continuously but often fail to teach clients. For example, a counselor might say, "Randy, I notice that every time I glance toward the arms of your wheelchair, you move your arms from your lap up to the chair arms. It almost seems as though you want to cover the chair. I just realized that my reaction is to avoid looking anywhere except at your face. Have you noticed this dynamic?" While the issue of their communication—nonverbal in this case—is important, this also provides a general opportunity to define and practice meta-communication skills. The counselor might say, "Whenever I bring up our communication, I'm doing what is called meta-communication. It means that we talk about what happens between us as if we're sports commentators. I do this, you do that, I do this, etc. It's an important skill because it helps two people deal with patterns and change them—if they want to—rather than getting stuck in repetitious cycles that aren't constructive." The counselor might then invite Randy periodically to meta-communicate his own observations. The skill of meta-communication can be particularly helpful to people who feel caught in unproductive patterns of communication, who are trying to understand their verbal and nonverbal behavior patterns better, or who are experiencing difficulty with conflict resolution. Group settings are ideal for modeling and practicing meta-communication skills.

PUBLIC SPEAKING

For many people, speaking in front of a group formally or informally is a frightening, anxiety-provoking experience. The thought of having to speak to a group is enough to prevent some people from pursuing activities or jobs that they otherwise might like to do. Although giving formal speeches to a large audience is a task that one could probably avoid indefinitely, other forms of group presentation may be avoided only at considerable cost. Participation in meetings, workshops, and even social events such as weddings often involves speaking in front of groups.

As an instructor of a college-level study skills course, I encountered many students who were afraid of public speaking. No class assignment provoked more resistance and anxiety than the four-minute speech that each student gave at the end of the semester. One student informed me that he was so nervous about speaking in public that he had fainted during his last attempt. He said to me that under no circumstances would he give another speech and embarrass himself in that way. Another student told me that she desperately hated giving speeches because she always started crying in front of everyone; she had never finished a speech. Even as she described her speech-giving history she burst into tears; she described herself as a "failure" and "a big baby," and begged me to release her from the assignment.

Both of these students, Darnell and Marilyn, had very low self-efficacy for public speaking. Both held irrational beliefs about the consequences of speaking in front of their classmates. Both had an internal litany of labels for themselves and negative statements about their abilities that they silently recited every time the topic of giving speeches came up. But both were willing, after some lengthy discussion, to attempt the four-minute speech.

Darnell was the only African American student in that particular class. He felt some pressure to give a superior performance to challenge any racist notions of Black inferiority that students might hold. At the same time, he was aware that students with racist attitudes would not be likely to change on the basis of his speech performance—that is, if he gave a good speech it would be attributed to something other than the fact that African Americans are as talented and capable as Euro Americans. Together we devised a strategy that maximized the chances of a successful experience. Darnell decided that I should explain his goal—not fainting during the speech—to the class. As an introduction to his speech, he explained that he would be pausing to do some deep breathing during his presentation, and, in a humorous manner, identified two nearby students as "catchers" in case he began to fall. This introduction established his sense of control over the situation and made him an active participant in the assignment rather than a passive, embarrassed victim of the assignment. He finished the entire speech with only two dizzy spells, both of which subsided with deep breathing and (silent) positive self-talk. Several students approached him after class to convey their respect for him, and one told him, "Maybe I won't be sick for my presentation after all."

Marilyn designed a similar strategy. She informed her fellow students that she had never before finished a public speech because she inevitably cried. She let the class know that her goal was to continue for at least one more sentence of her speech after she began to cry; she told the class how embarrassed she was about crying and received several spontaneous, "That's OK's." Marilyn began to cry as soon as she began her speech. At one point she started to sit down, but changed her mind and returned to the front of the room. When she finished, still in tears, the class gave her a standing ovation. A year and a half later she told me with great pride that she had just given her first dry-eyed speech. She had cried before class and immediately on returning to her seat after the speech, but not during the speech itself.

The key ingredients to both successes were (a) control of the decision when and if to terminate the speech prematurely; (b) self-generated definitions of a successful speech (not fainting, saying one more sentence after beginning to cry); (c) control over how and how much to tell their classmates about their goal and strategy; and (d) a relatively safe environment in which to give the speech. In the language of self-efficacy (see Chapter Three), these students' self-efficacy expectations for giving speeches were enhanced through direct experience and performance appraisals. Counselors can integrate these ingredients in a wide variety of environments.

Participation in many community organizations and businesses involves talking to groups, whether one is providing a summary of last month's meeting, sharing information learned at a seminar, contributing opinions and knowledge, or persuading people to take a particular course of action. To the extent that comfort with public speaking increases client willingness to participate in opportunities for collective action, training in public speaking can facilitate empowerment.

Powell and Collier (1990) warn that public-speaking classes usually fail to incorporate a multicultural perspective, resulting in ethnocentrically biased assessments of student performance. Counselors working with clients on public speaking must be aware of cultural variations in what constitutes effective and appropriate group communication. For example, Japanese speakers may prefer a style that is more indirect, includes metaphors, and draws on family affiliations to demonstrate credibility, while African American speakers may prefer a more dynamic and emotionally expressive style (Powell & Collier, 1990). Narrow definitions of "good" public speaking invariably will restrict clients.

PERSONAL SKILLS AND PARTICIPATORY COMPETENCE

Throughout Chapters Three and Four, a series of intra- and interpersonal skills have been discussed in the context of counseling for empowerment. These skills, and numerous others that could have been included here, assist clients in surviving and/or transforming their environments. While skill acquisition is not enough, it sets the stage for participatory competence and furthers the empowerment process.

Kieffer's (1984) description of participatory competence emerged from his in-depth study of 15 individuals who had become leaders and activists in grass roots community organizations. The transition of these individuals from silent bystanders to empowered actors followed a remarkably similar course that Keiffer conceptualized in terms of four "eras." Consider the parallel between these four eras and the evolution of the counseling relationship.

The *Era of Entry* is marked by some form of assault on the individual's sense of integrity. This assault goes beyond the person's daily experience of injustice, violating the individual's sense of pride or self-determination, or striking out against the person's family or community in a way that provokes a new kind of reaction. Though feeling essentially powerless, the individual is mobilized by the assault into some form of conflict with the "powers that be," resulting over time in a demystification of authority and the recognition that she or he is capable of challenging authority.

The *Era of Advancement* is characterized by the development of an influential mentoring relationship, entry into some form of collective effort, and increased critical awareness of the social and political environment. The individual joins the political efforts of others to effect some form of change, deriving support from peers, guidance from a mentor, and learning about personal and community resources through attempts, failures, and successes.

The *Era of Incorporation* is characterized by the integration of new skills and abilities, critical analysis of the environment with a self-concept of increasing competence, and a growing commitment to participation in the societal change process at some level. The final era, the *Era of Commitment*, is achieved with the successful integration of the individual's new sense of self and relationship with the sociopolitical environment. Although continuing to learn and sharpen skills and struggling to meet the everyday challenges of the real world, the person is fully committed to community action and participation.

Counseling for empowerment and the development of participatory competence are potentially very similar processes, with the counselor providing an "influential mentoring relationship." If the client is the Native American son of an alcoholic, the development of participatory competence might be construed as this adolescent's ability to analyze critically the effects of his mother's drinking on the family system and on his own self-concept; the development of skills for protecting his feelings; and the cultivation of support from other family members, peers, and tribal elders. His participatory competence may continue to evolve through his growing understanding of the history of the relationship between Native Americans and the U.S. government, awareness of Native American sovereignty rights, and increased participation in tribal activities. If the client is a depressed senior center participant, the process of developing participatory competence may be initiated when a much-enjoyed activity is permanently cancelled. It may continue to develop as she gathers information about her physical limitations and limitations imposed by the nursing staff. As she becomes critically aware of the center's policies and procedures, she might come to challenge limitations that are based on staff convenience rather than matters of health or safety, and work with her peers to form an advisory committee to the senior center's board.

CONCLUSION

The skills described in Chapters Three and Four can be seen as part of developing participatory competence and as integral to the empowerment process. These skills can be adapted for use with a wide variety of clients, in individual or group formats. A counselor who is aware of the client's culture and the systemic and structural barriers to empowerment experienced by the client will be in a better position to facilitate the client's development of new competencies. Case examples of skills training are provided in each chapter of Part III.

PART III

APPLICATIONS OF COUNSELING FOR EMPOWERMENT

The purpose of Part III of this book is to apply the previous discussions of empowerment and skills development to a variety of specific groups. Such an undertaking belies the vast heterogeneity within each group; no single chapter can address adequately the variety and complexity of the counseling issues relevant to any one group. Thus, the emphasis here will be on identifying several of the most critical issues for a given group in the context of counseling for empowerment. In recognition of the limited coverage possible in each chapter, numerous resources are provided for the interested reader.

The groups addressed in Part III include people of color (Chapter Five); gay, lesbian, and bisexual people (Chapter Six); people with HIV disease (Chapter Seven); people with disabilities (Chapter Eight); survivors of violence (Chapter Nine); older adults (Chapter Ten); adolescents (Chapter Eleven), and the "non-beautiful" (Chapter Twelve). With one exception, every chapter provides a general description of the group discussed, a personal statement that voices one or more persons' actual experiences with the issues addressed in that chapter, a discussion of barriers to empowerment often confronted by members of this group, and practical suggestions for facilitating empowerment. These practical suggestions incorporate the skills described in Chapters Three and Four. Chapter Twelve, "The Non-Beautiful," is organized in a slightly different fashion. The "non-beautiful" refers to people struggling with the explicit standards and pervasive societal messages regarding how women and men should look and behave. The personal statements in this chapter are drawn from published accounts of two women's personal struggles with physical appearance. Rather than a section on barriers per se, beauty standards and their consequences are described and analyzed in terms of gender role expectations.

Potential applications of empowerment to the context of counseling extend far beyond the particular groups discussed in Part III. However, these chapters should serve as a useful framework for counseling for empowerment with other client groups, such as children or people with addictions.

Chapter Five
PEOPLE OF COLOR

---

i am a child of milk and honey
i am a child of apple pie
i am a child of the land of glory
or am i just a child of the lie?

From "Child of the Lie," E.H.M.

INTRODUCTION

People of color have a long history of oppression and marginalization in the United States. From Native American and Mexican people living here long before any "settlers" arrived, to the African men, women, and children brought here against their will, people of color learned quickly that "The New World" was not to be the land of the free. After decade upon decade of struggle, we have transformed some aspects of our society. But counseling professionals cannot hope to work effectively with clients of color until we are deeply aware of what has not yet been changed, and are passionately committed to being a part of the change process.

Empowerment among people of color might include the following components: a positive ethnic identity; an awareness of the collective history of one's forebears; a critical understanding of the power dynamics influencing one's current life circumstances as an individual, a person of color, and a member of a particular ethnic group; group participation or collective action that supports the empowerment of others; and possession of skills and competencies for thriving and exercising control over one's life to the fullest possible extent.

WHO ARE PEOPLE OF COLOR?

By the year 2010, people of color will be the numerical majority in the United States. People of color include Black Americans, Hispanic Americans, Asian Americans, Native Americans, Arab Americans, and other groups. They include the vast numbers of people whose background is other than Euro American and who typically have been excluded from positions of power in our society. People of color may ascribe to the values and practices of the dominant Euro-American culture or to the values and practices of their particular ethnic group; the majority of people of color develop bicultural competencies to survive in contemporary society. Although current rhetoric embraces diversity and the richness of the many U.S. cultures, the reality is that racism and prejudice are institutionalized, and significant transformation must occur before concepts such as "equality" and "justice" are a part of the everyday reality of people of color.

The groups noted above often are characterized in global fashion, as if each were homogeneous. However, the diversity within these groups is wide ranging and significant. Black Americans include African Americans and Blacks from Haiti, Cuba, and Guyana. Hispanic Americans, or Latinos, include Puerto Ricans, Mexican Americans, and Cuban Americans, as well as people with roots in Central and South America. Asian Americans include Cambodian, Laotian, Hmong, Vietnamese, Korean, Japanese, and Chinese Americans; there are at least 58 subcultures within Asian culture. Native Americans include more than 500 different tribes (U.S. Senate Select Committee on Indian Affairs, 1985) with more than 200 distinct languages. Arab Americans may have originated in any of 20 different Middle Eastern or North African countries (Jackson, 1991), and hence, come from diverse cutural and ethnic backgrounds. In addition to being members of ethnic groups, people of color are many other things: heterosexual, gay, lesbian, and bisexual; temporarily able-bodied and physically disabled; young, middle-aged and old; male and female; they are AIDS-ree or have HIV disease; they are refugees or immigrants, or the great-grandchildren of refugees or immigrants, or their forebears were here long before the arrival of a confused Italian explorer; and infinitely more. Textbooks traditionally have subsumed counseling interventions for people of color within a single umbrella chapter called "Special Populations" or "Working with Minorities." This practice continues in various forms today and is a reflection of the dominant culture bias, signifying that Euro American middle-class attributes and norms are the standard to which all else is compared. Although this chapter focuses specifically on people of color, multicultural perspectives inform this entire book.

Before turning to the personal statement, some clarification is needed regarding terminology. The term "race" will only be used when referring to the work of others who employed this term, such as data from the Bureau of the Census. "Ethnicity" will be used throughout this book in recognition of the lack of a biological or genetic basis for racial distinctions (Montagu, 1972, 1974; Yee, 1983) and to emphasize the importance of the sociopolitical, historical, and cultural commonalities shared by members of an ethnic group. As noted above, people of color include all people residing in the United States except those of Euro American descent.

Jessie Garcia's story, below, reflects his own unique personal experience. He describes a developmental process common to many people of color, capturing the struggle, frustration, and ultimate sense of peace and pride he felt in achieving a positive sense of identity.

> I am the son of Mexican immigrants and the brother of three sisters. My parents made their home and raised their family on an Indian reservation in Arizona. Both of my parents spent most of their working lives as laborers. My father worked as an irrigator, all year-round, seven days a week; I rarely saw him as I was growing up. He spent most of his time in the fields (miles away from our mobile home), irrigating whatever crop was in season. My mother also worked in seasonal crops, but did not work one job per se. Depending on the crop, she would work as a picker and/or cutter of the crop or as a weed cutter. Mother would leave for work before dawn and would usually return at dusk, often too tired to stay up with her children. I am the first in my family to receive a college education.
>
> Early on, I never really questioned my identity. Whenever someone would ask what I "was," I would unhesitatingly say that I was Mexican. At that time, I thought that all people of Mexican descent were called Mexicans, and for that matter called themselves Mexican, especially those who spoke Spanish and who were of bronze complexions like me.
>
> It was during high school that I began to hear individuals of Mexican descent using terms other than Mexican to identify themselves. They began to separate into distinct groups: Those who were from Mexico and spoke little English, and who were probably residing in the U.S. illegally; those who were bilingual; those who only spoke English; and those who had assimilated into the White American groups. As each individual started to identify with a particular group, the individual also began to use different terms to identify his or her ethnicity.
>
> I, too, began to use a term other than Mexican to identify myself when I began to associate with the White American group. I remember calling myself "Latin" or "Spanish," but not Mexican, when I was part of this particular group. I resented being called Mexican, because "Mexican" had come to mean an uncivilized or dirty individual. Moreover, my White American friends increased my resentment of being called Mexican

whenever they would say that I was "not really a Mexican," or that I was different from the "other" Mexicans. Because of this, I preferred to be called anything but Mexican. Later in high school I began feeling uncomfortable about my resentment at being called Mexican. I began wondering if my White American peers really did accept me fully as their friend. I felt a little alienated from them and somewhat left out whenever we were together. Moreover, I felt that my peers perceived me as not truly an American.

These perceptions and this feeling of alienation has continued to puzzle me. Even though I am an army veteran as well as an American citizen with a college education, my White American peers to date do not fully acknowledge my "Americanism." Somehow I am not accepted as that "all-American boy" (even if I am one), simply because I am of Mexican descent.

Feeling not totally accepted as "one of the guys," I wanted to go to a country where I would be better accepted than in the U.S. During college I had an opportunity to study abroad as a foreign exchange student. I chose to go to Mexico, believing that I would be better accepted and less alienated than I had been in the U.S, since I was fluent in speaking, reading, and writing in Spanish and, most important, because I looked Mexican. This trip to Mexico was the beginning of my conscious effort to discover who I would better identify with—Americans or Mexicans.

When I first arrived in Mexico, I thought that I would fit in perfectly, or at least better than I did in the U.S. And at first I did—that is, in my appearance. I truly did fit into this culture by way of my skin color and my mannerisms; nobody even had the vaguest idea that I was American by birth. I easily camouflaged my "Americanness" in the crowds that had tan skin coloring closely matching mine. But once I started to speak, the difference between the Mexicans from Mexico and me started to be noticeable. Within a few sentences, the Mexican natives quickly recognized that I was not a native, in spite of my appearance.

As my peers from Mexico began to know me better, I again started to feel that alienation that I had felt in the U.S. Although I was Mexican by blood and looked like a Mexican, my new friends did not really accept me as a true Mexican. They would constantly state that I was not Mexican— for that matter, not even Mexican American—just American. I continually argued with them, telling them that I was only born in the U.S., that my parents were from Mexico, that I was fluent in their language, and that I expressed myself differently because I was educated in American culture. They listened to me and tried to understand, but they still did not perceive me as a "true Mexican."

The alienated feeling that I felt in the U.S. had rearisen in Mexico. I was fully accepted neither in Mexico nor in the U.S. *Where do I really fit?* I thought to myself.

In the midst of these feelings of alienation, I talked with several Americans of Mexican origin who were also studying in Mexico. Through those conversations and in my experiences since then, I have come to realize that we people of Mexican origin who are born in the U.S. have our own ethnic group, which can be termed Chicano, Mexican American, American, Latino, Latin American, Spanish, or whatever you prefer to call them. Our culture is neither fully "Mexican" nor "American." We are a culture and a people, whatever name we may use to identify ourselves, who have been discriminated against by both the Mexicans and the Americans. Yet, we are a culture with the unique advantage of taking the best from each culture to become one, which I have come to call the Mexican American one.

BARRIERS

Socioeconomic Status

Socioeconomic status is perhaps one of the most obvious barriers confronted by many people of color. More than half of all ethnic minority children in the United States are being raised in poverty (Horowitz & O'Brien, 1989). The job losses associated with the recessions of the early 1980s and 1990s have contributed to poverty rates, along with trends such as the shift in manufacturing employment from cities to outlying areas. Because African American and other ethnic minority families reside in inner-city areas in disproportionate numbers and are overrepresented in the blue-collar jobs that have been disappearing, they have been affected disproportionately by displacement and unemployment (Fusfeld & Bates, 1984; Simms, 1987). As of 1986, 8.6% of all White families lived below the poverty line, compared to 24.7% of Hispanic families and 28% of African American families (U.S. Department of Commerce, 1988). The unemployment rate for Native Americans remains consistently high, averaging about 30% on most reservations, with some Plains reservations reporting unemployment rates of more than 70% (La Fromboise, 1988; U.S. Senate Select Committee on Indian Affairs, 1985).

With respect to income, women of color face double discrimination. The median earnings of year-round, full-time female workers in 1986 was $16,843 compared to $25,894 for men (U.S. Department of Commerce, 1987). Male-female discrepancies are maintained within general racial/ethnic categories as well, with median year-round, full-time incomes as follows: White women $17,101, White men $26,617; Black women $14,964, Black men $18,766; Hispanic women $14,191, Hispanic men $17,008 (U.S. Department of Commerce, 1987).

Lower socioeconomic status frequently means substandard housing, poorer education (Kozol, 1991), and less access to resources. Children of color may internalize assumptions of inferiority or hopelessness when the lives they witness on television are so vastly different from their own.

Education

Attainment. Socioeconomic status has implications for educational *and* occupational attainment. Statistics compiled by Carter and Wilson (1993) indicate the current educational status of ethnic minority persons. High school completion rates among 18- to 24-year-olds in 1991 were as follows: White males 79.3%, White females 83.8%, African American males 71.8%, African American females 77.8%, Hispanic males 47.8%, Hispanic females 56.9% (U.S. Department of Commerce, 1991). Graduate educational statistics reveal even greater discrepancies between Euro Americans and people of color (National Research Council, 1991). Carter and Wilson (1993) indicate that although the number of ethnic minority students enrolled in higher education increased between 1980 and 1990, these increases lagged far behind the actual population increases among ethnic minorities. Further, large *percentage* gains in American Indian enrollment between 1980 and 1990 reflected only very small increases in *actual numbers*—for example, in 1990 there were only 10 or fewer American Indian students enrolled in professional institutions of higher education in 24 of 50 states. In these states, the addition of a single American Indian graduate student would constitute a dramatic gain in percentage. Given that education is generally a "necessary but not sufficient" condition for positions of power, lower educational attainment is a considerable barrier.

Quality. In the last decade, educational funding fell from 2.3% to 1.7% of the total federal budget (Shearer, 1990). Drawing from Goodman (1987) and Kimmich (1985), McWhirter et al. (1993) report:

> During the 1980's Ronald Reagan insisted that the Department of Education bring about educational reforms by "leadership and persuasion"—not by new programs or by allocating more funds to existing programs. In fact, during every year of his administration, Reagan requested level funding or budget cuts for programs that provided aid for disadvantaged children, bilingual education, and work-incentive child-care initiatives. (p. 65)

In his book, *Savage Inequalities*, Kozol (1991) provides a vivid description of public schools in America's inner cities. As he visited schools across the country he discovered the incredible gap between the "haves" and the "have nots." At one school, a seven-year-old informs him of her sister's rape and murder on school grounds just weeks earlier; at another, there are two or three study halls a day to save money on teachers; and at many schools, there is no toilet paper in the bathrooms and substitute teachers are the only kind of instructor the children ever see. A stark portrait indeed. Of the exceptional teachers he encounters—those who create positive learning environments against all odds and inspire their students to achieve—Kozol comments:

> It is tempting to focus on these teachers and, by doing this, to paint a hopeful portrait of the good things that go on under adverse conditions...these books are sometimes very popular, because they are consoling.
> The rationale behind much of this writing is that pedagogic problems in our cities are not chiefly matters of injustice, inequality or segregation, but of insufficient information about teaching strategies.... (1991, p. 51)

Children are able to identify differences between their lives and the lives of others at an early age. They have only to turn on a television or look through a magazine to know that other children don't walk to school through empty lots full of discarded chemicals; other children don't share 15-year-old textbooks with the first 25 pages ripped out; other children are not taught by a string of substitute teachers year after year; and other children learn basic mathematics and reading skills, without worrying about the walk home afterwards.

Climate. A variety of researchers have identified differential patterns of teacher-student relationships based on whether the student is Euro American or a person of color. For example, Trujillo (1986) found that Euro American students were asked significantly more complex questions, were pushed to enhance their responses, and received more time during the professor's response than did students of color. In other studies, students of color have reported that their professors tend to avoid contact with them (Burrell, 1981; Hall & Allen, 1983). Buriel (1983) found that elementary school Mexican American students received significantly less teacher affirmation for correct responses than their Euro American classmates, even with socioeconomic status, achievement, and English proficiency controlled. These not-so-subtle differences make for a discouraging classroom environment for students of color.

Another aspect of climate is the teacher's knowledge of student cultures. The National Education Association reported that only 3% of all public school teachers in 1991 were Hispanic ("More minorities," 1992); the proportion of teachers of color is uniformly low across ethnic groups. Without awareness of the cultural norms of the students in their classrooms, teachers may impose standards of behavior that are inappropriate, confusing, and uncomfortable for their students. Teachers may seat Asian American children next to each other for comfort without realizing that their respective countries of origin have been at war for years. Clearly, teacher "sensitivity" is not enough to provide a supportive climate in our increasingly diverse classrooms.

Although many school districts are attempting to implement multicultural curriculums, the majority are not. In addition, multicultural curriculums are not necessarily of good quality. For example, McCarty, Lynch, Wallace, and Benally (1991) argue that researchers have perpetuated myths such as the Native American child's "need" for a nonverbal curriculum, without examining more closely the conditions influencing the "learning styles" evidenced by Native American children. They found that Navajo elementary students responded eagerly and verbally to a bilingual-bicultural curriculum, and contend, "The well-documented passive responses of Navajo and other Native American children in school must be interpreted as outcomes of... sociohistorical experiences, not as manifestations of an inherent disposition or a nonverbal, non-analytical 'style'" (p. 53). A multicultural curriculum based on the inaccuracies noted by McCarty et al. (1991) could perpetuate the problems of the status quo. The vast majority of students will continue to be exposed only to a Eurocentric curriculum that, however inadvertently, perpetuates stereotypes, promotes the continuation of structural and individual racism, and deprives all students of great richness (Payne, 1984). Columbus's "discovery" of America, the focus on the accomplishments of Greek civilization to the exclusion of the Incan and Mayan civilizations, and the absence of African American perspectives of slavery also typify what is wrong with or missing from Eurocentric education.

Occupational Attainment

Although occupational aspirations tend to be similarly high across ethnic groups, there are significant gaps between the aspirations and occupational attainment of people of color (e.g., Arbona, 1990; McWhirter, 1992). People of color are consistently underrepresented in higher skilled categories and overrepresented in lower skilled categories of the work force. It is important to note that within the major racial/ethnic categories, discrepancies among subgroups exist. For example, among employed Hispanic women, Mexican American women are significantly more likely than Cuban American women to be employed in service occupations (private household cleaners, child-care workers, waitresses, etc.), and significantly less likely than Cuban American women to be working in professional or managerial positions (U.S. Department of Commerce, 1988). Thus, Mexican American women are disadvantaged even relative to other Hispanic women.

Previously noted barriers related to socioeconomic status contribute to the lower occupational attainment of people of color. Lack of progress is perpetuated by educational barriers such as the low numbers of teachers of color, wide discrepancies in the quality of education, and disabling characteristics of our public schools. The socioeconomic, educational, and occupational conditions described above reflect the structural oppression experienced by people of color in the United States.

Racism

From organized hate groups to the ethnic slurs pronounced by school-children, racism pervades our society. The Ku Klux Klan continues to recruit followers and promote violence. For example, in a recent Labor Day gathering of several Klan groups, one Klan leader exhorted his followers that it was time to discard their robes, dress in camouflage, and "learn to kill not just one way, but 1,000 ways" (Boland, 1992, p. 31). Referring to a study of college campus hate crimes, Youngstrum (1991) notes that 20–25% of minority students had experienced "incidents ranging from name-calling to physical assault and arson, perpetrated because of the victim's race, religion, ethnicity or sexual orientation" (p. 38). The results of a another campus survey indicated that 33% of African Americans, 20% of Asian Americans, and 25% of Hispanics had been physically or verbally assaulted *in the previous year alone* (Youngstrum, 1991). Southeast Asian refugee elementary and secondary students report frequently being harassed, teased, mimicked, and punched by non-Asian students (Huang, 1989).

Children of Holocaust survivors, refugees from Southeast Asia, immigrants from Latin America, and Native Americans often experience secondary effects from racism experienced by their parents. Witnessing and/or enduring human brutality in the form of torture, rape, and murder will affect parenting just as such traumatic experiences filter into all other aspects of life. The behaviors and attitudes that help human beings cope with and survive terrible atrocities invariably will affect their children. This less obvious but powerful product of racism must be recognized by counselors.

One form of institutional racism is exemplified in court cases reviewed by Moreland (1988). In all three cases described, Native American plaintiffs brought suit against photographers who had taken pictures of them at their reservation homes and then published the pictures without permission. Traditional Navajo religious beliefs hold that the publication of one's picture can have very adverse effects. The courts deemed that this was not an invasion of privacy on the basis that "Traditional American Indians are not possessed with the ordinary sensibilities, feelings, and intelligence of reasonable people" (Moreland, 1988, p. 1). The words "ordinary" and "reasonable" take on sinister implications in this context: We can legally dismiss an entire people on the basis of their differing religious beliefs. Although many people recognize the atrocities committed against Native Americans in the past, fewer recognize the continuing usurpation and denial of their rights. It is important to acknowledge that although *some* overt forms of racism have been abandoned, many less obvious or noticeable forms have taken their place. We have yet to become a society that truly celebrates diversity.

Lack of Political Cohesion

Although some Euro Americans surely lose sleep at the thought of people of color gaining in both numbers and political power, the former is a reality while the latter is changing only slowly. The common issues of poverty, safety, and discrimination have not been enough to unite people of color politically. According to Shorris (1992), the lack of a national commitment to redress past injustices pits Blacks and Latinos against each other, battling over insufficient health care, economic opportunity, and educational resources. Even within broad ethnic minority groups, lack of political cohesion is problematic. Shorris (1992) notes that among Latinos, issues such as bilingual education are divisive rather than unifying, yielding extremes from those who favor maintenance of Spanish to those who oppose anything but the teaching of English. Latino stances on affirmative action policies demonstrate the same variation, with conservatives speaking out against affirmative action policies, and liberal and leftist groups strongly in favor. Shorris (1992) argues:

> Unless some great unifying issue can be found to unite rich and poor, Africa and indigenous America, this world and the next, Latinos are unlikely to have national political power consonant with their numbers. The political experts in Washington and New York will find it more advantageous to pit them against each other than to suggest that candidates attempt to satisfy their needs. (p. 26)

The harsh reality is that neither ethnicity nor the experience of being people of color in a White-dominated society has been enough of a basis for the kind of collective political power required for structural transformation. Members of the middle class across all ethnic groups may have more in common with respect to voting and political priorities than a multiclass group of same-ethnic people. The factions within and between people of color—factions produced by the structure of society and the allocation of resources—have effectively prevented large scale collective mobilization.

SUGGESTIONS FOR EMPOWERMENT

Counselor Knowledge

Ethnic identity development. All counselors, not just Euro American counselors, should have a sense of clarity regarding their ethnic identity and their values. White ethnic identity development and values were discussed in Chapter Two. Models of ethnic identity development specific to people of color have been proposed by numerous authors (Atkinson, Morten, & Sue, 1979; Cross, 1971; Sue, 1981). Only one model is described here; the reader is encouraged to explore others.

Atkinson, Morten, and Sue (1979) proposed the five-stage Minority Identity Development Model. Some aspects of this model are paralleled in Jessie Garcia's personal statement. Stage One, *conformity*, is characterized by a preference for Euro American cultural values over those of one's own ethnic group. Stage Two, *dissonance*, is characterized by growing confusion and awareness of conflict between the values of the dominant culture and those of one's own ethnic group; the superiority of Euro American culture is questioned. The resentment and sense of alienation from White high school peers that Jessie describes seems consistent with the dissonance stage. In Stage Three, *resistance and immersion*, the individual actively rejects Euro American values and immerses into the value system of his or her ethnic group. Jessie's decision to study in Mexico was perhaps not so much a rejection of Euro American values as an embracing of Mexican culture. Stage Four, *introspection*, is characterized by questioning one's exclusive participation in the culture of one's own ethnic group and conflict between feeling constrained and the desire to be loyal to one's own ethnic group. In Jessie's case, his immersion experience resulted in the same alienation he had experienced previously. The fifth and final stage, *synergetic articulation and awareness*, is characterized by a sense of integration and autonomy. The individual feels a strong sense of ethnic pride and identity, while adhering to chosen rather than prescribed values. Ultimately, Jessie's proactive and conscious quest for identity yielded the "discovery" of a distinct Mexican American culture. His final words reflect a pride and sense of belonging consistent with the fifth stage. As noted by Sue and Sue (1990), all models of ethnic identity development should be considered conceptual frameworks that only approximate what is a dynamic, nonlinear developmental process.

Ethnic identity development has implications for counseling. An African American client in the resistance and immersion stage, for example, may be unreceptive to feedback from a Euro American counselor. If the counselor is experiencing Helms's (1993) disintegration phase, her guilt and anxiety may compound the tension in the relationship. Whether the counselor provides a referral to an African American counselor or devotes more energy to establishing a basis for trust, it is critical that the counselor respects and honors the client's position. If they continue to work together, the counselor's nondefensiveness and support of the client's ethnic pride will constitute an important aspect of the intervention. Barbara, the Japanese American client described in Chapter Thirteen, embraces Euro American values almost exclusively at the onset of counseling. As counseling progresses, the counselor deliberately invites her to explore her ethnic identity and to clarify her value system. On termination, Barbara's identity is more consistent with characteristics of Stage Three.

Sociopolitical history. In addition to an understanding of ethnic identity development, counselors must have information about the sociopolitical history of clients of color (Sue & Sue, 1990). It is inappropriate to expect clients to serve as the sole source of information about their cultural norms and expectations. While using clients' expertise in a collaborative fashion and recognizing the clients' status as experts on their own lives and experiences remains critical, counselors also must be willing to do their homework. Clients may be unaware of the collective history of their ethnic group and may not proclaim any particular affiliation with members of that group. However, factual historical information can assist an individual in understanding present-day dynamics. For example, the grandson of a Chinese railroad worker might understand his father and grandfather better, as well as current family dynamics, after learning about the extreme prejudice and racially motivated violence faced by his grandfather's cohort of Chinese immigrant workers.

Acculturation. Counselor awareness of the potential influence of acculturation on the counseling process, as well as competence in assessment of level of acculturation, are critical factors in working with people of color. Knowledge of traditional attitudes toward counseling specific to various ethnic groups is an important backdrop to exploring the role of acculturation in a particular counseling relationship. Szapocznik et al.'s (1986) Bicultural Effectiveness Training (described in Chapter Eleven) is one model for integrating issues of acculturation and ethnic identity in the treatment of intergenerational family conflict.

Power Analysis

People of color operate in multiple systems, as do Euro Americans. However, the systems influencing their lives may be so different from the experience of Euro American counselors that power analysis can be misconstrued. For example, hard work does not necessarily yield success, but this belief is a cornerstone of many Euro Americans. Does a corporate lawyer "work harder" than a farm worker, or a person who cleans up construction sites, or a parent working at home to raise children? Who works longer hours? Who gets a vacation? How did the lawyer "earn" this vacation? Were the toils and strains of law school, the all-nighters, the occasional missed meals, and the stress of exams really so different that, on completing them, one *deserves* a better quality of life? Power analysis of class issues is essential when working with people of color, and counselors must be aware of how their own lives have been influenced by class status. This demands honesty and vulnerability; for Euro American counselors it requires confronting what Skillings and Dobbins (1991) refer to as the "great American double bind": "that although we never asked to be White, we enjoy certain privileges from that accident of birth that are delivered to us at the expense of other people's well-being within this society" (p. 210).

Power analysis with people of color must address racism and structural injustices in economics, politics, and education. For example, how has the client's education been influenced by racism? Lee (1991b) notes other important dynamics to integrate into counseling, such as those related to level of ethnic identity and acculturation, family influences, gender role socialization, religious and spiritual influences, and immigration experiences. Davenport and Yurich (1991) suggest that gender-stereotyped behavior often is influenced by the relative status of each gender in a society. Acknowledging the variation in gender roles across cultures, they nevertheless point out that within patriarchal societies there will be many similar themes in gender-prescribed behavior. Counselors can explore with clients: What does it mean to be a woman or a man in your ethnic group? What happens if you behave in ways that are inconsistent with these expectations? To what extent are expected gender roles modeled within your family?

Espin's (1993) description of feminist therapy with women of color integrates power analysis along with other aspects of empowerment. Identification of the effects of sexism, racism, and elitism is central, as well as validating the internal experiences of women of color by facilitating their understanding of the relationship between the external environment and their inner reality. Exploration of the power dynamics influencing acculturation will require learning about the client's family and extended family system, as well as understanding the pressures from the larger social environment to conform to Euro American behaviors. Power analysis is always a function of the client's situation and presenting problem.

Skill Application: Assertiveness Training

Assertiveness training, discussed in Chapter Four, can be an effective component of empowering clients of color. The case example below demonstrates the integration of assertiveness training—which drew upon the client's existing assertiveness skills—with other intervention techniques.

Louis sat rigidly in his chair across from the Euro American counselor. He listed the physical symptoms that his doctor had recently attributed to stress: stomachaches, headaches, muscular stiffness, and constant nausea. When questioned, he described his work environment in controlled, precise language, choosing each word carefully. He enjoyed the nature of his sales work, was successful at generating and keeping new clients, and invariably received positive evaluations. He enjoyed the relative independence of his job. His wife supported his career, was interested in discussing what happened at work each day, and frequently gave positive, constructive feedback on his strategies. His boss was flexible and did not pressure him to work longer hours, unlike other company managers. Other areas of his life appeared similarly positive.

To what did he attribute his physical symptoms? After the counselor posed this question, Louis became visibly stiffer and spoke more slowly. Returning to the topic of work, he explained that the physical symptoms largely began when he left the house each morning and subsided—except for the nausea—when he left work at night. He went on to describe, in a voice devoid of emotion, the glances, the questions, and the comments of his all-male, all Euro American coworkers. "Where did you get that suit?" "Guess you took the day off yesterday." "Nice shoes." Louis looked at his clenched hands as he relayed their statements. The counselor ventured, "Sounds like you have a bunch of racist coworkers." This was not a remarkable leap of intuition, but the reaction invoked was indeed remarkable. Louis's head shot up and he made sustained, direct eye contact for the first time. He had known the devil; he had not expected the counselor to name it.

In the emotional, energetic, and at times heated discussion that followed, he and the counselor exchanged vignettes of the racism that pervaded his workplace and was common to many others. The counselor also provided statistics on racism in the workplace, and validated his perception of his coworkers' messages: He was not supposed to dress well or succeed. He was supposed to be incompetent. Because the daily commentary was voiced in neutral tones, and no particular statement was blatantly racist, Louis felt unable to confront his coworkers without living up to their expectations that he would be a "troublemaker." And although he believed he was being subjected to racism, he had little hope that anyone besides his wife would recognize it. In fact, he had predicted that the counselor would tell him to "take it like a man" or something similar if he shared his perception of racism, so he had decided not to mention it at all. He felt trapped and powerless.

Beyond providing specific training in stress management techniques, the counselor's role became primarily that of a supportive consultant. Louis had lived in this overwhelmingly Euro American community for only one year, and had devoted his time to this job and to his nuclear family; extended family and friends were across the country. Louis determined that his children would be facing similar racist attitudes very soon if they weren't already. He decided to focus his energy in two areas. First, he generated a list of cities to which he could possibly transfer, cities with large African American communities. Second, in consultation with the counselor, he developed a series of statements to use in response to his coworkers' remarks. The statements ranged from mildly sarcastic ("So now you're a wardrobe consultant") to directly confrontative ("I have never heard you comment on Jim's new shoes; do you think Black men shouldn't dress so well?"). Although Louis was assertive in dealing with other aspects of work, he had not used these skills with coworkers. He and the counselor devoted session time to rehearsing the phrases, practicing various intonations, predicting possible reactions, and using deep breathing and positive self-statements to reduce his anxiety while using the phrases. Before using these responses, he established a five-day baseline so as to measure the effectiveness of his strategy. Within six weeks, Louis had accomplished the following: (1) He had requested and received a transfer (within the company) to another city with an established African American community and several African American employees; (2) he had obtained a direct apology from one coworker (3) he had reduced significantly the number of racist comments from other coworkers; and (4) he and his wife had recommitted themselves to participating in African American civic and cultural activities. Louis prepared a statement for his soon-to-be-former supervisor, documenting the nature of his coworkers' comments and their effect. He hoped that this would enlighten his supervisor and help future Black employees of that division of the company. As for Louis's physical symptoms, they had decreased significantly. As of the counselor's last contact, Louis had visited his new office and was eager to move. He indicated that his experience had taught him not only about his response to stress, but also about the importance of community and about his ability to "hit back" in a way that was nonviolent, educative, and consistent with his inner feelings.

Many clients will not be able to obtain transfers and move to a new environment, and this case example should not be interpreted as advocating this approach across the board. In addition, many details of the case were omitted, leaving perhaps a false impression of an "everything's coming up roses" ending. Louis still had feelings of hurt, resentment, and anger to integrate (not necessarily to resolve), and he recognized that this experience would by no means be his last personal encounter with racism. This case does illustrate several important issues, however. Louis had experienced an "initiating event," an assault on his integrity, and the physical consequences resulted in his seeking counseling. Although he initially experienced himself as powerless, the validation he experienced enabled him to mobilize and extend existing strengths (assertiveness) and develop new ones (stress management techniques). Louis recognized the effects of being far away from a supportive African American community, and took action to renew his own ties and to ensure that his children also would experience these benefits.

Group Participation

Although larger-scale efforts to unify around political issues have been less than successful, as noted above, grass roots organizations continue to produce leaders, united efforts, and successful attempts to effect social change. Richardson (1991) encourages counselors working with people of color to access the rich resources of religious institutions. Noting the importance of the church in the lives of many oppressed peoples, Richardson details many advantages of working in cooperation with the church in general and the African American church in particular. Support groups sponsored by the church or housed on church grounds may draw participants who otherwise would not consider counseling, and may facilitate the development of trust and cohesiveness. The African American church historically has been a strong voice against the oppression of African Americans and continues to serve as a foundation for many activist groups. *Communidades ecclesiales de base*, or Christian base communities, have offered a similar source of refuge, support, and strength, particularly for the poor of Latin America (McWhirter, McWhirter, & McWhirter, 1988).

In addition to groups led by professionals, self-help groups may be an ideal option for clients of color. Self-help groups are described by Katz and Bender (1976; cited in Kahn & Bender, 1985) as voluntary groups formed by peers for the purpose of overcoming a common barrier or problem and bringing about social or personal change. Kahn and Bender (1985) suggest that participation in voluntary group activities creates a potential for a variety of developments, such as individual and group empowerment, community change, and global social development. They note that self-help groups provide more than assistance in mutual problem solving, contending that self-help groups often diminish feelings of helplessness and provide "an arena for individuals to consolidate an identity, to promote a feeling of belongingness, to develop (coping) action skills, thereby strengthening the individual and giving him/her the permission and power to act on his/her own behalf as well as for the group" (p. 8). Many self-help groups are shifting from a focus on self-care and self-change to one that includes wider social change; as such, they provide a sense of membership, purpose, and direction that sets the stage for political action and empowerment (Kahn & Bender, 1985).

One of the primary benefits of using a group modality with people of color is that groups of common-ethnic membership provide the opportunity for developing and enhancing ethnic identity and the exposure to multiple perspectives in power analysis. Jordan (1991) describes a model for counseling African American women in groups. The eight-session group, facilitated by an African American woman, is designed to "heighten awareness and appreciation of the uniqueness and beauty of Black womanhood" and to provide the participants with a support network. Similar to other women of color, African American women typically experience the triple oppression of racism, sexism, and classism. Although Jordan's group cannot be described fully here, several aspects of the group will be detailed for illustrative purposes. Participants actively and cooperatively explore their identity by defining and redefining at each meeting, as a group, what it means to be African American women in this society. Each session has a specific topic, such as Recent Roots, Paying Family Dues, Physical and Spiritual Beauty, and Celebration. The women share family wisdom, self-perceptions, songs, views of beauty and attempts to change their natural looks, burdens and responsibilities, and their unique resources for confronting difficulties. In addition, readings by and about African American women are shared and discussed, such as a passage from Alice Walker's *The Temple of My Familiar* (1989). The group is an excellent example of empowering group participation because it integrates connection and group identity, skill building, critical analysis of power dynamics, and support of the empowerment of others.

RESOURCES

The works of Sue and Sue (1990), Katz (1985), Pedersen (1987), Lee and Richardson (1992), and Vargas and Koss-Chioino (1992), as well as the special issue of the *Journal of Counseling & Development* entitled "Multiculturalism as a Fourth Force in Counseling" (Volume 70, Number 1, 1991) are among the many valuable sources of information available to counselors. While factual and descriptive information is essential, counselors and other mental health professionals interested in learning about a culture different from their own will find another rich resource in autobiographical and fictional writing. Authors such as Maya Angelou, Alice Walker, Paula Gunn Allen, and Amy Tan provide intimate glimpses into the lives of women of color. Finally, *Guidelines for Providers of Psychological Services to Ethnic, Linguistic, and Culturally Diverse Populations* (American Psychological Association, 1993) provides a clear statement of the responsibilities of mental health practitioners. Additional resources relevant to people of color will be found in the resource sections of other chapters in this book.

CONCLUSION

Although this chapter describes only a limited number of barriers and suggestions for empowerment, the reader is invited to extrapolate from his or her own experience to identify other barriers and other interventions supportive of empowerment. The rich diversity within the cultural and historical heritage of people of color is perhaps one of our nation's greatest, and least cherished, resources. We cannot claim to celebrate diversity and to be sensitive to multicultural issues without simultaneously working for social change within our profession and throughout our society. To return to the verse that opens this chapter, passive acceptance of structural injustice and Eurocentric values condemns us all—and our children—to being *children of the lie*.

Chapter Six
PEOPLE WHO ARE GAY, LESBIAN, OR BISEXUAL

I'm not homophobic

I'm just not that comfortable around
it's only when I try to picture it that I get
whatever, I mean, if that's what you want
are you sure it's not just about your father
well I don't think we should hug but it's not
have you talked with someone about it, really
so what do you people do besides wave banners and
I figured you must have signals for each other
it's just that no one I've ever known has been
as long as you aren't one of the kind that
gee I'm glad you told me keep in touch
er, I mean, see you around

E.H.M.

INTRODUCTION

Gay, lesbian, and bisexual people have been persecuted and marginalized for centuries. Still often viewed with fear and hatred, many gays, lesbians, and bisexuals live with a very realistic fear of harassment, assault, job dismissal, and other discriminatory acts. In this chapter, some of the barriers experienced by gay, lesbian, and bisexual persons will be described, and suggestions for empowerment provided.

An empowered gay, lesbian, or bisexual individual might have the following characteristics: a critical awareness of the discrimination and injustices experienced by gay, lesbian, and bisexual people in the past and present; knowledge of the strengths, resources, and political activism of gay, lesbian, and bisexual communities, as well as the accomplishments rendered through this activism; awareness of the contributions of gay, lesbian, and bisexual leaders, artists, educators, scientists, etc., throughout history; a positive sense of identity and pride; recognition of the factors contributing to homophobia and heterosexism and skills for challenging these phenomena; a sense of community with supportive others; and participation in efforts to raise consciousness, enhance pride, increase support, share cultural and artistic talents, or otherwise promote the welfare of gay, lesbian, and bisexual people.

WHO ARE GAY, LESBIAN, AND BISEXUAL PEOPLE?

Human sexual orientation traditionally has been viewed as a bipolar characteristic: People are either gay or straight. More recently, however, sexual orientation has been reconceptualized as a continuum ranging from heterosexuality to homosexuality (e.g., Klein & Wolf, 1985). Further, this continuum is viewed as multidimensional and dynamic (DeCecco, 1981). Klein (1982) discusses sexual orientation in terms of seven components: sexual attraction, sexual behavior, sexual fantasies, emotional preference, social preference, self-identification, and lifestyle. Each of these components is viewed in terms of present, past, and ideal, to capture the dynamic aspect of sexual orientation. Such a perspective incorporates the sexual orientation of the many people who, for example, have primarily heterosexual behaviors and attractions, but who fantasize about same-gender sexual encounters and have same-gender social and emotional preferences. In addition, this multidimensional and dynamic perspective incorporates the notion of bisexuality not simply as a transitory phase but as a potentially stable and enduring orientation that is also multifaceted. For example, a woman may be bisexual in her sexual attraction, fantasies, social preferences, and self-identification, while having sexual relationships primarily with women as well as preferring women to fulfill her emotional needs. If over time her sexual attraction, fantasies, and behavior become more exclusively with women, she may or may not come to self-identify as lesbian.

Homosexuality was classified as a psychiatric disorder until 1973, when it was removed from the American Psychiatric Association's list of psychiatric disorders. At that time, 37% of the membership of the American Psychiatric Association opposed this action (Bayer, 1981). Because the term "homosexual" has been clearly and negatively associated with pathology, homosexuality has been increasingly replaced with the affirmative terms gay and lesbian. Although "gay" may refer to a man or a woman, lesbians have chosen a distinct term because of the invisibility inherent in using a term that reflects men *or* men and women (Cohen & Stein, 1986). Thus, the preferred terminology is "gay male" and "lesbian." The term bisexual refers, in general, to individuals who are attracted to both men and women, along the multidimensional continuum discussed above.

Sexual orientation is used instead of sexual "preference" because preference reflects the misconception that people choose to be gay, lesbian, or bisexual in opposition to an inherently heterosexual nature. It is important to note that we currently do not understand how sexual orientation develops; the goal of research efforts should be to learn how sexual orientation develops in all human beings rather than finding out "what happens to" or "what goes wrong with" gay, lesbian, and bisexual people.

Sexual orientation must be distinguished from gender role orientation and gender identity (Iasenza, 1989). Gender roles refer to stereotyped expectations within a cultural group regarding appropriate behavior for males and females. Gender roles traditionally have been described in terms of masculinity and femininity, with those traits associated with femininity being more desirable in women and unhealthy in men, and masculine traits seen as desirable for men but not for women. Gender identity refers to a person's inner sense of being male or female. People with same-gender sexual orientations are often presumed to have opposite-gender role orientations (e.g., lesbians are presumed to be more masculine) and opposite-gender identities (e.g., gay men are presumed to believe they actually are, or wish they were, women). These assumptions are inaccurate and reflect stereotypes rather than reality.

Determining the number of gay, lesbian, and bisexual individuals in the population has become a focal point for arguments as to whether homosexuality is "normal." The most common estimate has been that approximately 10% of the population is gay, lesbian, or bisexual. However, since it has been established that gay, lesbian, and bisexual people do not differ significantly from heterosexuals with respect to psychological maladjustment (Gonsiorek, 1982; Gonsiorek & Weinrich, 1991), focusing on numbers is an unnecessary sidetrack regarding the issue of "normalcy."

Gay, lesbian, and bisexual people are Korean American, German American, Puerto Rican, and African American; they are computer consultants, teachers, CEOs, maintenance workers, and athletes; they are temporarily able-bodied and disabled; they are adolescents and older adults; they are "out" to no one, to some, and to everyone; they are homophobic and gay, lesbian, and bisexual affirmative. In other words, gay, lesbian, and bisexual people cannot be characterized any more than

Italian Americans or people with disabilities; "they" are us. The following personal statement by Sue Morrow reflects both the uniqueness and the universality of one lesbian woman's life.

When I think of discussing my experience as a lesbian in this society, my first response is, "But I am anything but typical." Then again, what is a typical lesbian? So I will speak for myself. I am a middle-class, Caucasian, 49-year-old lesbian doctoral student in counseling psychology. My partner/lover of 17 years and I live together in a university town in the Southwest. She is a psychologist; I am a counselor and faculty associate in a university Women's Studies program. My two children have just begun their first year in community college.

I "came out" to myself when I was 32; I had been married for nine years and my children were 2 1/2 and five years old. I had lived happily until that time as a heterosexual woman; then I fell in love with a woman. The intensity and rightness of it all made me know that my heterosexual identity had been dependent upon "just not having met the right woman." Although at first my husband and I attempted to work out a peaceful separation with joint custody, his visit home to his parents resulted in his serving me with a custody suit upon his return. It was a bitter battle, filled with lies and deception by my husband and his attorney; and when I was threatened that the names of several lesbians in the community—some of whom were also lesbian mothers, as well as teachers and state employees in a state unfriendly to lesbians and gay men—would be given to the media, I gave up.

I had suffered abuse in my childhood, as well as the early death of my mother, but the loss of my children was beyond grief. "I couldn't live if I lost my children," several women have said to me. One can't but one does. One simply does.

The rewards? "Freedom's just another word for nothing left to lose." I have been open as a teacher, a graduate student in my master's and Ph.D. programs, a community activist, and a psychotherapist. Being honest about who I am—to myself and to others—is part of being congruent and healthy. I have received mixed reactions in my doctoral program, from full support and advocacy from both lesbian and nonlesbian faculty to sexual harassment based on my life-style by one male professor. For the most part, the reactions of my peers and my students have been positive.

My life is richer than I could ever have imagined. Lesbians have a beautiful culture of women's music, concerts, festivals, conferences, literature, dances, and other community events. I am a feminist and a political activist, working to change attitudes and raise consciousness about women and lesbians, along with other social and environmental issues. The intimacy I share with my lover is enhanced and deepened because of our mutuality and equality, as well as the unique bond that is characteristic of women's friendships. My children have an openness to diversity that has resulted from being children of a mother who is "different." In a society that is characterized by alienation and that would impose the worst isolation upon those people it considers deviant, I find myself in a community of women who love and support one another; I experience a greater sense of community than I ever have in the church or neighborhoods of my prior life.

The challenges are never-ending. We must do extensive legal work in order to be certain that one of us will be able to visit the other in intensive care in a hospital or that one will not have our shared possessions of many years taken by an angry family member when the other one dies. We experience the regular threats and harassment by anonymous telephone callers, never knowing if the harassment will extend into violence. We cannot hold hands in public as we celebrate birthdays or anniversaries without our private moment becoming a political act. Yet when I was asked in a class one day, "If there were a magic pill you could take that would turn you straight, would you take it?," I was astounded. For my life, since coming out as a lesbian, has been characterized by freedom, growth, and pride. I have already found the magic potion.

BARRIERS

Several of the primary barriers experienced by many gay, lesbian, and bisexual people will be discussed below. The profound effects of HIV disease on gay men, in particular, are considered in Chapter Seven.

Heterosexism

As a nation we often pride ourselves on the presumption of our legal system that people are "innocent until proven guilty." Guiding jury decisions and all other aspects of the justice system, it is an explicit presumption. Our society is full of other presumptions, most of which are far less explicit but which have similarly profound implications for our society. Heterosexism is the presumption that all people are heterosexual, and that heterosexuality is the normal, healthy, and preferred orientation of all human beings (Dworkin & Gutiérrez, 1992). Homosexuals are viewed as deviant and pathological or at least "abnormal." Heterosexism is embedded in our institutions, our mass media, our textbooks, our thoughts, and is rooted in a complex combination of religious and cultural norms.

The elimination of homosexuality from the list of psychiatric disorders has not eliminated perceptions of homosexuality as sinful, perverted, abnormal, and pathological. Gay, lesbian, and bisexual individuals are still often shunned or rejected by their families, unprotected by the legal system, and subjected to hate crimes. Traditional personality theories promote heterosexism in their descriptions of normal human development (Buhrke, 1989; Glassgold, 1992). Heterosexism is also obvious in our legal system (Bersoff & Ogden, 1991). As of 1989, housing and employment discrimination against gays and lesbians was legal in every state except Wisconsin (Herek, 1989). DeAngelis (1992) notes that although Kentucky's Supreme Court recently voted down the state's sodomy law (which banned oral and anal sex between homosexuals but not heterosexuals), seven states still have similar laws. Another 16 states still prohibit oral and anal sex between any consenting adults, regardless of the gender of the partners. As noted in Sue Morrow's personal statement, gay, lesbian, and bisexual parents may lose custody of their children solely on the basis of their sexual orientation. Further, since there is no legal recognition of gay and lesbian couples and families, gay and lesbian couples may be denied visitation rights in intensive care units, may not be permitted to care for chronically ill or dying partners, or may lose shared possessions to family of origin members on the death of their partner.

Homophobia

Homophobia is the irrational fear of gay and lesbian people (or people who *seem to be* gay or lesbian) (Dworkin & Gutiérrez, 1992). Pharr (1988) argues that homophobia serves to maintain sexism, because fear of being perceived as homosexual keeps women and men adhering to narrowly defined gender role behavior. Homophobia is manifested in people who avoid associating with people who they perceive as homosexual; they often hold and express extremely negative attitudes toward gay, lesbian, and bisexual individuals. People who are homophobic also may exaggerate their own gender role behavior so as to make it clear that they are *not*, themselves, gay or lesbian—even though most gay and lesbian individuals exhibit gender role behavior consistent with that of mainstream society. Bisexual individuals often experience homophobia within the gay and lesbian communities as well as the dominant heterosexual world (Dworkin & Gutiérrez, 1992; Wolf, 1992)

Homophobia may be overt or subtle, and individuals vary in their degree of awareness of their homophobia. Counselors, psychologists, and other mental health professionals are no exception (Garnets, Hancock, Cochran, Goodchilds, & Peplau, 1991) and often lack awareness of their own homophobic attitudes and feelings. The following excerpts from letters to the American Psychological Association's *Monitor* exemplify more overt forms of heterosexism and homophobia within the field of psychology:

> It is with great sadness that I am not going to renew my APA membership, and will resign from my state association. I strongly support APA.... But I can no longer continue to financially support an institution that takes

> moral and political stands that are opposite to my Christian values...I am speaking specifically to the homosexual issue in which it is considered unethical for a psychologist to view homosexuality as any kind of developmental arrest or pathology in any form.... (Daniel, 1991, p. 4)

> It is one thing for an adult to identify himself or herself as a homosexual; it is not only inaccurate and inappropriate to label so vast a number of other individuals, it is unthinkable to do it to *innocent* children and young people.... (Wyatt, 1992, p.4; emphasis added)

Internalized homophobia refers to self-directed negative messages about homosexuality among gays, lesbians, and bisexuals. It may begin with name-calling in elementary school. Children learn quickly that nonaggressive boys are somehow bad, and label them as "queers" and "faggots," while girls who hold hands or who don't show sufficient interest in boys are similarly labeled "queers" and "dykes" (Birle, 1993). Adolescents face similar stigmatization (Hetrick, 1988). The devaluation and condemnation of gays, lesbians, and bisexuals thus begins early, and the negative stereotypes continue for a lifetime. The strong social message that homosexuality is perverted, unnatural, immoral, anti-Christian, pathological, and unhealthy cannot help but affect the self-perceptions of gay, lesbian, and bisexual individuals. Most writers on the topic of counseling with gay, lesbian, and bisexual clients advocate routine investigation of internalized homophobia. Given the prevalence of homophobia in society, as well as the lack of information and negative stereotypes about gays, lesbians, and bisexuals, it is not surprising that moving beyond internalized homophobia constitutes a major task in a model of gay and lesbian identity development (Cass, 1979).

Hate Crimes

Gay men and lesbians are the target of more hate crimes than any other ethnic or nonethnic minority group in the United States, including African Americans and Jews (Finn & McNeil, 1987). Drawing from Finn and McNeil (1987), Herek (1989) defined hate crimes as:

> words or actions intended to harm or intimidate an individual because of her or his membership in a minority group; they include violent assaults, murder, rape, and property crimes motivated by prejudice, as well as threats of violence or other acts of intimidation. (p. 948)

Although public awareness has increased and there is a new federal mandate (the Hate Crimes Statistics Act) requiring the U.S. Department of Justice to collect data on such crimes (Lieberman, 1992), the problem of hate crimes is increasing. Lieberman (1992) cited findings that attacks on gay men and lesbians in each of five major metropolitan areas had increased 31% between 1990 and 1991. The consequences of antigay hate crimes include physical and psychological harm, the creation of a climate of fear in gay and lesbian communities, and, for those who have not yet come out, fear of exposure as a gay or lesbian person (Garnets, Herek, & Levy, 1990; Herek, 1989). In addition, Lieberman notes that in the past 300 years, gay Americans routinely have been imprisoned, fined, castrated, clitorectomized, forced to undergo psychiatric treatment, expelled from the military, and subjected to general social ostracism.

Although young males acting alone or in small groups frequently perpetrate hate crimes (Herek, 1989), organized hate groups such as the Ku Klux Klan regularly include gay, lesbian, and bisexual people along with their traditional target, Jews and African Americans (Caldwell, 1988). Two Klan leaders (Imperial Wizards) are calling for restraint among followers with respect to overt violence and racism, hoping to improve their image à la David Duke (Boland, 1992). However, these individuals have been labeled traitors by other Klan leaders. Some of the more radical Klan groups are recruiting actively from the country's approximately 3,000 neo-Nazi "skinheads"; these skinheads are "more consistently violent" and "increasingly well-armed" (Boland, 1992, p. 32). Although largely unreported, antigay violence and harassment also occurs within families (Gross, Aurand, & Addessa, 1988; cited in Herek, 1989).

Racism

Gays, lesbians, and bisexuals of color frequently experience not only homophobia and racism from the larger society but also racism within gay, lesbian, and bisexual communities (Gutiérrez & Dworkin, 1992; Icard, 1986; Loiacano, 1989). Struggling with identity development in two separate domains can be a difficult task, even within accepting communities (Morales, 1992; Chan, 1989, 1992; Espin, 1987). The history of exclusion and/or marginalization of people of color within the Euro American gay and lesbian communities makes this task even more difficult. Racism may be experienced in many forms: exclusion from activities; racial slurs; social rejection; being treated as "exotic"; exclusion from leadership roles; and the omission of efforts to eliminate racism through political agendas and consciousness-raising efforts (Chan, 1989; Loiacano, 1989).

Invisibility

Gay, lesbian, and bisexual people sometimes are referred to as an "invisible" minority because they have no external characteristics that indicate they are not heterosexual. Because textbooks and especially history books rarely indicate the sexual orientation of the people described (e.g., we were never told that Emily Dickinson was lesbian or that Michelangelo was gay), children and adults alike easily impose their heterosexist bias and assume that all the people about whom they read are heterosexual. Prime-time television and the mass media rarely depict gay, lesbian, or bisexual relationships; when such relationships are portrayed, they are often stereotypical and negative. Further, the consequences of open acknowledgment of one's gayness, lesbianism, or bisexuality can be so severe that many people choose to "pass" (to hide their sexual orientation) except among their closest friends. Thus, heterosexist bias goes unchallenged, and many gay, lesbian, and bisexual individuals in the early stages of sexual identity development experience intense isolation. The invisibility of bisexual individuals is even more profound. Even within the gay and lesbian communities, bisexuals frequently are viewed as people who can't decide or who haven't fully realized their sexual orientation yet (Wolf, 1992).

The process of "outing" has been embraced by some radical groups. "Outing" refers to exposing a person's gay, lesbian, or bisexual orientation without the individual's permission. The purpose of outing is to reduce invisibility and demonstrate that gay, lesbian, and bisexual people are everywhere—not merely in San Francisco—and that they are competent and trusted members of all professions—not only artists, hairdressers, and interior designers. Advocates of outing believe that violating the privacy of an individual is an acceptable means to the end of eliminating heterosexism and homophobia. Nevertheless, outing, regardless of its greater social aims, is disempowering to individuals, contributes to the existing climate of fear, and is ultimately unjustifiable. Coming out and establishing a positive gay, lesbian, or bisexual identity is difficult even when individuals consciously self-direct each step of the process. The imposition of an externally determined timetable, with or without warning, reinforces the notion of powerlessness and of being less than capable of determining one's own life course.

The influences of heterosexism, homophobia, racism, internalized homophobia, and invisibility often lead gay, lesbian, and bisexual people to seek counseling.

Lack of Counselor Training/Sensitivity

In 1969, the police raided a section of New York City's Greenwich Village known to be home to many gay and lesbian individuals. The subsequent uprising on Stonewall Street marked the gay and lesbian community's first public resistance to ongoing police discrimination. The "Stonewall resistance," the surge of gay activism in the '60s and '70s, strong nationwide advocacy on the part of gay, lesbian, and bisexual task forces, and the AIDS epidemic "should" have been sufficient to bring sexual orientation into the forefront of counselor training. However, just as counselor training programs will vary with regard to the integration of multiculturalism (D'Andrea & Daniels, 1991), there is programmatic variation in counselor preparation to deal effectively with issues of sexual orientation. As such, gay, lesbian, and bisexual clients may receive services that are inappropriate, offensive, and even destructive.

The need for counselor training related to gay, lesbian, and bisexual issues is clearly recognized (Dworkin & Gutiérrez, 1992). Reviewing the literature on counselor attitudes toward homosexuality, Rudolph (1988) concluded that there remains a great deal of ambivalence among counselors. This ambivalence is reflected, for example, in the concurrent endorsement of statements that lesbian women may be mentally healthy *and* that lesbian women usually have a history of disturbed relationships with both parents, particularly with respect to issues involving sexual maturation. Rudolph (1988) argues that counselors must be "vigorously self-conscious" of their attitudes toward "homosexuality, homosexual behavior, and homosexual persons" (p. 167). The extent to which counselors in training are actually directed and encouraged to do so is questionable.

House and Holloway (1992) discuss the supervisory process as a vehicle for promoting gay and lesbian affirmative counseling. Frank and open discussion of heterosexism and homophobia is critical; supervisors also can model affirmative behavior by making educational materials available to supervisees (House & Holloway, 1992). When supervisees are unwilling to examine their own biases, or when they engage in counseling practices that are detrimental to their gay, lesbian, or bisexual clients, supervisors' first responsibility is to the client. House and Holloway (1992) explore these and other issues through case examples and analyses.

Although information regarding sexual orientation and gay, lesbian, and bisexual issues may not be integrated formally into counselor training programs, an abundance of information is available. For example, Buhrke (1989) provides readings for counselors in training in the following categories: general information about lesbians, gay men, and bisexuals; counseling issues; personality and human development; marriage, family, and couples counseling; career counseling; multicultural counseling; and assessment. Recent issues of mainstream counseling journals have focused on the mental health and development of gay, lesbian, and bisexual individuals (e.g., Dworkin & Gutiérrez, 1989). In addition, extensive resource lists are available from sources such as Dworkin and Gutiérrez (1992). Finally, above all else, counselors must recognize that the problems of gay, lesbian, and bisexual clients do not occur *because* of their sexual orientation. Problems emerge for a multiplicity of reasons, but always in the context of a heterosexist, homophobic, and racist society. This point can be illustrated in part by contrasting the implications of the following two statements: "I was attacked by two young men because I am gay," versus "I was attacked by two young men because they are violently homophobic." Preparation to work with gay, lesbian, and bisexual clients will reduce the likelihood that counselors will impede rather than facilitate the empowerment process.

SUGGESTIONS FOR EMPOWERMENT

Information

The provision of information can be extremely useful in helping gay, lesbian, and bisexual individuals examine power dynamics at work in their lives, develop a sense of group identity, become involved in activism, and support the empowerment of others. For gays, lesbians, and bisexuals of color, power analysis of the dynamics of racism and homophobia within gay and lesbian communities may be particularly relevant to their struggle. Exposure to efforts such as *Project 21*, a national alliance for achieving accurate curriculum and textbook inclusion of the achievements of gays, lesbians, and bisexuals (Birle, 1993), can introduce clients to the proactive stance of their peers, alert clients to their own heterosexist assumptions, and provide a means of getting involved in transforming society. Learning the history of society's treatment of gays, lesbians, and bisexuals provides a context for understanding the significance of specific events such as the Stonewall resistance. The emergence of the gay rights movement, gay/lesbian/bisexual task forces and collectives throughout the country, and the instrumental role of gay, lesbian, and bisexual people in calling attention to the seriousness of the AIDS epidemic, are important aspects of the history of the gay, lesbian, and bisexual communities.

Identification of local support groups and exposure to cultural, educational, and recreational events within the local gay, lesbian, and bisexual communities may assist in the enhancement of a group identity, as well as providing a source of positive role models, mentors, and companions. Finally, there is a wealth of written resources available for addressing a wide variety of concerns specific to gay, lesbian, and bisexual clients. For example, Katz's *Gay/Lesbian Almanac* (1983) and *Gay American History* (1976) document some of the contributions of prominent gay, lesbian, and bisexual historic figures.

Advocacy

Counselors have an ethical responsibility to be educated with respect to gay, lesbian, and bisexual issues; those who believe they don't have any gay, lesbian, or bisexual clients probably have not created an atmosphere in which coming out is safe. Participation in task forces, professional meetings, and community activities that promote the well-being of gay, lesbian, and bisexual individuals is not the sole responsibility of gay, lesbian, and bisexual counselors. In addition, all counselors have an obligation to confront homophobia and heterosexism as it emerges in staff meetings, case conferences, educational activities, and agency policies. Of course, advocating for the rights of gay men, lesbians, and bisexuals means possibly being perceived as gay, lesbian, or bisexual; as such, it offers heterosexual counselors an opportunity to confront their own homophobia and heterosexism as well as to experience some of its consequences.

Identity Development

The counselor's ability to provide information and suggestions regarding the development of positive gay, lesbian, and bisexual identities is essential. Having a positive gay, lesbian, or bisexual identity is related to psychological adjustment (Miranda & Storms, 1989). It is not always necessary to educate clients about specific models and stages; sometimes just being able to assess the client's stage and supporting the client's movement through that stage is of greatest help. Clients need to know that the development of a positive identity is a process that is both common and unique relative to the identity development of other gays, lesbians, and bisexuals.

Cass (1979) proposed a six-stage model of homosexual identity formation. The first stage, *identity confusion*, corresponds with the onset of questions regarding one's sexual orientation. Previous assumptions of heterosexuality are examined now in light of recognizing attractions to members of the same sex. The second stage, *identity comparison*, involves recognition that "I might be gay" (or lesbian or bisexual). Individuals in this stage experience feelings of social alienation and separateness from previously comfortable subgroups. In the next stage, *identity tolerance*, the person begins developing alliances with other gay, lesbian, or bisexual people, but maintains a high degree of secrecy regarding his or her sexual orientation. Stage Four, the *identity acceptance* stage, is characterized by the selective sharing of one's sexual orientation. People at this stage may come out to family members and close friends who are heterosexual, and begin to view their sexual orientation as normal and valid. Stage Five, *identity pride*, is characterized by greater pride and involvement in gay and lesbian cultures and communities, often to the exclusion of activities with heterosexual friends. Individuals in this stage are very aware of the negative stereotypes of gay, lesbian, and bisexual people that pervade the dominant culture, and may devalue heterosexuality themselves. Finally, in *identity synthesis*, sexual identity is integrated with other aspect of the personality. During this sixth stage, individuals may pursue friendships and activities within and outside of the gay/lesbian community. Cass's (1979) model and others typically characterize the process of developing a positive gay, lesbian, or bisexual identity as a series of nonlinear and potentially reoccurring stages (O'Connor, 1992).

For gays, lesbians, and bisexuals of color, the process of developing a positive ethnic identity may happen concurrently and even conflict with the development of a positive sexual identity. In his qualitative interviews with African American gay men and lesbians, Loiacano (1989) found three common themes in their process of gay/lesbian identity development: the search for validation among gay and lesbian communities; the search for validation in the African American community; and the integration of these identities. The racism present in the largely Euro American gay, lesbian, and bisexual communities contributes to what Espin (1987) calls a fundamental dilemma. She argues that Latina lesbians fear stigmatization from the Hispanic community and loss of their Hispanic identity within the Euro American lesbian community. Similar to Loiacano's (1989) findings with African American gay men, Espin (1987) found that her study participants sought validation in both communities. Perceptions of gay, lesbian, and bisexual individuals varies by ethnic groups. Chan (1989, 1992) notes that homosexuality is largely denied within the Asian American community; gay and lesbian Asian Americans may be perceived as rejecting their families and reflecting their parents' failure to transmit the foundational values of Asian culture. Thus, coming out as gay, lesbian, or bisexual may be experienced by Asian Americans and/or their families as bringing great shame on the family. Chan (1989) found that the majority of gay and lesbian Asian American participants in her study had not come out to their parents, and were more strongly identified as gay or lesbian than as Asian American.

The counselor's validation of the multiple identity struggles of the gay, lesbian, or bisexual client of color is critical. Morales (1983, 1992) integrates models of ethnic and gay/lesbian identity development and provides suggestions for counselors assisting Latino gays and lesbians in their process of identity integration. For example, gay Latinos and lesbian Latinas may experience a conflict allegiance and feel compelled to choose between their identity communities. Morales (1992) suggests that exploration of the nature of the support available in each community, as well as establishing the individual's priorities, can help in the recognition and appreciation of multiple and nonexclusive identities. Certainly one of the most important sources of support can be developing relationships with gays, lesbians, and bisexuals of similar ethnic backgrounds. Several of Loiacano's (1989) gay and lesbian African American study participants were active in forming organizations and support groups specifically for Black gays and lesbians. Counselors' knowledge of the developmental processes associated with ethnic and sexual identity will enhance their effectiveness and helpfulness to clients; client participation in supportive groups can further enhance their identity development process.

Family of Choice

Unfortunately, many gay, lesbian, and bisexual individuals are rejected by their families after they come out. Others may opt to create distance between themselves and a family that excludes lovers from family gatherings; refuses to acknowledge their gay, lesbian, or bisexual identity; or in some other way demonstrates a lack of support for or rejection of the individual. In addition to helping clients move through a grieving process for the loss of support, connection, affection, or whatever their changed family relationships represent, counselors can introduce the notion of a family of choice. Playing off the old adage, "You can't choose your relatives," many gay, lesbian, and bisexual people have established families of choice. These families have no set characteristics other than an agreement to provide emotional and perhaps other kinds of support. Sometimes specific roles such as sister, mother, and brother are clarified among members of a family of choice; at other times no such distinction in roles is made. The family of choice represents a proactive step toward receiving and providing the positive nurturance, companionship, and loyalty that families of origin did not, or no longer, provide. Hawxhurst and Morrow (1984) offer excellent, practical suggestions for building a feminist community that could easily inform the process of creating a family of choice.

Skill Application: Communication

Communication skills training facilitates empowerment by enabling clients to voice their feelings and perceptions, ask for what they want, and identify their limits. People able to communicate effectively have a better chance of being heard and having their needs met. In addition, they provide a healthier environment and better role models for the people around them than those who do not communicate well. In the example described below, communication skills training facilitated the coming out process of a young bisexual woman.

Kelly was a 19-year-old Euro American woman who sought counseling to "deal with my mother better." Kelly informed her counselor in the first session that although she got along with her father "alright," she and her mother had had a rather stormy relationship since Kelly was 13 years old. She described her mother as nosy, demanding, religious, and nervous. Her father was "pretty cool" and "an intellectual, hippie-used-to-be type." She reported that she could talk with her father about many topics, but her mother would "freak" when Kelly expressed a strong opinion or a liberal viewpoint.

Kelly began the second session by announcing, "Well, I'm 'bi' and it's just fine," as she sat in her chair. The counselor simply said, "OK," and sat silently for a few minutes. Kelly became agitated: "What do you mean, 'OK'; we have to talk about this, I'm not just kidding around." As the session unfolded, the counselor learned that Kelly's father—who considered her to be lesbian—had advised her not to tell her mother; he thought Kelly might "grow out of it," "find the right man," and never need to tell her mother anyway. Kelly was angry about "hiding" this part of herself, but she also agreed with her father that her mother would "probably have a heart attack." She didn't believe she would grow out of her feelings; she had been aware of being attracted to males and females since she was 13 years old. She had been in a sexual relationship with a close girlfriend for two years. Prior to this she had had several shorter romantic relationships with boys. Currently her other friendships were fairly superficial and no one else knew she was bisexual.

Kelly demonstrated a protective attitude toward her father; he was "so good about the whole thing" and if it helped him to believe she might change, that was acceptable to her. But she resented feeling as though she had to protect her mother constantly from her own thoughts and identity. She was tentatively planning to inform her mother just as she had informed her counselor; "Guess what, Mom; I'm bisexual!"

Although Kelly appeared confident and comfortable with her sexual orientation, the counselor suspected that she would benefit from having a wider support network than her father and girlfriend. In addition, the counselor noticed that Kelly frequently made dramatic, "bombshell" statements and then reacted with disappointment when she failed to startle the counselor. The counselor shared her concern that Kelly should develop a group of friends who could support and validate, rather than simply tolerate, her bisexual identity. They also processed Kelly's "bombshell" style. Kelly discovered a pattern in her family's communication: Her sudden statements would upset her mother and gain her father's attention; her father would react initially by soothing her mother, relieving Kelly of her protector role; later, her father would come to "talk sense into her" and they usually would have an intimate conversation. Although this style was adaptive,

Kelly realized that she was getting tired of "going in circles." She and the counselor established the goals of (1) finding support, (2) working on communication skills, and (3) formulating a "coming out" plan.

Over the next several sessions, Kelly and the counselor discussed different options for finding community. After talking to one of the participants on the phone, Kelly decided to try joining a support group for lesbian and bisexual women. With respect to communication skills, they focused on the perception-feeling-want triad and meta-communication (discussed in Chapter Four). After role-playing conversations in which Kelly and her counselor took turns being her mother, Kelly tried meta-communicating with her mother about staying out late. She described to her mother how she felt when her mother stayed up waiting for her, and how she (Kelly) would get angry in response to her mother's questions. She let her mother know that her mother's concern felt good, but the degree of concern did not. Then she asked her mother, "How can we fix this?" Although the ensuing conversation ended with an angry exchange of words, Kelly was intrigued by her mother's initially calm response. Kelly stated, "Maybe there's hope; at least I know I can do some things to make the situation potentially better."

With respect to her third goal, Kelly decided to postpone coming out to her mother until she felt more comfortable and consistent in using her new communication skills. Her first support group meeting was "scary and wonderful; I thought they would all be weird, but they're pretty cool." She invited her girlfriend along to the next meeting. When Kelly terminated counseling three months later, she had begun to socialize with women in the lesbian community and was expressing strongly positive attitudes about being bisexual. Her relationship with her mother was developing into one characterized more by tolerance than anger. Kelly was taking more risks with both of her parents in terms of sharing her feelings, and at the same time seemed slightly less vulnerable to their negative or neutral responses. She felt much more aware of her family dynamics, and viewed herself as making healthier decisions about how to relate to her parents.

RESOURCES

A growing number of resources are available for those interested in increasing their awareness of issues related to gay, lesbian, and bisexual people, as well as resources for community participation and political action. These include *Counseling Gay Men and Lesbians: Journey to the End of the Rainbow* by Dworkin and Gutiérrez (1992); *Living Our Visions: Building Feminist Community* by Hawxhurst and Morrow (1984); *Loving Someone Gay* by Clark (1977); *Gay Parenting: A Complete Guide for Gay Men and Lesbians with Children* by Schulenberg (1985); and *The Lavender Couch: A Consumer's Guide to Psychotherapy for Lesbians and Gay Men* by Hall (1985).

In a special issue of the *Journal of Counseling and Development*, Hetherington and Orzek (1989) list more than 30 professional associations and resources for lesbians, gays, and bisexuals. These organizations include National Gay and Lesbian Task Force Gay Organizations Mailing List, 1517 U Street, N.W., Washington, DC 20009, (202) 332-6483; Association for Gay, Lesbian, and Bisexual Issues in Counseling (AGLBIC), P.O. Box 216, Jenkintown, PA 19046; and Federation of Parents & Professionals for Friends of Lesbians & Gays, P.O. Box 24565, Los Angeles, CA 90024. Organizations listed by Dworkin and Gutiérrez (1992) include Black Gay and Lesbian Leadership Forum, 3924 W. Sunset Boulevard, Los Angeles, CA 90029; CALM: Custody Action for Lesbian Mothers, Box 281, Narberth, PA 19072; Gay Asian Pacific Alliance, 1841 Market Street, 2nd Floor, San Francisco, CA 94103; Gay Fathers Coalition, P.O. Box 19891, Washington, DC 20036; LLEGO Nacional, P.O. Box 44483, Washington DC 20036; and SAGE: Senior Action in a Gay Environment, 208 W. 13th Street, New York, NY 10011, (212) 741-2247. Additional writings and organizations of interest may be found in the resource sections of other chapters in this book.

CONCLUSION

In this chapter, some of the barriers experienced by gay men, lesbians, and bisexuals have been identified. Understanding the sociopolitical context in which gay, lesbian, and bisexual individuals live—a context of heterosexism and homophobia—is critical to counseling for empowerment. As counselors, we are obligated to identify our own heterosexist and homophobic attitudes so that we can provide appropriate, respectful counseling services. We also have an important role to play as advocates within our profession and in the larger society; to ignore this role is to become a part of the barriers faced by gay men, lesbians, and bisexuals in the development of a positive self-identity.

Chapter Seven
PEOPLE WITH HIV DISEASE

---

as if magic whispered
called forth this calamity
as if the devil initiated
rather than ignored its devastation
as if molokai
were locked in history
never again, we said again
as if your weakening embrace
were a death threat

E.H.M.

INTRODUCTION

The human immunodeficiency virus (HIV) poses a major personal and professional challenge to all helping professionals. The shocking prevalence of HIV infection, the absence of a cure, the stigma associated with the infection and AIDS, and the hysteria that has accompanied society's slow response to this lethal illness all combine to make the role of professional helpers absolutely vital. While the personal and professional caregivers for people with HIV disease also require attention and professional support, the focus of this chapter is on empowering people who have contracted HIV disease.

In the context of a diagnosis of HIV, full empowerment might incorporate the following: understanding the nature of HIV and its

---

Note: The personal statements in this chapter are based on an open-ended interview with four gay men with HIV disease. The verbatim reflections of Joseph Conrad, Rodney Shuey, Fritz Bally, and Scott DiStefano of the Nebraska AIDS Project are interspersed throughout this chapter.

progression; understanding medical options; an ability to deal assertively with medical personnel; proactive participation in treatment decisions; understanding the nature of the stigma of HIV disease and how this stigma has influenced research and prevention efforts; affiliation with a supportive community; some form of activism that supports the empowerment of those with, or at risk of, HIV disease; hopefulness with respect to a cure or with respect to the remainder of life; and preparation for impairment and death.

WHO ARE PEOPLE WITH HIV DISEASE?

Following the terminology employed by Keeling (1993), HIV disease is a chronic, progressive disorder caused by the human immunodeficiency virus. The disease passes through a sequence of predictable stages and culminates in the condition called acquired immune deficiency syndrome (AIDS). Currently, although the amount of time between testing seropositive for HIV and receiving an AIDS diagnosis is lengthening, all those who have HIV eventually progress to the final stage of AIDS. As of June 1992, more than one million people in the United States were infected with HIV, and there were 230,179 diagnosed cases of AIDS (Centers for Disease Control, 1992).

Commonly perceived as a disease of gay and bisexual white males, HIV disease increasingly claims the lives of IV drug users, heterosexual women and men, and adolescents. People of color represent a large proportion of those infected. Keeling (1993) states:

> The factors of social and economic class, poverty, and urban despair that produce overrepresentations of people of color in the population of injecting drug users will continue to result in an increasingly disproportionate impact of the epidemic on African American and Hispanic people during the second decade of HIV; it is worth emphasizing as strongly as possible that these disproportions occur not because of the biologic reality of race, but because race is a "front" for class, socioeconomic status, and poverty in this context. (p. 264)

Rates of heterosexual transmission of HIV among adolescents and young adults are rising dramatically, especially in urban areas and among runaways, homeless, and disadvantaged youth (St. Louis et al., 1989). HIV infection among homeless adolescents is 2% to 10% higher than rates for other adolescent samples (St. Louis et al., 1989). Due to needle sharing and increased rates of heterosexual transmission of HIV, women and their infants are the two fastest growing categories of people with AIDS (Centers for Disease Control, 1992). Women made up 9% of diagnosed AIDS cases in 1988 (*AIDS Weekly Surveillance Report*, July 4,

1988), and 77% of women infected via sexual transmission are Black or Latina (Guinan & Hardy, 1987).

As the number of people with HIV disease increases, and as HIV affects an increasingly diverse group of people, we must be prepared to respond whether our setting is a college counseling center, an inner city agency, or a private practice. We are, in the words of Kain (1989), "no longer immune."

BARRIERS

Physical Health

The progression of HIV disease has been documented fairly well. There are four major phases of the disease: primary HIV disease; chronic asymptomatic disease; chronic symptomatic disease; and advanced disease, or AIDS. The following descriptions are drawn primarily from Keeling (1993). The first phase of HIV disease is characterized by a short period of minor illness occurring just after the person has been infected with HIV, but before standard testing for antibodies would yield positive results. During this phase the individual is most likely to pass on the virus. This phase is usually identified only retrospectively, since the symptoms correspond with those of a wide variety of common illnesses. The second phase, chronic asymptomatic disease, is characterized by a lack of overt symptoms while the disease continues to reduce the capacity of the immunological system. The presence of the virus can be detected through testing during this phase. The chronic asymptomatic phase terminates, on average, between six and 11 years after the initial infection with HIV; on rare occasions it lasts less than one year or more than 12 years.

The third phase, chronic symptomatic disease, marks the beginning of overt physical symptoms. A person in this phase may experience fever, intense night sweats, excessive fatigue, loss of appetite, and weight loss. These symptoms may come and go, and may appear in conjunction with secondary infections.

> I mean it comes in spurts.... Like a month ago I was on nine pills, I'm down to two today. I went from nine to two. It's like now I'm feelin' great but there was a period four months ago...

> I was in the emergency room in February and I swear to God...I was feverish, I couldn't breathe, and my partner was there with me holding my

> hand and I said I can't keep going through this, I can't. And I was so sick,
> I felt so bad…. But two weeks later after you get out you feel better, and
> you're able to tolerate food without being nauseous from one of the drugs
> you're taking or just the illness, and you feel better and then you say, yeah,
> okay I can get along with this. I'll keep goin' until the next thing happens.
> But you've always got that cloud above you.

Problems with the skin (hair follicle infections, dermatitis, shingles)
and mucous membranes (canker sores, thrush, and chronic vaginal
infections) often occur during the chronic symptomatic phase. The
fatigue that often accompanies this phase is potentially the most debili-
tating physical symptom; people may have difficulty fulfilling their
normal responsibilities as workers, parents, partners, and friends. As
they attempt to maintain routines in the face of reduced energy, they
may be less able to invest effort in the potentially empowering activities
of community involvement and activism.

People generally are diagnosed with AIDS, phase four of HIV disease,
when they manifest symptoms consistent with one of four major
categories of illness: opportunistic infections (such as tuberculosis or
pneumocystis carinii pneumonia); neoplasms (most often Kaposi's sar-
coma, which may result in purple lesions on the face and neck, or
lymphomas, which are tumors in the lymphoid tissue that frequently are
resistant to treatment); neurologic disease (typically AIDS dementia
complex); and wasting (the loss of large proportions of weight and lean
body mass). Opportunistic infections are the most dangerous and account for much of the hospitalization, disability, and death associated
with HIV disease.

> I haven't had a serious illness, I haven't really been sick in a long, long time.
> But my mental part of HIV right now is I'm waiting for the shoe to drop,
> I'm waiting for the "big one" I call it. Boom. The big OI we call it,
> opportunistic infection. Which one is it gonna be?

AIDS dementia complex is characterized by memory deficits, difficulty concentrating, apathy, emotional lability, and psychomotor retar-
dation. These illnesses result in increasing physical restrictions prior to
the person's death. Ultimately it becomes impossible for the individual
to fulfill familial and occupational responsibilities, resulting in loss of
important, self-defining roles.

Underlying all issues of physical health is access to health care. Many
people with HIV disease cannot afford the high cost of medical care and
are without health insurance. Many of those who do not yet require
hospitalization have no one to care for them in the advanced stages of
the illness; they may end up in hospitals prematurely because they have
nowhere else to go. Even low-cost counseling is beyond the means of
many people with HIV disease.

Psychological Health

For the vast majority of people with HIV disease, receiving the initial diagnosis is devastating. The diagnosis usually results in physical and psychological trauma. Insomnia, depression, heightened emotional distress, and fatigue are common responses to the crisis precipitated by the diagnosis, and adjustment disorders are not uncommon. Some people feel guilty or ashamed about their life-style. Many feel they have received a death sentence, are fearful of potential pain and disfigurement, or feel dirty and damaged (Martin, 1989).

> I fully expected the test to be positive and when he told me it was, it was a shock even though I was ready to hear it. You know it was still kind of a shock and my reaction wasn't one of anger or real fear at the time except for the fact that the doctor told me I would be dead in 18 months and ah, you know, I just basically went home and cried. I withdrew from my friends and then from my job and from society, really, I just withdrew myself. I decided that I was just gonna go off and die. That's how I chose to handle it at first. I waited six months to tell anybody, which was a mistake.

> I found out last July that I was HIV positive through one of the local plasma centers. I was going in and giving my blood, and the next time I could give they said they lost my files. They found them within a half hour so they called me into this little room and told me I was HIV positive. There was no kind of counseling or anything done with it so I didn't know where to go with it. I was suicidal, severely depressed, it was rough and you know, I mean, I didn't know who to talk to. My dad lives out of state and my mom was here but I just didn't know if I wanted to share it. Depression goes on, as far as where I sit even today. Dealin' with it is pretty hard.

> I remember I was thinking, give me my negative test results I gotta go, gotta go. And she opened this folder and said, "Well your test did come back positive." And I just looked at her and I laughed at her. That was my response. I don't know, when I get nervous about something I laugh. So I laughed at her. And I got up and walked around, paced back and forth around the room a couple of times and she was trying to give me these facts and figures, and "that doesn't mean you're gonna die tomorrow," and I didn't hear any of it.

Interpersonal conflict may increase (Frigo et al., 1986) and relationships may be terminated in the aftermath of a diagnosis of HIV disease. People may reevaluate their values, life goals, and relationships in light of their diagnosis and begin grieving their loss of the future; such reevaluation takes a psychological and physical toll.

Denial is a common, natural reaction to the HIV disease diagnosis. Although denial provides an initial buffer against the traumatic knowledge of one's certain (barring a cure) difficult death, denial also can prevent people from obtaining useful information, informing sexual partners or taking precautions, developing and enhancing their support network, and taking a proactive stance with respect to their illness.

> I had ideas that I was going to be positive. I mean I broke out with shingles over a year ago and was doing drugs and sharing needles, you know, it was bound to happen. But you know the denial...

Anxiety and fear may produce similar consequences; people may isolate themselves from potential sources of support and information for fear of the stigma associated with the HIV disease diagnosis. Self-directed anger and anger at partners is another common response, although certainly not inevitable.

> I don't know, there are sometimes when I'm really like, you know, the "why me" kind of thing, but then it's well, why not? I was involved with all kinds of things during that whole window period where no one knew anything was going on so you weren't careful, you weren't protected, and I didn't have a lot of relationships, but it only takes one. And who knows where. I can honestly say I'm really not angry over whoever it was who transmitted it to me, 'cause I have no idea how many people I may have transmitted it to before I knew. So today we just deal with one day at a time, and get as honest as we can each day and go from there.

As the disease progresses and the number of physical symptoms increases, depression and fear become increasingly common. People may be immobilized by depression prior to the impairment brought on by physical symptoms alone. Anxiety typically accompanies the onset of AIDS dementia complex; as dementia becomes more pronounced, anger and efforts to fight the dementia tend to be replaced by apathy and withdrawal (Tross & Hirsch, 1988). Because the psychological consequences of an HIV diagnosis—and all that comes afterwards—prevent individuals from drawing upon community support, actively participating in their treatment, incorporating healthy life-style changes, and supporting the empowerment of others, they detract from empowerment.

Stigma

The stigma associated with HIV disease is twofold: HIV disease is a chronic, lethal illness, and it is perceived to be an affliction of groups (gay men, IV drug users) that are viewed with great negativity already (Herek & Glunt, 1988). Similar to other fatal illnesses, HIV disease confronts people with thoughts of their own death and mortality. The stigma associated with fatal illnesses often results in withdrawal of social support, denial of the illness, and victim blaming. People with HIV disease are viewed as placing other people at risk and as bringing the disease on themselves. Further, AIDS has been defined socially as a disease of marginalized groups; Herek and Glunt (1988) write, "AIDS has become a symbol: Reactions to AIDS are reactions to gay men, drug users, racial minorities, or outsiders in general" (p. 887). The following statement by a Ph.D. candidate in a college of education reflects some of these attitudes:

> I'm not judging anybody's life-style—do what you want to do, that's my philosophy. Hey, my cousin is gay and I really like him, but as I tell him to his face, I think his life-style is morally wrong. I mean, maybe it's not your fault if you have those inclinations, but you can choose to act on them or not. And all this gay rights stuff is just a big attempt to make us feel guilty about their problems. You know what? I would never give a penny to AIDS research. They're killing *themselves*. They want us to believe that AIDS research is underfunded but it isn't, and other curable diseases are being ignored because AIDS research is getting all the money.

Shilts (1987) illustrates the effect of this stigma using the *New York Times* as an example. Shilts notes that six stories on AIDS appeared in the *Times* between 1981 and 1982, none of which was on the front page. At that time, 634 Americans had been diagnosed with AIDS and 260 people had already died. During 1982, however, 54 stories (four on the front page) were published in the *Times* regarding the poisoned Tylenol capsules that resulted in seven deaths. Herek and Glunt (1988) cite a variety of other examples of AIDS stigma, ranging from general public beliefs that AIDS is a "punishment from God" to political campaign rhetoric and institutional policies. The increasing number of antigay hate crimes has been linked with fear of AIDS (Kim, 1988).

The stigma associated with AIDS results in interpersonal and societal ostracism of people who have, or who are perceived to have, HIV disease. This ostracism takes many forms, from interpersonal violence to institutional apathy. Further, this stigma has limited the effectiveness of prevention efforts (Herek & Glunt, 1988). Given the relationship between stress and the body's immune system, (cf. Knox, 1989; Kiecolt-Glaser & Glaser, 1988), the stress associated with stigma and its consequent effects on prevention programs seriously harms people with HIV disease as well as those at risk of the disease.

Public acknowledgment of HIV disease among admired sports figures such as Arthur Ashe and "Magic" Johnson may help reduce some of the stigma associated with AIDS as well as the "invulnerability" felt by many heterosexual women and men. In a sample of African American clients at an inner-city clinic for sexually transmitted diseases, participants interviewed *after* "Magic" Johnson's announcement that he had HIV disease differed significantly from those interviewed *before* his announcement in several ways (Gleghorn, Kilbourn, Celentano, & Jemmott, 1993). Specifically, they viewed themselves as more vulnerable to AIDS, as more capable of refusing to participate in unsafe sex, and were three times more likely to say that they intended to use condoms all the time.

Prevention

William F. Buckley, Jr. (1986) argued that prevention should focus on the identification of people with HIV disease; he called for tattooing of all people with AIDS on the upper forearm (to warn IV drug needle-sharers) and on the buttocks (to warn gay men). This perspective of prevention is hardly uncommon, even among mental health professionals. For example, a psychologist proposed using a social quarantine via the facial tattooing of people infected with HIV (Family Research Institute, 1987, cited in Croteau & Morgan, 1989). Similarly, some prevention efforts target the "innocent victims" of AIDS, presumably as opposed to those who are *guilty*.

It is generally agreed that information about behaviors placing individuals at risk for AIDS should be a fundamental part of prevention efforts; it is also clear that information alone is not enough to reduce the incidence of risky behaviors (Baum & Nesselhof, 1988; Stall, Coates, & Hoff, 1988). Due to the "socially unacceptable" sexual behavior associated with the gay life-style, and reluctance to address sexual behavior openly even among heterosexual partners, preventive measures have been hampered by restrictions on content. Existing sodomy laws, discussed in Chapter Six, put safe sex campaigns in the position of advocating "illegal" activity (Herek & Glunt, 1988). AIDS education materials are often homophobic; some contain negative messages about lesbians and gay men, while others fail to mention or acknowledge lesbians and gay men in their materials, thus rendering them "invisible" (Croteau & Morgan, 1989). Materials directed to heterosexual people sometimes treat gay and lesbian people as "others" or fail to mention them at all. Guidelines for safe sex practices may exclude behaviors associated with same-sex couples. For example, anal sex using latex condoms reduces risk, as do oral sex using condoms or dental dams (5- by 5-inch squares of latex used for oral surgery). Some pamphlets fail to acknowledge these "safer" options, however (Croteau & Morgan, 1989), and advocate only abstinence or sex with a committed, long-term partner. Finally, many of the prevention materials are distributed via channels that are inaccessible to or unlikely to reach gay men of color and IV drug users of color (Mays & Cochran, 1988; Peterson & Marin, 1988). Thus, prevention efforts are not uniformly helpful or effective.

SUGGESTIONS FOR EMPOWERMENT

Counselor Knowledge

Counselors working with people with HIV disease should know facts regarding contraction, progression, treatment, and prognosis of the disease. Professional partnerships with medical personnel can provide counselors with up-to-date information regarding treatment and related medical procedures. The professional literature provides a growing number of resources for counselors and other mental health practitioners, such as Kain's (1989) *No Longer Immune: A Counselor's Guide to AIDS*. Others are listed in the resources section at the end of this chapter.

Knowledge of the history of AIDS and the response of the medical community and society at large is particularly helpful in conducting a power analysis with clients. The differing stigmas associated with having HIV disease as a gay white male, a gay man of color, an IV drug user of color, or a mother must be recognized. Traditional modes of therapy will have to be modified in responding to the AIDS crisis (Cochran & Mays, 1991). Counselors and other helping professionals should be prepared to visit clients in their homes, hospices, or hospital rooms. To discontinue counseling when people with HIV disease cannot attend office appointments reflects the same general abandonment and withdrawal that they may experience with nonsupportive friends or family members. Counselors also must be sensitive to economic issues. As HIV disease progresses, people likely will be unable to work and maintain an income. Those without insurance or some other source of financial support will have difficulty paying for counseling. The difficulty of qualifying for Medicare makes it unlikely that those experiencing a reduction of symptoms will give up their benefits to return to work temporarily. The following suggestions and opinions about counselors were offered by the men interviewed:

> When I deal with a counselor, a therapist, I want somebody, if this room's a fuckin' mess and there's shit all over the floor, I need a counselor to get down on their hands and knees with me and help me get honest with myself enough to clean it up. I see people coming here, major alcoholics, and nobody has the guts to say get the fuck off the booze and clean it up and stop the bullshit. I want someone in counseling who is willing to call a spade a spade, if they see a spade call it and don't avoid it just because the person has AIDS.

I would want counselors to be less patronizing and condescending towards you. I've had counselors that are so wrapped up in sympathy that they don't get past their own demons with HIV.

If I walked in as a 28-year-old man to a counselor now, and I wasn't HIV, she could say, "Wow, if we can get you straightened out by the time you're 38 we're doin' pretty damn good." But now we don't have that, we don't know that we have 10 years, so we need to get this shit together quick and make a little expressway here.

I just wouldn't let my ego think I even needed anyone to talk to. And one day I finally realized I did. She's been really good because we deal with immediate issues. It's very funny, we can start the session going and I may kind of pass over something that's really important. She picks up on it. I mean I may try to make it so unimportant, but she knows how to pick up on it.... Now it's gotten to the point where I can let people know when I'm hurting about something or I have questions or doubts about something, and not feel like I can't let anyone think I'm that stupid that I can't work through this. You know, the stupidity was not admitting, not letting, making it seem like I did know everything where I didn't really know anything.... At times, as I said, she'll pull out things that I'm like oh God, and I mean I'm sitting there and everything is always videoed. And I'm sitting looking at myself on a big screen as we're talking, I mean it's in front of me, and I can see myself 'cause I know certain expressions and certain ways that I'll act when I'm squirming. And I know that when I'm doin that, that's what we need to talk about.

Finally, counselors must be prepared to help people with HIV negotiate life-style changes that will prolong the quantity and quality of time remaining. All of the men interviewed reported changes in their lifestyles.

...it made me stop and look at some of the abusive things I was doing. And now I have changed my life-style... I don't drink, I stopped all the abusive prescription drugs, I stopped the late hours. I got really a better life. And a more comfortable life, things got more balanced.

You know I just needed to learn that if I am gonna sleep 15 hours, fine. And if I've got two hours that I'm out, able to do some things, fine. And then if I have to go back home and go to bed I will. That's the hardest part because I've been wanting to be always on the go. I closed the office, my career kind of ended at one point. But then it really picked up again because I learned a new balance.

Group Participation and Support Networks

One of the counselor's first tasks when working with someone with HIV disease is to explore the person's support network. The presence of a supportive community can be of enormous help in dealing with the psychological and physical consequences of HIV disease. Gay men who have not yet come out when diagnosed with HIV disease may feel unable to use the support of family and friends who don't know they are gay.

> I hate keepin' the secret, it's hard, and my older brother doesn't even know. And dealing with that on a daily basis, you know when I see him and he just, something deep down inside of you is saying, "Tell him," and then another part of you is saying "No, not yet," 'cause of his wife and baby, and fear that she wouldn't want me around the baby...they're real closed-minded about anything. I mean they were talkin' about AIDS one night and they're totally off on the subject, they just don't know. And then I'd say something about what they're sayin' and correct them, and they look at me, and as much as you'd like to share right then and there, you just don't know when the right moment is.

Among those with HIV disease, heterosexual women and men, gay men of color, and IV drug users may have greater difficulty establishing a social support network than gay Euro American men. Although knowledge about HIV disease has grown significantly within the gay White community, concomitant increases have not occurred among other groups. Gay men of color drawing primary support from their ethnic community may feel compelled to conceal their HIV status; the political, cultural, and social communities enjoyed by many gay men and lesbians are unlikely to be paralleled among IV drug users; and similarly, women with HIV disease are less likely to be in contact with other women with HIV or people with knowledge of and sensitivity to HIV disease issues (Cochran & Mays, 1991). Thus, development of a supportive and knowledgeable social network may be more difficult with these groups.

Feelings of anger, shame, or being "dirty" may keep people from seeking out the companionship and support of others. Guilt and fear regarding sexual partners is also common; people with HIV disease sometimes delay informing partners for fear of having infected them already and losing the relationship.

> I kept tryin' to figure out how to bring this up and I couldn't. Finally one night we were laying in bed talking and I kept saying things like, what do you think about AIDS or how do you feel about this, or just trying to get

his view, because we were both very young and we didn't have any experience with AIDS and I didn't know anybody that had AIDS. I was just trying to feel for how he was gonna react when I shared that news. And I remember we were laying in bed and he said, "I would never date anybody that's HIV positive, it would be like playing Russian roulette." Well I was really emotionally involved with this person so my whole hell started basically that night when I decided to tell him. We didn't live together. I said, "Now I have to tell you something and you have to promise me no matter what that you're not gonna leave me, that after I tell you this that you're gonna spend the night like every night." "Okay, okay." So I told him and he freaked out, he started crying and he wasn't able to handle it and so he tried to call his mom. And I remember 10 minutes after I told him, I'm layin' there and he said, "I gotta go, I've gotta go, I can't stay here tonight." And so he left, it was over. I didn't want anybody to know but this person went around and told people and so the next thing you know I was being outed.

Counselors can help people with HIV disease decide with whom to share their diagnosis and how to tell them. Certainly counselors and other mental health professionals have ethical and legal obligations with respect to protecting specific others from infection (for extended discussions of ethical and legal issues related to HIV disease, see Green, 1989; Melton, 1991; Melton & Gray, 1988). Given the stigma of HIV disease, the decision about whom to tell must be made carefully. Supportive communities may consist of family (of origin or of choice), partners, spouses, friends, members of groups active in HIV education and prevention efforts, self-help or therapy group members, church groups, co-workers, and others.

Only when other people know of the HIV diagnosis will they be able to provide the needed emotional and physical support. The supportive community can function in a number of other very important ways, including finding information, providing companionship, enhancing self-esteem, and supporting an other-oriented focus. With respect to information, supportive communities involved in HIV-related activism may be able to direct the person with HIV disease to sources of current information regarding the contraction, progression, and treatment of the disease. Even those uneducated with respect to HIV disease can encourage and support information seeking by accompanying the person with the disease to libraries, clinics, or educational events to obtain more information. Supportive others also can listen attentively to all that the person with HIV disease learns from these sources. People with serious illnesses often have to deal with large amounts of new and frightening medical information. Processing this information with others can facilitate its assimilation, provide recognition of the affected person as a responsible and active learner, and reduce anxiety through open acknowledgment of the potential effects and complications associated with the illness.

Companionship can offset feelings of alienation and serve as a buffer during crisis phases. Voicing fears of pain, disfigurement, disability, and isolation to receptive, respectful, and empathetic listeners can be extremely helpful.

The stigma associated with AIDS can combine with preexisting negative feelings regarding one's membership in a minority community (being gay, an IV drug user, a member of a lower socioeconomic class, being a person of color, or any combination of these) with the effect of decreasing self-esteem. Participation in or exposure to supportive communities involved in efforts to reduce this stigma can enhance self-esteem. Role models who demonstrate pride and positive feelings can have a similarly beneficial influence on self-esteem; this is particularly important in light of evidence suggesting that gay men who are more comfortable and secure in their gay identity are more likely to practice safer sex behaviors (Fisher, 1988).

Supportive communities often help people with HIV disease focus on others in their environment. Although people with HIV disease of necessity must focus attention on themselves as they assimilate vast amounts of new information and learn new behaviors, it also can be helpful to put energy into others' problems and issues. Providing support and encouragement to others can reduce one's personal focus in a way that decreases stress and tension.

Another important role of supportive communities is that they can support the practice of safer sex behaviors and health-related behaviors associated with delaying the onset of the chronic symptomatic phase of HIV disease. Prevention efforts more likely to be successful include those that target changing community norms. When safer sex practices are expected, risky sexual behavior is less likely to occur (Fisher, 1988; Morin, 1988).

Therapeutic support groups for people living with HIV disease can serve to bolster hope and reduce depression. Getzel (1991) describes such support groups as helpful in the process of making self-discoveries, developing new living skills, and taking a proactive stance with respect to health. Counselors and other mental health professionals engaged in such work can help people with AIDS develop "solutions" to the fear and anxiety triggered by living with AIDS. Getzel (1991) describes four common solutions that emerge among people with AIDS: (a) the *beneficent* solution is characterized by the desire to act lovingly and kindly with what is left of one's life; (b) the *heroic* solution is characterized by viewing AIDS as a personal assault that must be faced and battled with courage; (c) the *artistic-spiritual* solution is characterized by viewing the disease as providing a transformative potential that allows the individual to transcend death; and (d) the *rational-instrumental* solution is characterized by "living one day at a time and approaching choice and conflict through knowledge, precedent, convention, and expertise" (p. 8). Counselors can facilitate the empowerment of group members by helping them identify a solution or combination of solutions that enable them to maintain the greatest degree of well-being and hopefulness (Getzel, 1991). The development of a positive "solution" may enhance the quality of the individual's life as well as prolong it.

Coming to Terms with Loss and Death

Loss is a primary and pervasive issue among people with HIV disease. Losses begin with the initial diagnosis: loss of certainty, of invincibility, of a future with one's children, family, and partner, loss of time. To prevent the infection of partners, sexual behaviors associated with great pleasure and intimacy, such as anal and oral sex, may be given up altogether or modified with the use of condoms. As the disease progresses, people with HIV disease experience multiple losses related to health, including the loss of energy, freedom from pain, concentration, and/or mobility. Longtime friends may withdraw to avoid confronting their own mortality, or they may be so burdened with the multiple losses of other friends or family members that they are less able to provide emotional support. Family members may keep their children away because of unfounded fears of infection. The children of people with HIV disease may be targeted for verbal abuse and ostracism at school and in the neighborhood. Coworkers may become distant, impatient, even hostile. And for gay men in particular, they face these losses even as they cope with the progressive illness and death of close friends and partners; their supportive community (Tross & Hirsch, 1988).

> I've been to many, many funerals. I came up here not knowing anybody, I didn't have any history of living here, and slowly as I meet new people and I make new friends the same thing's happening that happened there. My support group had nine or 10 people in it, and it ended up with two of us left 'cause we haven't died. I thought maybe here it would be a little bit different, but no, it's not so.

> You just get to know somebody, get to like them and to talk to them and they're gone, they're gone and it's so, so difficult to deal with. I started this collection of funeral cards; you know, when you die then you have the little cards at the funeral home. I started this collection and it hasn't been

that long but every time I pull out my checkbook one of them pops out and it's just a constant reminder of death.

I usually get frustrated 'cause most people with AIDS at some point give up. And it's real frustrating to deal with that because you don't feel like they feel, so you don't really understand. Like [Jerry] just gave up. So I went to his funeral and everything but still to this day the family calls me sometimes and I can't deal with his family because they have no clue what his life was about, they have no clue what he went through. And they want to sit around and talk about this person and you don't even recognize the person they're talking about. You know, you were there and watched him, I watched the shit hit the fan and his family all stood around and they're like, "Jerry did this," "Jerry was that," and you're like, this isn't the Jerry that I knew...like they kept saying he fought so hard until the end. Jerry gave up four months before he ever died. He climbed into bed and told everybody, "I'm dying." And it's real hard for me to sit there with the family feelin, "Yeah, Jerry fought until the last second."

...that's the thing I caught myself doing when [William] died. I was there at the hospital when he died and so it was very, very hard for me, and for three or four days after that and after the funeral I would just call his house to get his recording so I could hear his voice. And the thing that really hit me hard was when I called and the phone had been disconnected so then you really realize that it's over, that it's done.

Each loss requires a separate grieving. The death and dying literature can be very useful, but counselors must incorporate attention to the additional issues of stigma, as well as the loss of community for gay men in particular. As pointed out by Cochran and Mays (1991), much of the existing literature attends to single instances of death; in the age of AIDS, multiple losses are the reality with which clients often are confronted. It is also critical to recognize that grief, and grief resolution, is a culturally constructed phenomenon (Stroebe, Gergen, Gergen, & Stroebe, 1992). In other words, the so-called healthy way to deal with death varies across cultures and across time. Gergen et al. (1992) argue that Western views, such as those embraced in the work of Kubler-Ross (e.g., Kubler-Ross, 1969), suggest that resolution requires letting go of the relationship with the person who has died. They contrast this perspective with the view that maintaining a relationship with the deceased is healthy and important. "Maintaining the relationship" may be in the form of communicating with the spirit of the deceased, naming children after them, prayer, or hopeful anticipation of a reunion in the afterlife. They suggest that counselors convey to clients that "there are many goals that can be set, many ways to feel, and no set series of stages that they must pass through—that many forms of expression and behavioral patterns are acceptable reactions to loss" (p. 1211).

Ironically, the losses accompanying a diagnosis of HIV disease may serve as a springboard for discoveries and gains. Several of the men in the support group experienced profoundly positive changes in their lives:

> ...and I said alright, you're dying or you might die, what is it you want to accomplish? And there were two things about me. One is, I didn't know about my afterlife because I was raised in a very fundamentalist religion and they basically said all gay people were going to hell. So I thought, well you know, I had to somehow address that because I was having nightmares about dying and stuff. And then the next one was I never liked myself, and I thought what a shame to leave this earth like that. They always said in order to be a good friend you have to be a friend to yourself and in order to love somebody you have to love yourself. And I always thought, you know, I don't love myself. Ultimately I have lots of bad images of myself and I play lots of shit back to myself. And so those are the two things: I want to decide where I'm gonna go when I die, and I want to look in the mirror and really be OK, really be at a good place with who I see there. And that was a year and a half ago. And since then I've made so much progress it's just incredible.

> ...see and the thought of never reaching a retirement age of 65 kind of affects you as well, because people with HIV and AIDS end up having to quit their jobs and if they don't have insurance go on Medicaid, and I just recently went on Medicare. So at 35 or 34 years old that's kind of ah, you know, 30 years premature as far as I'm concerned. Something my grandparents used when they were in a nursing home. And it forces you to look at life a whole lot differently. I remember one particular day when I was in San Antonio, and I had gotten over the feeling-sorry-for-myself stage and I was into the let's-see-what-life-has-to-offer stage, and I noticed in the front yard of the house a huge yellow dandelion. And I thought, God, that is just the most gorgeous flower or weed, whatever you want to call it, that I've ever seen in my life, and I probably walked by millions of dandelions but I've never had time to look at them. And if you can see beauty in something like a weed, at this particular point in my life then I think that I'm getting somewhere finally, I'm finally learning what life is really all about.

> Those other things we say that are real positive—I think we should probably preface that with all of us are in decent health now, I guess we would call it. Sometimes if you got us when, if we were doing this tape when we were in bad health you might get a little bit different view...

> Yeah, like now I don't feel sick, so if you ask me if I'm gonna die from AIDS I'll tell you no. But wait till I'm down 20 pounds and feelin' like shit, or havin' a bad day, and then ask me if I'm gonna die and I'll be like yeah fuckin' tomorrow.

Finally, counselors and other mental health professionals must be aware of their own issues related to loss and death. As indicated in some of the personal statements, people with HIV disease don't have time to work with counselors who avoid critical issues. Counselors have the responsibility to refer elsewhere when a client issue is beyond their expertise or when they feel unable to respond therapeutically to the client. However, counselors and other mental health professionals also have the responsibility to self-examine their reasons for referral and to address biases or weaknesses that emerge from such self-examination.

> I had a therapist turn me down; I went to see her because I heard really good things about her. I wanted to work with her and stuff so I went and did an initial consultation with her, and she told me she wouldn't work with me because she couldn't make that kind of an investment, just to lose me.

Dealing with Medical Personnel

Ideally, people with HIV disease work with trusted physicians who encourage their active participation in the treatment process and provide ample information regarding options, procedures, and prognosis. In the real world, however, many physicians are uncomfortable and unaccustomed to proactive patient participation in health care. Physicians working with patients with HIV disease are not necessarily less likely to be homophobic.

> The kind of procedures he did, he had to know I was gay, but he never mentioned a thing. How could you say nothing with AIDS like it is? That was before I knew. Another doctor, after I knew, I told him I had AIDS and he had to know I was gay but he never said a word, no information about safe sex, nothing.

Counselors can assist people with HIV disease to identify priorities as they choose a physician. Location, cost, preferred modes of treatment, and willingness to enroll patients in experimental treatment programs are all important criteria (Chavez, 1993). Some people may value scheduling ease over bedside manner, while others may want to work with a gay physician. Many clients will not have a choice of physicians; in this case, counselors can play a valuable role by encouraging assertive behavior, role-playing related confrontational skills, and helping clients to identify strategies for participating as fully as possible in their treatment.

Many of the medical treatments and procedures accompanying an HIV disease diagnosis and subsequent health problems can be painful and frightening. Martin (1989) suggests that counselors provide emotional support and use relaxation and guided imagery to increase client comfort during these procedures, and prepare clients for other aspects of treatment, such as bringing a pad and pencil for communication with medical personnel for procedures during which they will be conscious but unable to speak. The counselor's basic knowledge of medical procedures will be a distinct advantage in developing appropriate and helpful images and relaxation strategies. In addition, sensitivity to the frustration and anxiety that may accompany the frequent trips to the doctor is important.

> You never know, I mean every time you're sitting in that waiting room and the doctor opens the door, you know at some point he's possibly gonna walk in and hand you your death sentence but you never know when.

Finally, women with HIV disease experience different symptoms from those of men (Reese & Thomas, 1993). Opportunistic infections in female medical patients frequently are unrecognized as such because doctors are less likely to consider the possibility of an HIV disease diagnosis in women. This is in spite of the fact that AIDS is the leading cause of death among women age 25–29 in New York City (Kristal, 1986). Invasive cervical cancer, vaginal candidiasis, pelvic inflammatory disease, and genital ulcers are among the conditions that must be monitored more closely among women with HIV disease. In addition, because of traditional power inequalities between doctors and patients as well as between men and women, women sometimes have to exert greater assertiveness to obtain medical information. Women with HIV disease are largely women of color (Mays & Cochran, 1988), who may have been socialized to view doctors as all powerful (Banzhaf, 1993). Banzhaf (1993) describes strategies for dealing with medical doctors used by women with HIV disease; one woman blocked her doctor's fast exits by setting her chair in front of the door and not moving it until all of her questions were answered. Another woman refused any injections or prescriptions until she was provided with explanations of a drug's use and its potential side effects. *Positively Aware* provides a resource/reading list about HIV and women to those who send a self-addressed, stamped envelope to the address listed in the resource section.

Skill Application: Public Speaking

Activism must be defined within the context of stigma, fear, and homophobia. One common form of activism related to HIV disease is speaking to groups. The men whose words are included in this chapter speak publicly to a variety of groups, including elementary, secondary, and college students; health professionals; business organizations; and the general public. Speaking to groups about HIV disease and acknowledging one's personal experience of AIDS involves a continuous reliving of the emotions related to the initial diagnosis and subsequent events. To acknowledge having HIV disease is to risk losing one's job, privacy, and even personal safety. Educating friends and family members is another form of activism; simply revealing one's HIV disease diagnosis is an act of courage that involves risking the loss of contact and support. The *PWA Coalition Newsline* is a monthly publication of interest to activists because it includes outreach and networking activities (see the resource section for an address). Kain (1989) provides a listing of HIV/AIDS resources in communities in every state.

RESOURCES

Counselors and clients alike may benefit from periodical publications such as *Positively Aware* (published monthly by the Test Positive Aware Network, Incorporated 1340 W. Irving Park Road, Box #259, Chicago, IL 60613, 312-472-6397). *Positively Aware* provides treatment updates, recommended readings, resources, a host of practical suggestions for people living with HIV disease, and other information.

Other resources for people with HIV include *Seasons*, a quarterly newsletter of the National Native American AIDS Prevention Center (U.S. American AIDS Prevention Center, 3515 Grand Avenue, Suite 100, Oakland, CA 94610, 510-444-2051); *Positive Woman*, a national bulletin for women with HIV/AIDS (The Positive Woman, P.O. Box 34372, Washington DC 20043, 202-898-0372); *The Common Factor*, a newsletter by and for people infected with HIV through blood and blood products (The Committee of Ten Thousand, c/o The Packard Manse, 583 Plain Street, Stoughton, MA 02072, 617-344-9634); and *Body Positive*, a monthly newsletter for HIV-positive individuals that also has limited availability in Spanish (Body Positive, 2095 Broadway, Suite 306, New York, NY 10023, 212-721-1346). The *PWA Coalition Newsline* is a monthly publication that includes outreach and networking activities (31 W. 26th Street, New York, NY 10010, 212-532-0568).

Books of interest include Kain's (1989) *No Longer Immune: A Counselor's Guide to AIDS* and Jennings's (1988) *Understanding and Preventing AIDS: A Book for Everyone*.

CONCLUSION

HIV disease has changed our society and our world irrevocably. We have lost forever the talents, the love, the support, and countless other aspects of the thousands of people who have died of AIDS, and we will lose far more in the years to come. The hatred and fear that form a part of the context of people with HIV disease, as well as the profound personal and communal losses, demand that counselors and other mental health professionals be prepared to work with people with HIV, their families, and their friends. Empowering people with HIV requires that we confront and deal with our own issues related to IV drug use, homosexuality, and death. Professional activism—educating our own families, partners, spouses, friends, and especially colleagues, on issues pertaining to HIV disease—must be incorporated into our empowerment efforts. When counselors and other mental health professionals assume these efforts of education, activism, and continued professional and personal development, we will be far better prepared to respond to people with HIV disease in a manner consistent with empowerment.

Chapter Eight
PEOPLE WITH DISABILITIES

when doors open, elevators run
signs have sounds, sounds have movement
when there is no need
to go on the rampage for ramps
when we don't have to call ahead to restaurants
when my children are taught
by women and men using chairs and dogs
then you can use words like equality
like justice like equal opportunity
but for now: what is the true nature
of disability?

                                                    E.H.M.

INTRODUCTION

The Americans with Disabilities Act (ADA), passed July 26, 1990, offers protection for people with mental and physical impairments, including protection for people with HIV disease and people receiving treatment for drug and alcohol problems. Under this act, discrimination in the areas of employment, public service, public accommodations, and telecommunications is prohibited. Some aspects of the ADA went into effect immediately, while others are being implemented with longer time-tables. For example, with respect to transportation, all new buses and train stations must be accessible; all existing rail systems must have one accessible car per train by July 1995, and all Amtrak stations must be accessible by July 2010. Passage of this legislation marks a step forward in achieving equality for people with disabilities; however, it is only one step, and many others remain to be taken.

This chapter focuses on issues related to people with disabilities. Empowerment among people with disabilities might include the following components: establishing a positive self-concept and identity; recognition of how society's ignorance of, inattention to, and reluctance to address issues related to disabilities contributes to limitations experienced by the individual; recognition of how factors in the more immediate environment (e.g., family and coworker attitudes, accessibility) contribute to limitations experienced by the individual; understanding the nature of one's specific disability; advocacy for oneself and others in medical, employment, and other arenas; and a positive sense of shared identity, purpose, or experience with other people with disabilities. Development of critical awareness of one's situation and assertion of control over factors affecting one's health are also characteristics of empowerment noted in nursing literature on chronic illness (Gibson, 1991; Jones & Meleis, 1993). These components are relevant here because many forms of chronic illness are disabling.

WHO ARE PEOPLE WITH DISABILITIES?

More than 43 million people in the United States live with some type of disability. In essence, for every human ability there is a disability. The term "disability" has been defined in accord with medical, economic, and sociopolitical models in the past 100 years (Hahn, 1988). In this chapter, disability is defined relative to the sociopolitical model, in which disabilities are viewed as a multifaceted product of the interaction between the individual and the environment. The medical model defines disability in terms of individual limitations, while the economic model focuses on the individual's functional limitations. Only the sociopolitical model emphasizes the disabling features of the environment.

The economic and medical models of disability arise out of our modern-day cultural assumptions regarding disability. These include the assumptions that disability is synonymous with needing help; that disability is central to a person's self-concept and self-definition; that disability is a fact of biology alone; and that people with disabilities, as victims of biological rather than social injustice, must change their personal behavior rather than their social context (Fine & Asch, 1988).

I. King Jordan (1992), the first hearing-impaired president of Gallaudet University, refers to "people with disabilities" as well as to those who are "not yet disabled" and the "not-so-noticeably disabled"; his terminology reflects the multidimensional nature of disabilities. In a most general sense we are all disabled, and those not currently experiencing disability are temporarily able-bodied. This notion is critical. Society tends to view people with disabilities as "them" rather than "us." This offers protection from the idea that "it could happen to me." Treating people with disabilities as "less than," as "different," as "super-heroes," or as "special" helps to keep *them* distant. As a consequence of the competitive nature of our society, we view having a disability as bad luck, a disadvantage, and something that the individual alone is responsible for overcoming. The heroic efforts of some people with disabilities are held up as standards for *all* people with disabilities; "They made it; so should you!" In the past, society has borne little responsibility for responding to disability issues. The ADA confronts this mentality, charging society with the task of providing truly equal access and opportunity.

It is important to note that "disability" and "health" are two unrelated concepts. Although a person may have a disability and ill health, this is certainly not the case for most people with disabilities. Emerging definitions of health as a process of becoming and a realization of health *potential* means that even people with chronic illnesses may be considered healthy (Jones & Meleis, 1993). However, many healthy people with disabilities are required to interact with medical professionals on a regular basis. Clients with disabilities may or may not enter into counseling with issues related to their disability. The following personal statement by Cynthia Milum voices one woman's experience of living with a disability.

> It has been 11 years now. At the age of 27, I went from being a person with excellent vision to being a person with no vision at all within a period of six months. I do not consider myself adjusted or accustomed to this situation. Eleven years ago, after I ruled out suicide, I felt I had two choices. The first was to go forth with my life and make the best of it. The second was to become a recluse, hide from the world's curious eyes, and stop growing. I might have chosen the second; however, I was already sensing the devastating effect this was having on my family, who loved me very much. I felt my condition had broken each of their hearts. I decided that if I could go ahead and make a success of my life, then perhaps their hearts could mend and they could again find some semblance of joy. So I chose to try my first choice. This short piece is about my personal thoughts and experiences. I would never presume to speak for all visually impaired people.
>
> When after four major eye surgeries and thousands of laser burns, my doctor said more surgeries would do no good, my physical body spun in. There had been hope up until then, but once that was gone, even the flesh became weak. I was admitted to the hospital with the nebulous diagnosis of: Reaction to Traumatic Event. When I was released one week later, I returned to my apartment where I had lived alone for nine years. It took me months to stop reaching for the light switches, thinking they would shed some light on the matter.
>
> When I first received the news that my blindness was permanent, I knew immediately that I wanted a dog guide. It was the only thought that gave me even a hint of happiness. So I set my first goal; to get that dog.

During the initial months of surgeries and the waiting, I had refused to go places where I was known or to have friends visit me. Then when I became aware that this was a permanent situation, I cut off all my friendships and close relationships outside of my family, with the exception of three very special people. I did this because I felt so far inferior to them. In fact, I felt inferior to any and everyone. My relationships with the three special people—who I thought would remain close forever—disintegrated. It was devastating.

During those first five years of blindness, I depended on others to take me where I needed to go. I did not like doing this, but I thought that as soon as I got my dog, this would stop. The waiting list to get into either of the best dog guide schools was about a year and a half. When I received word that it was my turn, I really felt that my time had come. However, three days into the 28-day program I fell and broke my ankle, so I was not able to keep my dog. I felt horribly betrayed for the second time. I became obsessed with doing everything perfectly so that I could get back to the school and get my dog back. It took me several years and two more broken ankles before I returned and completed the training program. I finally had my dog! That experience was the best one I have had as a blind individual. The people at the school were some of the finest people I have ever met. They treated everyone there with a great deal of dignity.

It has been my observation that the sighted treat the unsighted in one of two ways. Either they treat the blind as being almost magical because they can do something as simple as tying a shoe, or they treat them as if they can do anything they want, just because they want to. Neither is realistic or helpful to the sight-impaired individual. Everyone treats you like you are their best friend. I find it very irritating to be treated nicely just because I happen to be blind.

Transportation is often a problem, especially if the public transportation where one lives is poor, which is the case in many communities in the United States. It gets very old having to depend on someone else to always take you where you want to go. And often, nobody is available to take you where you want to go. Cabs are very expensive! Another problem for the visually impaired is isolation. I can be in a large crowd of people and yet still be very much alone. I can pass groups of friends and yet, unless they speak to me, I will never know they are there.

I must admit that it is a supreme compliment when someone says out of the blue that they forgot I was blind, or that they never think of me as being blind. On the other hand, unless someone takes it upon themselves to tell me that my hair is not looking good, or my makeup is smudged, or that I have a spot on the clothes I am wearing, I have no way of knowing these things. I feel that it is very important for one's appearance to be at its best. It has been my experience that a great many people feel it is kinder to keep these things to themselves in order not to hurt my feelings. I would plead of these people to please *tell* me. It is the only way I can compete in this very competitive world.

My best friends are those who literally do not seem to be aware that I am different from them in any way. Luckily I have met just such people; they mean the world to me.

The people I have encountered in public places have, in general, been honest where an exchange of money has been involved. Cab drivers have been extremely fair with me. The main problems I have had with people out in public is that they think I need help when I don't. Once I learned how to use a white cane well enough to get around independently, I used the bus system to go back to school for a master's degree, and made a three-hour round trip daily. I could be walking along having absolutely no problems, nor looking as if I were lost; suddenly from out of nowhere I would hear a voice or feel a hand on my arm or shoulder, telling me which direction I needed to go. It took me many months to ignore those voices, and I got sure and fast at extricating myself from those grabbing hands. I always ended up lost when I tried to follow their directions.

This brings up another very important issue for me in this world of blindness: independence. I was a very independent person before I lost my sight, and to have as much of that independence back is extremely important to me. My dog helps in that area a great deal. Being willing to go slower and not give in to impatience has a great deal to do with unlocking this puzzle. I am lucky in that my family has put aside their own worries and anxieties and let me keep as much independence as possible. Anyone else who gives me that freedom is greatly appreciated.

As I said in the beginning, I feel neither adjusted nor accustomed to this situation. Some days are particularly frustrating, and some of those days roll into weeks. I don't think it is something that anyone ever gets used to; however, it again comes down to choices. So I made my choice to just keep going and try to make the best of things. It seems to work for me. The love of family and friends works too. "Thanks" to them, and much love back to them.

BARRIERS

Not every barrier described in this section is confronted by every person with a disability, nor do the barriers described represent an exhaustive list. However, barriers that a large number of people with disabilities are likely to experience have been selected for inclusion.

Culture

Societal attitudes toward people with disabilities are shaped by Euro American culture; a culture wedded to the notions (if not the practice) of "individualism" and "equality." The values of self-reliance, autonomy, freedom, and responsibility are similarly integral (Fowler & Wadsworth, 1991). Thus, attitudes toward people with disabilities generally reflect the medical and economic models; the person is deficient and the environment is neutral. The sociopolitical model of disability is countercultural in that individuals are not *blamed* or held responsible for disabilities they may have. Furthermore, structural inequalities are targeted for intervention along with the exercise of individual initiatives. Boden (1992) articulates the distinction between mainstream assumptions and assumptions consistent with the sociopolitical model of disability:

> People with physical disabilities and chronic illness live in a world where the values, ideals, and goals of the dominant culture are based on what I refer to as an "able-bodied assumption"—a world in which physical limitations are seen as the exception, viewed as problematic, and often judged pejoratively. In an environment with a "disabled assumption" physical differences are the norm. The assumption is that all situations require some modification both for physical access and for effective communication. (p. 159)

In reality, rugged individualism is a myth; people with disabilities are merely more obviously interdependent. The privilege of the wealthy is *dependent* on the presence of an underclass. Those who "did it alone" presumably did not diaper and feed themselves as infants, provide themselves with their own formal education, and produce their own food supply. Our imposition of acceptable categories of interdependence ("Well, people don't grow their own food anymore") serves to minimize the ways in which we are dependent and emphasizes aspects of "independence" that are often less available to people with disabilities. As a consequence, people with disabilities are viewed as needy and helpless, as inferior, and as objects of pity when they do not demonstrate the type and degree of independence that Euro American and other cultural groups value.

The lack of employment opportunities has compounded the emotional and monetary consequences of having a disability. In spite of great sums of money being poured into federal, state, and private career education and job placement programs, people with disabilities are largely unemployed or underemployed (Lombana, 1989). As stated by Fowler and Wadsworth (1991), "Laws do not change basic attitudes" (p. 21). The passage of the ADA is only a beginning; Fowler and Wadsworth note, "Within North American cultures, people in general place a high value on the principle of equality, but research in political science suggests that when applied to specific situations, tolerance is significantly reduced" (p. 20). In other words, we support equality and opportunity when it doesn't cost anything. People with disabilities live in a culture that blames biology and holds individuals solely responsible for resolving any difficulties they encounter; counselors become a part of this barrier when they reflect and perpetuate these attitudes. For example, counselors reflect a blaming, individualistic attitude when they emphasize a client's "physical limitations" rather than the "environmental limitations" with which the client must contend.

Environment

The environment reflects the culture and determines, to a large extent, the degree of impairment experienced by a person with a disability. For example, a person using a wheelchair in East Los Angeles will experience more difficulty getting to the store than his or her counterpart in the suburbs. There are simply fewer working elevators in apartment buildings, fewer curbs with ramps, poorer sidewalks, and fewer modern stores with wide aisles in East L.A. than there are in Beverly Hills or Orange County. A deaf person working for a company that actively transforms the work environment to incorporate more visual cues will experience less impairment than a deaf person working at a company that expects individual compensation—such as constant visual surveillance of the environment—to the exclusion of environmental modification. Riger (1992) describes affirmative environments—those with Braille signage, wheelchair modifications, etc.—as "refreshingly liberating," especially given the personal and collective history of devaluation, marginalization, and exclusion experienced by people with disabilities (p. 4). It is extremely important that counselors do not presume that the Americans with Disabilities Act will reduce our need to consider environmental barriers to the empowerment of people with disabilities.

How might the day-to-day confrontation with cultural, attitudinal, and environmental barriers affect people with disabilities? Riger (1992) leaves no room for doubt:

> Continual frustration because of unavoidable architectural barriers creates feelings of shame, alienation, victimization, hurt and outrage that can be as strong as the emotional sequelae of physical or sexual assault. Architectural barriers diminish the self-esteem of people needing access by highlighting their defects and conveying that they are unworthy of belonging. (p. 4)

Loss of Control

People with disabilities may experience a loss of control associated with the onset or progressive impairment related to their disability. For example, people with spinal cord injuries may go from being relatively able-bodied to being quadriplegic in a matter of seconds; they are likely to experience the loss of control of body functions and movements as a very profound and devastating loss of power. In their discussion of the empowerment of survivors of cancer, Gray and Doan (1990) write:

> The power exercised within "helping" systems, including the health care system, is most often covert. The effect of covert power is for people to become apathetic and convinced that there is nothing they can do to make a difference...covert power involves a powerful group treating a less powerful group as if the former understood the needs of the less powerful group better than its constituents.... Patients often express a feeling of having to be passive recipients of expert consultation. They come to consider their opinions and subjective experiences about their own health and needs as irrelevant. (p. 35)

Physicians and other medical staff may support the patient's right to information in theory but may not provide such information in practice. In a study of surgeons' attitudes toward patients with breast cancer, for example, only 10% of the doctors viewed patient consultation as a key aspect of their therapeutic role (Ray, Fisher, & Wisniewski, 1986); unquestionably such attitudes are conveyed to patients. The experience of loss of control may be intensified when information is difficult to get and decisions are made without consultation.

The use of such terms as "cancer victims" and "wheelchair-bound" embodies the perception that a person with a disability has, indeed, little control. Pity and protectionism on the part of caregivers and observers also help to create an environment conducive to feeling out of control. Recall, for example, Cynthia's personal statement above; uninvited "helpers" often hampered Cynthia while she was going about her business competently.

The loss of control experienced by some people with disabilities may evoke a variety of reactions. Miller (1992a) reviews psychological reactions associated with chronic illness that may also accompany other types of disability. People's sense of body intactness and competence may be threatened, and may be accompanied by a loss of self-esteem. Fears may become pervasive, such as fear of losing control of body functions, of losing independence, of strangers providing intimate care, and of pain. People may fear that greater dependence on others will result in a loss of love and approval. If hospitalization or nursing home care is required, people may feel anxious about being separated from familiar environments and loved ones. Finally, people may feel guilty about how their disability affects family members, spouses or partners, and friends (Miller, 1992a). Many of the losses discussed in Chapter Seven are experienced by people with disabilities related to chronic illness.

The Nature of the Disability

The nature of a disability may be a barrier to empowerment. Pain may restrict movement and limit a person's ability to concentrate. Disabilities that restrict oral communication, such as a brain injury, make connecting with others and expressing feelings and thoughts very difficult. Fatigue, decreases in time and energy, and fear and other strong emotions accompanying the disability may serve to limit social participation and interaction. Loss of cognitive functions that occur in conjunction with Alzheimer's disease, AIDS dementia complex, strokes, and other conditions can severely impair an individual's awareness of the environment, ability to understand and respond to others, and decision-making ability. The nature of the disability often interacts with the environmental and cultural barriers discussed above to limit individual empowerment. For example, the difficulties confronted by a person recovering from a stroke may be compounded by caretakers who overprotect rather than encourage, or who fail to support the person's developing self-care capacities because it is more "efficient" to provide care themselves.

SUGGESTIONS FOR EMPOWERMENT

Counselor Knowledge

Counselors will be in a better position to facilitate client empowerment when they possess at least basic information with respect to disability issues. In addition to critical awareness of power dynamics surrounding issues of disability in our society, working knowledge of the Americans with Disabilities Act is a bare minimum (see the resources section in this chapter). Further, counselors should actively seek information on the disabilities experienced by clients on their caseloads. The social services section in the local telephone directory will provide counselors with a host of resources; 10 phone requests for information could begin a counselor's personal resource library in only 20 minutes.

The intersection of disability with ethnicity cannot be ignored. Unfortunately, there is little information available that specifically addresses people of color with disabilities. Smart and Smart (1991) summarize the literature on acceptance of disabilities among Mexican Americans, but fail to be consistently critical of the studies they review. Their recommendations for family involvement in counseling, use of home visitation, and integration of religious/spiritual beliefs are similar to recommendations offered in counseling literature bearing on Chinese Americans (Chan, Lam, Wong, Leung, & Fang, 1988) and Native Americans (Marshall, Martin, Thomason, & Johnson, 1991) with disabilities.

Even when clients do not experience their disability as an area needing focus, counselors should research the issue independently or seek the input of colleagues to develop sensitivity to possible underlying issues and to increase awareness of what the client may be experiencing. For example, people with disabilities often are treated as if they are asexual (Duffy, 1981); sensitized counselors will be careful not to overlook sexuality issues in exploring client concerns. Specific information about disabilities can be integrated into interventions such as imagery exercises or assertiveness-training role-plays. The counselor's willingness to expend energy learning about the realities of the client's disability can be very validating and conveys a sense of respect for the client's experience.

Information

Counselors can facilitate client empowerment by encouraging and supporting the client's efforts to take an active role in information seeking. Simply finding out what clients do and do not know with respect to their disability can help clarify directions for inquiry. Counselors can provide subtle and overt messages that clients have a right to be involved in any medical and treatment decisions associated with their disability. Role-playing telephone or in-person conversations with medical personnel may help reduce client reluctance or timidity in the face of "experts." Role-playing and rehearsal will be especially important for clients with cultural expectations of doctors as superiors, or for clients for whom English is a second language. Counselors can support clients by exploring their emotional responses to the information gathered, and by encouraging clients to share their growing expertise in sessions. These efforts also help to minimize the traditional power imbalance in therapy.

An individual's desire for detail about his or her disability will vary; for example, some will wish to read professional literature while others will prefer to know only the basics. Gray and Doan (1990) make a vital point: "Optimal empowerment may depend not so much on the absolute amount of information or decisional control made available but rather on allowing [the person] to control how much information s/he will get, and to what degree s/he will participate in decision making" (p. 38). Counselors have to respect an individual's readiness and willingness to hear information. Most individuals, however, will want to develop considerable knowledge in the area of their disability.

Clients who understand their disability and its implications are in a better position to participate actively in decision making related to treatment or environmental modifications. For instance, I frequently encountered students with learning disabilities as an instructor of a university study-skills course. All students with learning disabilities were required to explain the nature of their disability to me before I approved the specific accommodations (e.g., a private testing room, an oral test, etc.) that they requested for the class. Almost without exception, the students were unable to do so without returning to their academic counselor and requesting further information. In an environment often suspicious or indifferent to "invisible" disabilities, it was essential that students could advocate for themselves by providing a brief, clear description of the nature of their disability and their environmental requirements. One student remarked, "My mother always handled teachers in the past; I never actually understood what was happening in my brain before—it's really interesting!"

Power Analysis

Frank discussion of the cultural and environmental barriers noted above can be a transforming experience for clients with recent disabilities and clients who have not had contact with advocates for people with disabilities. People with disabilities may possess able-bodied assumptions similar to those of the dominant society; they may feel it is entirely their own responsibility to adapt to the environment and they never consider society's responsibility for change. Exploration of societal and personal assumptions of responsibility can result in a decrease in internal pressures and an increase in self-esteem.

Disempowering aspects of the larger society usually are mirrored in the interpersonal lives of people with disabilities. For example, Anna was a 26-year-old Korean American woman who had been paralyzed from the waist down in an accident when she was five years old. Throughout her elementary and secondary education, her father had told her, "You must try harder than everyone else; no one will think a girl in a wheelchair can be smart" and "There is nothing wrong with your mind, just your body." While these messages enhanced her academic self-efficacy, Anna also internalized assumptions that her body was faulty. When she expressed her belief to an insightful medical doctor that she "obviously" could never marry or have children, she was referred to a support group for women who used wheelchairs. In the context of this group, she explored how her self-perceptions were shaped by familial and cultural assumptions, and how these assumptions contributed to her feelings of powerlessness and inadequacy. Thus, power analysis should always include cultural and familial views of disability. Visible disability may be viewed as a mark of parental wrongdoing, as something to hide, as a sign of weakness and need for protection, or as an opportunity to rise to a challenge; families will demonstrate unique perspectives within and across cultural groups. Within a single family, members may ignore, dramatize, minimize, or hide the fact that a family member has a disability. Power analysis can help clients identify how their self-perceptions and choices have been influenced, and sets the stage for establishing new self-perceptions and making different choices if desired.

Skill Application: Self-Esteem

People with high self-esteem are more likely to participate actively in efforts to maintain their health and well-being. They will be more confident that their opinions and feelings are of value and be more likely to express themselves to medical and other professional personnel. People with low self-esteem will be more likely to attach negative connotations to people's responses to them, for example, attributing an indifferent interpersonal response to unattractiveness or to a lack of worth as a person with a disability.

One framework for enhancing self-esteem among people with disabilities is offered by Wright (1983). Wright's framework has four components. First, the person recognizes existing abilities and learns to value the outcome more than the style of participation in activities. For example, an individual may learn to value sexual activities leading to emotional intimacy and physical gratification even though some pleasurable movements, techniques, and options are not or are no longer possible. In Anna's case, her parents would not have discussed sexuality even if she was not paralyzed; but perhaps to protect her from rejection, they never even acknowledged the possibility that Anna could marry and have children. Had her doctor ignored Anna's remark that she "obviously" could not do these things, or if the doctor had simply contradicted her by saying, "You are medically capable of having children," Anna would never have joined the support group and discovered that many women who use wheelchairs are sexually active, enjoy sexual intimacy with their partners, and have children.

The second component of Wright's framework is "subordination of the physique." The individual works to reduce focus on physical attributes and appearance, and invests in self-definitions extending beyond physical aspects of the self. For Anna, who already experienced herself as intelligent and a valuable member of her family and community, this component would have been less important. She had never considered her body's beauty, capabilities, or functioning before, so for her the physique was an unexplored territory that deserved greater attention. Wright's third component involves "containing" the disability, or limiting it to one aspect of identity rather than viewing it as an all-important and central aspect of identity. Although Anna's self-perception included identification beyond her disability, such as being Korean

American, a woman, a daughter, and a competent worker, she had excluded the roles of wife and mother from potential aspects of her self-identity. The addition of these potential roles was a source of excitement, apprehension, and hope. Wright's fourth component involves learning to avoid comparisons between current and past performance or activities, as well as avoiding comparisons between self and others. The person focuses on valuing and accepting self and others. Because Anna identified strongly with her Korean American community and many traditional Korean values, she already felt a genuine acceptance of herself and others as parts of a unified whole, and generally did not compare herself with others on issues of mobility or physical activity.

Group Participation

Chesler and Chesney (1988) advocate self-help groups as a means of empowerment for people with disabilities and parents of children with disabilities. They identified a number of components that benefit the participants: promoting disclosure of the disability; networking with others; sharing emotional experiences related to the initial diagnosis and ongoing response to the disability; identifying new sources of information; developing coping skills; discovering resources; contributing to the welfare of others by providing support, companionship, and information; and developing the means and strength to take collective action on behalf of others. One excellent source of information on self-help groups is described in the resources section of this chapter.

When barriers associated with chronic illness or disability are combined with barriers associated with being a person of color or a member of a nonethnic minority group, group participation can be particularly empowering. For example, a national survey of self-help groups for people with sickle cell anemia and their families (Nash, 1989) identified the following characteristics associated with empowerment: the direction and responsibilities for the group remained in the hands of the group members; a mental health professional helped facilitate a climate of sharing and respect; the common experiences of pain, unpredictability, and shortened life expectancy often associated with sickle cell disease served as focal points for bonding among group participants, as well as the shared history and culture of African Americans; physicians were invited to meet with the groups for informal discussion and information sessions; and members provided each other with mutual support against negative societal perceptions associated with being African American and chronically ill with a disease primarily affecting African Americans.

The invisibility commonly experienced by gay men, lesbians, and bisexuals may be compounded in the presence of a visible disability that leads to being "looked at but not seen." An example of a therapeutic group led by a professional is offered by Boden (1992). She describes the efficacy of a group for lesbians with physical disabilities, noting that physical differences experienced as defects often produce shame and self-loathing. By offering group therapy in the context of a "disabled lesbian assumption," that is, a context in which being lesbian and having a disability are not viewed as defects or differences but are viewed as the norm, she creates an atmosphere in which shame, fear, and self-hatred can give way to pride and self-acceptance.

Finally, group participation can serve as a vehicle for developing specific skills. Tobias (1990) describes the development of self-advocacy skills in the context of a problem-solving group for chronically mentally ill adults living in a therapeutic community. The problem-solving group was formed in response to ongoing resident complaints. Although residents had many valid concerns, the system for voicing and dealing with problems was not working. Through structuring and focusing problem discussions on one issue at a time, and consistent validation of residents' feelings and experiences, the social worker helped create a norm for listening to and discussing each problem systematically. The residents felt validated by her attention to and focus on participants' viewpoints. By resisting the temptation to speak on behalf of residents, she supported the residents' self-efficacy for voicing complaints and suggestions for improvement to the rest of the staff. Ultimately, group members initiated and independently followed through with several changes designed to enhance their social lives, including a weekly social on Friday nights. Important features of this group experience included the social worker's genuine respect for the residents' perceptions and trust in their abilities. The group's initiation and follow-through with social activities is clear evidence that self-advocacy skills were achieved.

RESOURCES

For detailed information about the Americans with Disabilities Act, contact the ADA Information Line at (202) 514-0301, or the Office on the ADA (320 1st Street, N.W., Washington DC, 20530, 202-307-2222).

One of the best national sources of recent information on self-help groups is the American Self-Help Clearinghouse at St. Clares-Riverside Medical Center, 29 Pocono Road, Denville, NJ 08734-2995, 201-625-7101. Among other materials, they sell *The Self-Help Source Book* for $10 (published by Hazelden Educational Materials in Center City, Minnesota). This book provides suggestions on how to organize self-help groups and lists a wide variety of resources. The U.S. Department of

Education Clearinghouse on Disability Information (708-205-8241) recommends this book for people with disabilities who are interested in finding out more about local support groups.

Bass and Davis's (1988) reading list includes inspirational and educational writings for people with disabilities, including *Despite This Flesh: The Disabled in Stories and Poems* edited by Miller (1985); *With Wings: An Anthology of Literature by and About Women with Disabilities* edited by Saxton and Howe (1987); and *No Apologies: A Guide to Living with a Disability* by Weiner (1986). Finally, Miller's (1992) *Coping with Chronic Illness: Overcoming Powerlessness* is an excellent source of information.

CONCLUSION

People with disabilities are a diverse group of individuals representing all socioeconomic, ethnic, sexual orientation, and age groups. Although counselors rarely are required to take coursework in the area of disabilities, our clients will always include people with disabilities. We cannot facilitate the empowerment of clients with disabilities when we overlook the power dynamics that influence their lives. We reflect the biases and able-bodied assumptions of the larger society when we work in inaccessible buildings, treat the need for client accommodations as "special" circumstances, assume the client's central identity is that of a "disabled person," or fail to recognize and confront our own biases and assumptions about disabilities. The Americans with Disabilities Act is a single step toward transforming our society into one that is responsive and responsible; our knowledge of the ADA should be accompanied by active participation in efforts to become a society truly characterized by equal opportunity.

Chapter Nine

SURVIVORS OF VIOLENCE

He smiled in the wine section
and commented on the weather
He lingered in the ethnic foods aisle
took ten minutes to choose a loaf of bread
looked over and smiled again in the checkout line
just a friendly guy
on a sunny day
He offered me a ride
what with my packages and all
he drove past four times
while I walked faster and faster and
kept thinking, it's broad daylight, it's OK
I ran into a complex but it looked so deserted
and who would answer the door; somebody worse?
So I ran out and he was waiting in his car
my packages bounced
sweat streamed down my temples
it had to be OK
I ran out of options, ducked into my complex
prayed he missed my last movement
ran panting to my apartment
dialed 911 cried into the phone

The officer said, He's right downstairs
(watching you walk up here?)
What were you wearing, honey?
(why are you asking me this?)
He laughed at my defensiveness
At least you've got an admirer
We'll tell him not to bother you anymore
I did not know if he was the vengeful type
if he knew which apartment was mine

if he had a gun, bad habits
if he was out there somewhere
if he would be waiting
tomorrow next week
I did not know

E.H.M.

INTRODUCTION

We live in a society marred by violence. From the overt violence of murder, rape, and physical assault to the more insidious violence of poverty, none of us is invulnerable. While suburbia provides "refuge" from many difficulties, it is no protection from violence: white-collar drug deals go bad; rapists and stalkers do not concern themselves with neighborhood boundaries; and depressed people strafe restaurants with gunfire in any part of town. If we don't hear of violent incidents from the newspaper, radio, or television news in the morning, we witness them in the form of "entertainment" in the evening, in a barrage of dramas, graphic murder mysteries, and reenactments of actual rapes, assaults, and murders. Movies made to "call attention to the issue" (e.g., the horror of child pornography) advertise scenes that degrade women and attract viewers with the same combinations of sex, violence, and powerlessness that they supposedly are trying to eliminate.

Empowerment in the context of survivors of violence might include the following components: a critical awareness of the cultural, social, and economic forces that create a climate in which violence is likely to occur; recognition that individuals do not *cause* others to treat them with violence; possessing a sense of control and power over one's life course while recognizing that some factors cannot be controlled; having and using the skills to assert one's rights to respect and dignity; and participating in efforts to empower others.

WHO ARE SURVIVORS OF VIOLENCE?

Survivors of violence are people who have lived through an episode or series of episodes of violence. This includes survivors of incest, rape, domestic violence, and other forms of assault; witnesses to murder and assault; people targeted by hate crimes; survivors of wartime violence; and people whose lives have been threatened by others, such as hostages. Survivors of violence include children and older adults; a disproportionate number are young African American men and women. Refugees have frequently witnessed and been subjected to extreme violence. Torture is a specific type of violence that usually involves the infliction of extreme physical pain and deliberate psychological manipulations designed to humiliate, terrorize, and produce subservience or information. Torture may occur in the context of domestic violence, ritualized abuse, or war. Women are far more likely to experience violence related to sexual assault; men and women are about equally likely to experience other forms of physical assault. The vast majority of perpetrators of violence are males.

The frequency of violence is staggering. One in four women in the United States will be raped at least once as an adult (Worell & Remer, 1992). Thirty-eight percent of a representative sample of California women reported having been sexually abused in childhood by an adult male (Russell, 1986). A compilation of other evidence indicates that one in three girls and one in seven boys are sexually abused by the time they reach age 18 (Bass & Davis, 1988). It has been estimated that as many as four million Americans may be the victims of physical abuse and neglect each year (Goldstein, Keller, & Erne, 1985). Data reported to the American Psychological Association's Commission on Violence and Youth indicate that 17% of a sample of Washington, D.C., fifth and sixth graders reported having been shot, stabbed, or raped (Youngstrom, 1992). African American adolescent males are more likely to die of gunshot injuries inflicted by a friend or an acquaintance than from any other cause (Fingerhut, Ingram, & Feldman, 1992; National Center for Health Statistics, 1992). The second leading cause of death among 15- to 19-year-olds in the United States is firearms homicide (Fingerhut, Ingram, & Feldman, 1992). Violence in the workplace is also on the rise. Stuart (1992) reports that workplace mass murders have increased 200–300% in the last decade, usually involving employees who have been laid off, passed over for promotions or demoted, their spouses, or enraged customers. While these figures do not present a comprehensive picture, they are illustrative of the scope of the problem.

People who have survived victimization by violence experience a different world from those who have never been victimized. The world of the survivor is more dangerous and less predictable, more realistic and less naive. Meg vividly portrays her experience of this world in the following paragraphs.

> I can't even begin to calculate the number of times that I've said "What if" or "If only" since that June evening back in 1968. Because for so many years—really until only about eight years ago when I started therapy—I never knew that it was okay to talk about what happened, let alone to begin to sort through it all.

I was only 14. I had just started my menstrual periods a couple of months before. My mother had given me a book to read about my body changes and growing up, but there was never any discussion. When that man appeared in front of me from out of nowhere, sticking a knife in my stomach, I only knew that I was going to die, and die a painful death. I thought it would be a physical death, though, not an emotional one.

The idea of rape never even occurred to me. My little sister, who is three years younger than me, was with me. She tried to run. I stood there frozen, so afraid that if he caught her, and I was gone, he would kill her instead. He made us both disrobe. She was forced to sit with her back to us, as he held the knife to my throat, and a gun in my side, while he raped me. I just kept waiting to be killed and at the same time thinking about my little sister— how I had failed to protect her from all of this while she sat there and had to listen to every disgusting thing he said, and my crying through it all.

From the time my parents arrived home, all the way to the hospital to be examined, and until the days my mother and father died, the incident was only discussed in legal and medical terms. Never in the sense of how I felt about it, what had happened to me inside, or how it might impact my decision process in the future. My father was a prominent attorney and the only concern on the part of my parents was to protect the family name. The neighbors were not to know about it. I found out years later that my older sisters living away from home were not even told about it. My father even had all the details altered so that the account in the newspaper would not identify our family. The police were the only ones to ever hear my story, and that was during the numerous trips to the police station to look at line-ups and mug shots, or to give descriptions to police artists.

This wasn't supposed to happen in good families. I had brought shame on the family. And the feelings of guilt on my part only got worse when the police would bring suspects to our home in a squad car and line them up in our driveway for identification. I believe something inside my mother died every time that happened. More than a year after the rape, the man was caught. He had committed numerous other rapes, those of women who worked at a nearby medical center. Ironically, what helped police catch the man was a photograph of my brother-in-law. I had a difficult time putting into words an accurate description of the man for the police artist, but the picture of my brother-in-law, a long-haired, wild-eyed drug addict, looked just like him. He was standing next to my sister in the photo, and I remember my mother cutting the picture in half so that they would only have his photo, and not my sister's.

My mother tried to "buy" back my innocence throughout my high school years, giving me all kinds of things. Never a hug; never telling me if she felt pain for me; never just telling me that I was still okay in her eyes and her heart.

By the end of my sophomore year I began to drink heavily. I didn't date a lot. I was terrified of boys unless I knew and trusted them as friends. I knew by my senior year that my drinking was different than that of my friends, and I had a reputation as a drunk. I married right after high school, throwing away a full academic scholarship to a Jesuit college, and by the grace of God, 21 years and four children later, am still married to the same man. He stood by me through alcoholism, spending addictions that put our family on the brink of bankruptcy, years of screaming and flashback nightmares, and my fear and confusion about emotional and sexual intimacy that kept a wedge between us.

I believe that for me, the act of rape was not nearly as traumatic as how it was dealt with. The burden of shame that I carried for so many years was *so heavy*. The first time anyone ever told me that it wasn't my fault was in therapy. The burden of silence was even greater. The first time I ever even talked through it with anyone was in therapy. I know today that so many of my decisions and my behaviors were the result, directly or indirectly, of the rape itself, but even more so of the way it was dealt with in my family. For so many years I had the battle inside of me of coming from a family who thought they were better than anyone else, and yet I never thought I was as good as anyone else. How could I be, after all the pain and shame I had brought to my parents because of my being raped?

I know today that I want to be more than just a survivor of rape. While I can never get back the innocence that was stolen from me, today I have the tools to know that it never has to be like that again.

BARRIERS

Economic and Cultural Context

An economic system that creates and maintains distinctions between rich and poor, and particularly a system that requires the existence of an underclass to maintain the life-styles of a small upperclass, is an economic system that promotes and perpetuates violence. We are used to categorizing acts of rebellion, such as riots and revolutions, as acts of violence. We are less likely to consider ongoing oppression through denial of health services, education, and political power as acts of violence. The fact that the United States has the highest infant mortality rate of *any industrialized nation in the world* speaks to the vast inequities of our society: Most of the babies that die are not middle- or upper-class Euro American babies. If we are to understand *why* our society is violent, we must understand *what* violence is, and view conditions of poverty—conditions that promote hopelessness, despair, and a profound sense of inferiority and powerlessness—as constituting violence, just as surely as the firing of guns.

It is also important to understand how economics influence violence even beyond our national borders. The international child pornography industry, which earns more than $10 billion a year, is one graphic example. In Asia, profound and widespread poverty is a backdrop to the stealing and selling of children into virtual slavery (Witt, 1993). "Sex tourists," chiefly from the United States, Canada, Western Europe, Australia, and Japan, go to Asia to avoid child protection laws in their own countries; estimates of the number of child prostitutes in Asia are 400,000 in India; 20,000 in the city of Manila, the Philippines; 72,000 in Taiwan; 800,000 in Thailand; and 20,000 in Vietnam (Witt, 1993). Economic issues are inseparable from the violence that permeates the lives of these children, and the 500,000 to one million children in the United States (Bass & Davis, 1988) who are brutalized by the child pornography industry. This example highlights another aspect of the context in which violence occurs: the acceptance of dominance and submission as a valid means of organizing society and relationships within society.

Worell and Remer's (1992) analysis of the cultural context in which rape occurs has implications for other forms of violence against women as well. Drawing from the work of Sanday (1981), Weis and Borges (1977), and others, they reviewed rape myths, gender role socialization, and the power differential between men and women as factors in the incidence of rape. Sanday (1981) argues that the prevalence of rape in a society is a function of gender role socialization and of hierarchical power relations in which men dominate women. Characteristics of gender role socialization that lead to rape-prone societies include encouragement for men to be aggressive and dominant over women, devaluation of women's roles as nurturers and caretakers, and men's uninvolvement in child care.

Weis and Borges (1977) contend that women are set up to be victims by such gender role prescriptions as be kind, gentle, and nonaggressive; do not be physically strong; always be polite; be dependent on men, passive, and childlike; be responsible for controlling men's sexual behavior; accept men as protectors. Men are likewise set up to be rapists by prescriptions such as the following: be aggressive, powerful, and controlling; initiate sex and dominate women; be the boss; "no" means "maybe"; to protect a woman is to rightfully possess her; women are sexual objects; dates are to be paid for and reimbursed sexually. There is a growing body of literature that supports these contentions. For example, Giarusso, Johnson, Goodchilds, and Zellman (1979) found that more than 50% of the high school males surveyed indicated that in some circumstances it was acceptable for males to use force to achieve sexual intercourse; a similar percentage of female high school students *agreed*. Malamuth (1981) found that 51% of male students who read a rape scenario indicated that they might commit the rape in the same situation if they were sure they wouldn't get caught.

In her qualitative study of survivors of childhood sexual abuse, Morrow (1992) describes relationships of dominance and submission between adult and child as forming part of the cultural context in which incest is likely to occur. Other contextual conditions include the constant possibility or threat of violence, the abusive treatment of adult women in the immediate environment, and denial by adults that abuse could be occurring. Russell (1986) argues that the increasing sexualization of children in advertising and pornography contributes to the rising incidence of child sexual abuse.

Another aspect of the context in which violence occurs is our society's almost exclusive reliance on domination to resolve conflict. Our media heroes, male and—increasingly—female, are those who resolve conflict by killing, beating up, or otherwise violently treating those with whom they disagree (Whitaker, 1989). From American Indians to Iraqis, the identified "bad guys" change, but the method of resolution remains the same: We eliminate them. In family situation comedies, conflict is dealt with by put-downs, name calling, and silent treatments. Most conflicts are "resolved" without ever discussing the original issue. In soap operas, characters are unable to resolve conflicts because no one would bother to watch the next day; instead, people lie, omit information, or make accusations and slam doors before any communication occurs. Physical, verbal, and emotional domination are modeled as the way to deal with conflict.

There are estimates that children will have witnessed thousands of acts of violence on television by the time they reach adolescence. The debate about television violence and aggression continues, with some studies failing to find (e.g., Harris, 1992; Messner, 1986; Wiegman, Kuttschreuter, & Baarda, 1992) and others finding relationships between watching violent television shows and aggressive behavior (e.g., Comstock & Strasburger, 1990; Friedrich-Cofer & Huston, 1986; Lukesch, 1989). Focusing on specific individuals and their TV viewing habits, however, seems to leave out the more profound effect of the cultural context. The general cultural context in which dominance ends conflict and violence is a means of entertainment is a part of the fabric of everyone's lives, not simply those who watch violent television. The roles of men as actors and aggressors and of women as reactors and submitters permeates everything from textbooks to billboards.

Pervasive and highly visible economic discrepancies, cultural acceptance of domination and violence as legitimate means of resolving conflict, and gender role socialization all contribute to the incidence of violence in our society and serve as barriers to empowerment. In the words of Goodman, Koss, and Russo (1993), "Although traditional therapeutic approaches may provide some help for women in [violent] circumstances, it is clear that intervention and prevention programs that address the social and cultural forces that promote violence must be part of the therapeutic vision and professional roles of psychologists" (p. 128).

Critical Incident Stress and Post-Traumatic Stress Disorder

Critical incident stress occurs in response to traumatic events. A traumatic event is defined by Figley (1985) as "an extraordinary event or series of events which is sudden, overwhelming, and often dangerous, either to one's self or significant other(s)" (p.xvii). Normal responses to critical incident stress include but are not limited to the following symptoms: tearfulness, shakiness, nightmares, insomnia, irritability, isolation, hypervigilance, panic, headaches, and gastrointestinal upset. In addition, emotional reactions such as depression, apathy, anger, and extreme fear are common. Critical incident stress may evolve into post-traumatic stress disorder (PTSD) (American Psychiatric Association, 1987), which is characterized by an alternating sequence of intrusive images and avoidance of the event that endures for longer than one month. The intrusive images may be in the form of nightmares or flashbacks in which the event is reexperienced vividly. Avoidance of behaviors, feelings, or activities associated with the traumatic event, memory loss, withdrawal, and emotional numbing are buffers against the intensity of the experience. It is now recognized that PTSD symptoms frequently occur in the aftermath of physical and sexual violence (Goodman, Koss, & Russo, (1993).

Janoff-Bulman (1985) contends that three major assumptions are violated by traumatic events: belief in one's own personal invulnerability; seeing oneself in a positive light; and belief in a meaningful, orderly world. McCann, Pearlman, and Abrahamson (1988) contend that the following assumptions are also countered by incidents of violence: safety (I can protect myself from physical and emotional harm, injury, or loss); trust (I can rely on my own perceptions and judgments and on other people); power (I can control my own thoughts, feelings, and actions, and the future outcomes of my interpersonal relationships); esteem (I am of value and worthy of respect, and so are other people); and intimacy (I can enjoy time alone, comfort myself, and I can connect with others in a meaningful and personal way). Violation of these assumptions is psychologically devastating.

Goodman, Koss, and Russo (1993) review five models of women's reactions to physical and sexual assault. They note that while none of the models accounts for all the symptoms of PTSD, each incorporates the critical role of survivors' thought processes in the development of PTSD symptoms. Specifically, individual and sociocultural factors such as family history, prior trauma, personality, sexual orientation, and community attitudes influence survivors' evaluations of the personal significance of the event. Their evaluation of significance, in turn, influences the severity of their reaction. Thus, Goodman, Koss, and Russo argue that counselors must explore the survivors' personal meanings of the violence and their perceptions of their coping strategies to understand survivors' psychological responses to victimization. They note, for example, that the "passive" behavior of a battered woman may also be a resourceful, purposeful response designed to protect her children. The way in which survivors view their behavior and the behavior of perpetrators will influence the severity and duration of PTSD.

The symptoms of critical incident stress and/or PTSD are barriers for survivors of violence for several reasons. First, survivors often do not know that these symptoms are normal responses to violent events and may believe they are sick or going crazy. Second, the negative affect associated with these symptoms may increase survivors' sense of isolation and reduce the likelihood that they will reach out for support. Finally, the symptoms can interfere significantly with normal functioning, reducing survivors' sense of mastery and efficacy and increasing their sense of powerlessness.

Blaming the Victim

Meg's personal statement poignantly articulates the consequences of blaming the survivor of violence. Society's tendency to blame victims (Ryan, 1971), and our consequent tendency to blame ourselves, creates enormous difficulty for all survivors. Loved ones and acquaintances may feel very threatened as they hear of someone's experience of violence; believing that the victims *caused* the violence, or did something to bring it on themselves, creates the illusion that "It couldn't have happened to *me, I* won't be victimized like that." In other words, it allows others to maintain their assumptions of safety, trust, and invulnerability. By the same token, if I am a survivor of violence, believing that I contributed to the occurrence of violence helps me feel a false sense of control and power; "Now that I know better, I can prevent violence from happening to me again."

Counselors must be sensitive to self-blame veiled in statements such as "I was walking through an unfamiliar neighborhood—I was too uncomfortable to ask for a ride home—and I was assaulted." A woman making this statement may well have been deciding between two risks; driving with someone she did not know well (and potentially being assaulted) versus walking by herself. Either situation involves risk; we could "blame" her for making either choice and argue in retrospect that the other choice would have been safer. We could also blame her for going out at all; if her ride home fell through at the last minute, she never should have left the house. If her ride home never showed up as planned, she should have brought money for a taxi home; if she didn't bring the money, well, she should have known better. We want to think of a million ways that the woman could have prevented being victimized because it reduces our terror regarding the obvious fact: The perpetrator made a choice to be violent. We may learn to exercise behaviors that reduce our likelihood of being targeted for violence, but we cannot learn behaviors that *prevent* victimization. And failure to exercise these behaviors is *never* a cause of violence.

When members of stigmatized groups are victims of violence, they are more likely than others to be blamed. Gay men and lesbians subjected to violent hate crimes, for example, are told, "You were targeted because you are gay," with the implication that their sexual orientation *evoked* the attack. Those who are in the early stages of the coming-out process may have greater difficulty healing because they probably have had fewer positive experiences associated with their sexual orientation; are less likely to have established a positive gay, lesbian, or bisexual identity; and are less likely to have a wide support network in place at the time of the attack (Garnets, Herek, & Levy, 1990). Members of the gay community may blame victims of antigay violence by targeting "obvious" gestures or clothing as the cause of the attack, thus attempting to minimize their own sense of fear and vulnerability.

Blaming the victim is a form of revictimization that may occur when the survivor reports the incident to the police or brings charges against the perpetrator. Although many police departments are making efforts to educate officers and provide more sensitive responses to survivors of violence, there is still a strong tendency to blame victims. The experience depicted in the poem at the beginning of this chapter is common to many women who report sexual harassment or assault: They are questioned about their clothing. The implication, of course, is that certain clothing *causes* men to lose control and rape. In addition, defense lawyers in rape trials may attempt to put the accuser's life on trial. Current sexual relationships may be subjected to scrutiny; the survivor may not feel emotionally ready to confront the perpetrator in the courtroom; the survivor usually has to repeatedly describe—and relive—the event to police officers, attorneys, and other officials; and finally, the survivor often feels very out of control due to the nature of the legal system (Rindt-Wagner, 1992). Thus, reporting a crime and prosecuting the perpetrator can be an overwhelming, frightening, and revictimizing experience.

Repeated violent victimizations leave women—and presumably many men—less likely to be able to protect themselves and may leave them more likely to be targets of additional violence (Agosta & Loring, 1988; Herman, 1981; Koss & Dinero, 1989). Without understanding the complex interplay of factors that contribute, for example, to the frequency of women returning to abusive partners, counselors easily fall into blaming clients: "Not the first time, but *afterwards* she *should have known better*."

Shame

One of the most powerful consequences of being victimized by violence is shame. In her review of the literature, Gardner (1992) notes that shame is experienced as a threat to the core identity, a sense of degradation and failure to live up to internalized standards that is almost unbearably painful. The pain and sense of exposure associated with shame make the experience isolating and alienating. Shame is intimately linked with feelings of inadequacy, inferiority, and unlovability. Perpetrators of violence often cultivate shame responses by deliberately humiliating victims with name calling, demanding the performance of certain behaviors, or by telling victims they deserve or wish to be victimized. Violence in the context of hate crimes—that is, violent acts in which the perpetrator(s) specifically indicate targeting of the person because of some group membership—creates a powerful negative association for survivors among violence, shame, and their group identity. Perpetrators of domestic violence and childhood sexual abuse often convince survivors over time that they are unlovable and worthless. Society's proclivity for victim blaming compounds the shame evoked by the violence, and clients are likely to hide their feelings of shame. Gardner writes:

> Shame is traumatic, and the responses to it are variants of the flight, fight, or freeze responses to other kinds of trauma. Flight manifests as denial, suppression, repression, avoidance, intellectualization, not knowing, and displacement. Fight presents as anger, hostility, shaming others, and depression. Freezing manifests as silence, dissociation, and becoming passive. With a high index of suspicion for shame when we see these defenses, we will be better able to work with our [clients] to help them identify and work through shame issues. (p. 24)

The counselor with an unresolved history of victimization by violence may avoid or "not notice" the client's shame; Gardner recommends that counselors thoroughly examine their own issues around shame.

The extremely painful nature of shame means that clients must feel safe before revealing this aspect of their experience. Counselors usually will have to combine gentle persistence with empathy and acceptance to draw out the client's experience; the counselor's empathy and genuine acceptance can powerfully contradict the client's sense of failure. Because shame is tied to the person's intimate view of him or herself as inadequate, counselors must often assist the client in extricating the self-concept from the shaming experiences. Even clients who were very aware of societal power dynamics before their experience with violence usually will need help putting their experience in context and eliminating self-blame.

Male survivors of violence often experience profound shame. In accord with their gender role socialization, males are supposed to be powerful, dominant, and in control. Males battered by their partners are unlikely to go to the police; when they do so, the police may disbelieve or humiliate them. Approximately 10% of rape victims are male. Brownmiller's (1975) documentation of rape in society includes the prevalence and stigma associated with male rape. Men who rape men are predominantly heterosexual; similar to the case with women, it is a crime of violence and domination rather than one of sexual desire.

SUGGESTIONS FOR EMPOWERMENT

Counselor Reaction

When clients share the fact that they are survivors of violence, two counselor reactions are of particular importance. First, counselors should accept the client's story. Although there may be instances in which an experience is constructed artificially, the overwhelming evidence is that clients do not lie about abuse. An incest survivor probably will have tried to tell someone about it in the past, and just as probably will have been punished, ignored, disbelieved, or silenced. The consequences of charging someone with incest or rape are still so overwhelmingly negative for the accuser that there is little to be gained from making it up. The more extensive the abuse, the greater will be the client's fears of being disbelieved. In the case of childhood sexual abuse, clients often do believe that they are crazy or that they must have made it up, particularly when memory loss is present (see Bass & Davis, 1988). The counselor's willingness to believe the client is a critical step in the healing process.

The second important aspect of the counselor's response is to retain composure. Counselor reactions of horror or overidentification with the client are not empowering. A counselor who cries as the client reveals the story may send a message to the client: "Your pain is overwhelming me." Survivors of violence often cope with the experience by suppressing their own feelings and caretaking for others (Bass & Davis, 1988; Morrow, 1992). When the counselor's reaction calls attention to the counselor's emotional state and invites such caretaking, the client is ill served. It is not unusual or unnatural for counselors working with survivors to experience vicarious traumatization (McCann & Pearlman,

1990). For example, a counselor at a rape crisis center may have nightmares and increased fears of assault after working with survivors of particularly violent attacks. However, counselors have an ethical obligation to address and resolve their symptoms outside of the session.

Finally, the negative effects of a counselor's heterosexist bias may be compounded when working with gay and lesbian survivors of violence, especially sexual assault. Counselor exploration of current relationships ("Are you using birth control in your sexual relationships?" "Do you have satisfying sexual relationships with women now, Dave?") will quickly convey heterosexist assumptions and may reduce the client's feeling of safety and acceptance (Orzek, 1989). Similarly, assumptions that the perpetrator was male can alienate clients who have been victimized by women.

Information

Information about survival can help survivors deal with the trauma. Discussion of PTSD symptoms helps normalize what clients may be experiencing, and reassures them that they are not "crazy" but are having normal responses to abnormal events. Bass and Davis's (1988) characterization of stages in healing has been extraordinarily helpful to both male and female survivors of childhood sexual abuse, as well as to survivors of other forms of violence. They portray healing as a process of cycling through some or all of a series of stages, not necessarily in a particular order. Their stages include Remembering, Believing It Happened, Breaking Silence, Trusting Yourself, and 10 others.

In the case of violence related to specific, time-limited incidents, such as a date-rape, witnessing a murder, or a one-time physical assault, stage models can help clients to organize their aftermath experiences. One six-stage model of rape response described by Remer (1986) is helpful in describing recovery from other incidents of violence as well. Stage One, *pre-rape*, refers to the social context existing at the time of the rape. It includes all the life experiences of the survivor, as well as gender role socialization and cultural norms. This stage also characterizes clients who have not been victimized but live in fear of being raped. Stage Two is the *rape event*, and includes the events immediately preceding, during, and after the rape. The survivor's perceptions, feelings, and behaviors, as well as the behaviors of the perpetrator, are important to explore. Worell and Remer (1992) recommend that therapists listen for how clients' myths about rape and gender role socialization influenced their actions; when clients understand these connections they are less likely to self-blame. Exploring with clients how they coped with the rape as it happened—that is, by dissociating, pleading, struggling, remaining motionless, etc.—in the context of gender role socialization and the threat of increased violence, helps reduce shame and guilt, and honors their method of survival.

Stage Three, *crisis and disorganization*, involves the time period immediately after the rape and may last for hours or up to a year. This stage is characterized by feelings of helplessness, shock, confusion, guilt, and/ or numbness. Blaming reactions from others intensify the negativity of this period and increase the difficulty of healing. Stage Four, *outward satisfactory adjustment and denial*, reflects the survivor's attempt to return life to normal. The survivor uses avoidance strategies such as minimization of what happened, blocking out the memory of what happened, denying the rape occurred, or repressing details of the rape. Although the client may say he or she is doing "fine," symptoms such as depression and nightmares are common. People may continue in this stage indefinitely. Stage Five, *reliving and working through*, begins when denial breaks down, and may occur in response to a movie scene, a smell, a comment, or some unidentifiable stimulus. In this stage, the survivor often relives the experience vividly, has flashbacks and intense nightmares, and generally reexperiences the crisis stage that occurred immediately after the incident. Survivors are especially likely to be disturbed by this stage and question whether they are "going crazy." Stage Six, *resolution and integration*, is characterized by integration of the experience into the life of the survivor. The person no longer self-blames. Survivors at this stage accept that the experience occurred and that it is a part of their personal history. They appreciate their own personal strengths that helped them to survive the experience, and frequently participate in organized efforts to prevent rape or to help other survivors. Many survivors will recycle through stages five and six several times, each time achieving a higher level of integration and post-rape functioning. Although survivors of violence cannot return to "life as they knew it," post-violence life can still be a richly rewarding experience: Survivors need to know this. Hearing this information from other survivors, whether in person or through literature, can be a source of hope and empowerment. Knowledge of this or similar models can be a source of validation and hope for survivors who are feeling unable to control their reactions.

Finally, for women survivors, counselor and client knowledge of feminist identity development models may be helpful. Downing and Roush (1985) suggest that this developmental process parallels that of Black identity development. Beginning with *passive acceptance* of sexism and second-class citizenship, women move to a *revelation* stage. This stage is characterized by the crises that emerge from repeated confrontation with sexism and discrimination. In *embeddedness-emanation*, friendships with women become an intense and primary source of social support. *Synthesis* occurs when women evaluate men on an individual basis and transcend gender role prescriptions. Ultimately, women consolidate their positive feminist identity and enter the stage of *active commitment.* Men are considered equal to (though not the same as) women, and women are commited to meaningful forms of social involvement. A positive feminist identity seems consistent with several components of empowerment such as the awareness of power dynamics, sense of shared identity, and support for the empowerment of others.

Reducing the Isolation

Survivors of violence often feel alone and isolated. The stigma of victimization prevents many from sharing their experience with others, and as a result, the survivor may feel as though no one else has ever gone through a similar experience, or that no one has had the feelings he or she has have experienced. In the example below, the counselor was very green and the client was experiencing a very complex set of problems. When her profound sense of isolation was reduced, however, the client began healing herself.

Veronica was a 29-year-old African American mother of five. She worked in a school cafeteria during the day and had a second job two nights a week and on weekends. Her husband had a bad back; he drank all day and "looked at" the children; she reported he only fed or changed them if they cried. Veronica prepared all the meals and did all the cleaning, shopping, and laundry. She weighed nearly 300 pounds, and standing at work all day caused chronic pain and swelling in her feet. Veronica had come in for help with depression: She wanted to go to sleep and never wake up.

Veronica could not remember large portions of her childhood and adolescence. She knew that her stepfather had forced her into having sex with him at least by the time she was five years old, maybe earlier. She moved out of the house and broke off all contact with her family when she was 17 years old, shortly before giving birth to her oldest child, her stepfather's daughter. She assumed that her mother, four sisters, and three brothers all knew that she had been "having sex with" her stepfather all her life. While she didn't really think it was her fault initially, she was deeply ashamed that she had been unable to stop his advances as she became older. Typical of many incest perpetrators, he had rewarded her with money and special privileges, and convinced her that she "seduced him" into having sex with her. She could not remember ever being held by her mother; she could only picture her mother as angry and screaming at everyone. But mostly, she couldn't remember anything at all.

Veronica was not actively suicidal, but she was becoming so apathetic that it frightened her. She spoke as if she were dreaming, with a heavy and faraway voice, for the first three sessions. She seemed largely unaware of the counselor's presence. Each of these sessions was simply devoted to telling her story, crying, and experiencing her overwhelming pain. The counselor listened, held her hand, and occasionally reflected on Veronica's endurance, or strength, or determination. The counselor didn't think anything was happening.

But something was happening. Veronica came to the fourth session with an idea: She could move in with a girlfriend, the girlfriend would watch all of their children, and Veronica would pay the bills. Veronica made eye contact with the counselor; she said she had deliberately picked a fight with her husband. She had just a little bit of energy. The counselor sent her home with copies of three women's stories from The Courage to Heal—*the stories most closely resembling Veronica's life—not sure if Veronica could or would read them.*

During the fifth session, Veronica exploded. She literally sat down and began screaming, cursing, and punching the arms of the couch and her thighs. Then she began to moan, rocking back and forth and seeming to chant; for a long time, the counselor couldn't understand what she was saying. Finally, she recognized the phrase, "I'm not dead yet." Veronica eventually became still and startled the counselor with a broad grin. She said, "I'm a big woman, I'm a strong woman, and my husband is a skinny little shit. I'm gonna do my thing now; I'm a good mother." And she got up and walked out.

Veronica came back one more time. She hoped to be in a new place with her girlfriend by the end of the month. Although still depressed, Veronica was back in touch with the strength she had used to survive all her life. She told the counselor, "Nobody has listened to me for years. No one ever held my hand." But the most powerful experience for her was reading the stories of the other incest survivors. She pulled the pages out of her purse just before leaving. "I take them everywhere. I read them over and over. They made it out of there. *They didn't give up. These pages are my bible now. These are my hope-words." Two weeks later, her phone had been disconnected. Veronica made it out of there.*

Group experiences also can be empowering. In *The Courage to Heal*, Bass and Davis (1988) suggest that telling others about past abuse can be a transformative experience for many reasons. Specifically, it may bring people out of the isolation of secrecy and shame, draw people out of denial by acknowledging the truth of what happened, open doors to receiving understanding and help, allow people to be more in touch with their feelings, allow people to see themselves through the compassionate eyes of a supportive other, reduce barriers to intimacy, help establish people in the present moment, allow people to become models for other survivors, and, ultimately, help people feel strong and proud of having survived.

Group experiences may be helpful to partners of survivors, who experience a secondary form of victimization. Even when partners know how to be helpful and supportive, they may need support for the frustration, anger, fear, and other emotions that they experience during their partner's healing process.

Self-Advocacy

Participation in groups and organizations that support survivors, work for societal change, and raise public consciousness about violence and survivor issues can be empowering for survivors. Such participation can take many forms. For example, one group of women survivors of sexual assault and abuse organized a "Take Back the Night" march through a college campus to raise awareness about sexual assault. The marchers included survivors, partners, spouses, and friends of survivors, and other concerned members of the community. They were accompanied by trained counselors, whose purpose was to provide support to marchers experiencing trauma or flashbacks, and to deal with harassment from bystanders. The marchers converged in a central campus location to hear speakers share information about the scope and causes of the problem, as well as personal experiences and words of hope and encouragement. As one participant expressed very simply, "This is what *good* power is all about."

One important component of surviving is the restoration of a sense of personal competence, mastery, and wholeness. The loss of one's view of the world as safe and relatively benign is traumatic and threatens many aspects of life. Participation in a group that actively works to reduce violence and support survivors can facilitate healing by providing survivors with a community of people who understand, a rich source of role models, and the power that comes from using one's skills to benefit others.

Bass and Davis (1988) and Davis (1990) provide a series of resources for survivors of violence. For example, VOICES in Action, Inc., is a national self-help network for survivors and partners and friends of survivors that provides free national referrals, an annual conference, a newsletter, and information regarding more than 100 special interest support groups (e.g., survivors who were abused by their mothers, survivors of ritual abuse/satanic cults). The resources section of this chapter provides a variety of other sources of information, support, and advocacy.

Skill Application: Imagery Training

As noted in Chapter Three, imagery training can facilitate empowerment by enabling clients to recreate and transform past experiences, to resolve unfinished issues, and to provide self-nurturance and healing encounters with oneself or others. The case below illustrates the use of imagery training with a survivor of violence.

Manuel was a 35-year-old Mexican American man who entered counseling because he was dissatisfied with his career. He was married to Susana, his high school novia, or sweetheart, and they had four children: daughters of two, five, and seven years of age, and an 11-year-old son. Manuel had worked at a local manufacturing plant since dropping out of high school, and had been a supervisor for the previous two years. He reported that he and his wife were still in love with each other; they were close to their children and active in their Catholic parish. He described his relationship with his parents, siblings, and in-laws as close; all of his family lived nearby, and Susana's family members lived within 200 miles. Manuel was experiencing feelings of depression, difficulty sleeping and eating, had little energy, was irritable, and had lost all enjoyment in his work. During the first several sessions, Manuel and the counselor, a Euro American female, explored the nature of his work and his dissatisfaction.

When discussion of Manuel's work situation failed to clarify the source of his discouragement, the counselor began exploring other possible sources. By this time, Manuel had begun to trust the counselor and to feel slightly more comfortable about being in counseling. As they reviewed Manuel's family life, Manuel revealed that he had cried "like a baby" the night of his son's 11th birthday party. He was unable to talk about it with Susana, and attributed his outburst to "drinking too much." Because this event seemed to coincide with the onset of Manuel's depression, the counselor asked Manuel to describe his own life at age 11. Manuel related several stories about school, fighting a group of boys with his brothers, and trying to hide the smell of cigarette smoke from his mother. He related these stories with a studied nonchalance and told the counselor he had to leave the session early. He cancelled the next session by telephone and did not reschedule. When the counselor contacted him, Manuel explained that he was feeling a little better about his job and saw no need to continue counseling.

Two months later, Manuel scheduled an emergency session with the counselor. He showed up for his appointment in an agitated state and paced the floor. The counselor said, "Sometimes we try to forget things that happened when we were children, but it isn't so easy. I think maybe something very painful happened when you were about 11 years old, and you are having a hard time forgetting about it." Over a period of 2 ½ hours, Manuel told the counselor that he had been gang-raped by a group of teenage boys when he was 11 years old. They had come upon him alone in a park and began taunting him. In a show of bravado, he accused them of being homosexual, maricones, and tried to run away. They caught him and spent what seemed like hours humiliating him, forcing him to perform oral sex, and raping him anally. They told him that he was the maricon, that he wanted them to perform these acts, that he was just a "bitch in heat." During the entire episode they waved a knife in front of his face and threatened to castrate him if he made any noise. They finally let him go when someone thought he heard voices. They told Manuel they would do the same thing to his sister if he ever told anyone what happened. Manuel reported that he felt numb for weeks afterwards. He did not remember dressing, walking home, or getting into bed. No one treated him differently the next morning, so he assumed that his family did not know what happened. He never told anyone and managed to forget for long periods of time.

Manuel's experience of violence threatened his view of himself as a man; men are supposed to be strong and self-sufficient. He viewed homosexuality as a perversion and saw homosexual men as weak and effeminate. He went through a period in high school in which he obsessed about what had happened, and coped by lifting weights, drinking beer, and regularly getting into fights. When he began seeing Susana, he gradually reduced his drinking and fighting and began forgetting again. It wasn't until the night of his son's 11th birthday that the memories resurfaced with great intensity. Since then, he used an enormous amount of energy to keep the memories from "taking over." He seemed more able to forget when at home, but at work, whenever he became involved in tasks requiring little concentration, the memories overwhelmed him.

The final portion of the emergency session was devoted to deciding what to tell his wife. Manuel decided to see the counselor at least one more time before telling her. Although he "knew" she would accept him, he feared that she would see him as less of a man if she learned about his past. In Manuel's subsequent therapy, issues related to gender role socialization, societal emphasis on dominance and submission, Mexican American culture, Catholicism, and manhood were addressed directly and indirectly. The counselor provided information on male survivors of sexual abuse and assault as well as on the nature of counseling to help reduce Manuel's feelings of shame and isolation.

One of the most painful elements of the experience was Manuel's sense of humiliation and shame both during and after the assault. Gentle exploration of his feelings revealed a "secret wish" that Manuel also regarded with great shame: He wanted his father to hold him, comfort him, and tell him that he was brave, that he was still a man. This wish seemed completely contradictory to Manuel. If he was a man, he would not need such reassurance. Besides, his father never would have responded that way; at best, his father would have told him to forget about it. At worst, his father would have asked, "Why didn't you fight back? Are you just a baby or are you a man?" Although Manuel's family was very close—a closeness that probably contributed to his ability to have healthy relationships with women and men as an adult—their predicted reactions would have been consistent with those of many families.

Through the use of imagery exercises, Manuel experienced a powerful and healing encounter between his 11-year-old self and his father. In this experience, his father demonstrated the comfort and support that Manuel knew his father would have wanted—though probably was unable—to provide. His father explained that his attackers could never be men and could never be good fathers the way Manuel would be one day; he said that he was proud of Manuel's bravery and ability to endure pain; he held Manuel and told him the physical pain would not last long, and that he would grow to be a stronger and more compassionate man after this horrible experience. Because Manuel's father modeled a masculine figure that was compassionate and at times emotional, these images of Manuel's father were only uncharacteristic in that they were verbalized.

Manuel continued seeing the counselor for 10 months. On termination, he had decided that with the exception of his wife (who had been included in later sessions) he would not tell anyone about his experience; he shared with his family only that he was "consulting a career counselor." Nevertheless, he felt that his relationship with his father had grown stronger since he had experienced his father's compassion through the imagery exercises. In addition, his depression had lifted and he felt that his "inner strength" had returned. Although he did not want to participate in a male survivors' group, Manuel did join a neighborhood safety group of parents from his son's school. The group met once a month to discuss ways to prevent their children from getting involved with drugs or gangs.

Manuel's story illustrates the use of imagery training to reconstruct the past and provide nurturing experiences. The privacy of imagery work enabled Manuel to access his father's compassion without risking exposure and possible negative reactions. Some issues went relatively unaddressed; for example, the counselor modeled positive attitudes and perceptions about gay men but did not confront Manuel's homophobia directly. The clarification of Manuel's definitions of manhood and masculinity, and how these perceptions were influenced by society, culture, and family, were consistently woven into their discussions.

RESOURCES

VOICES in Action, Inc., can be reached at P.O. Box 148309, Chicago, IL 60614. Other important resources provided in Bass and Davis (1988) and Davis (1990) include annotated bibliographies for survivors of violence, including such works as Lew's (1990) book for male survivors, Bear and Dimock's (1988) book for male and female survivors of childhood sexual abuse (To order, send $12.95 to Safer Society Press, Shoreham Depot Road, RR #1, Box 24-B, Orwell, VT 05760-9756), and Evert and Bijkerk's (1988) book for survivors of abuse by their mothers. In addition, they provide numerous other resources for women survivors, parents of survivors, parents who are survivors, and partners of survivors. These works include autobiographies, self-help books, poetry, and fiction, and they range from sources of facts and statistics to creative and inspirational works.

CONCLUSION

Counselors working with survivors of violence must have far more information than what is available on these pages. The primary purpose of this chapter is to alert counselors to some of the barriers confronted by survivors of violence, to highlight the importance of analyzing societal and cultural dynamics when working with survivors, and to provide some recommendations for empowerment. Counselors and other mental health professionals have an important role to play in bringing about social changes that will make society violence-free for all girls, boys, women, and men.

Chapter Ten
OLDER ADULTS

Mama Quilla*, we share a secret;
that the same voice lives inside,
the same heart
these hopes, fears, moods
are yesterday's daughters.
For all the seasons
we endure
all of our waxing and waning
is a trick of light
we look upon the world
newborn and ancient
with the same eyes.

E.H.M.

INTRODUCTION

Counselor training programs often overlook or minimize attention to the mental health concerns of older adults (Moses, 1992; Waters & Goodman, 1990). Although older adults traditionally have used mental health services much less than younger adults, this trend appears to be changing. Waters and Goodman (1990) note that the current population of older adults possesses higher levels of education, has been exposed to more normative views of counseling, and is more likely to seek counseling services than its predecessors. The counseling literature is just beginning to recognize and address the counseling needs of older adults (Gross, 1988; Moses, 1992).

---

* Mama Quilla is the Incan goddess of the moon.

Empowered older adults might have the following characteristics: hopefulness; a sense of purpose in life; recognition and rejection of ageist beliefs and attitudes; awareness of the collective political power of older adults; a sense of community with others; an ability to advocate for one's own rights and the rights of other older adults; participation in decisions related to one's health, living situation, and legal issues; and the skills to assert one's wishes and needs as desired.

WHO ARE OLDER ADULTS?

Since all human beings who do not die before the age of 55 can be considered older adults, this group of people is more heterogeneous than any other discussed thus far. Older adults include people of all ethnicities, all sexual orientations, and every variation of health and disability status. Twelve percent of the population of the United States is made up of older adults, and the fastest growing subgroup consists of people over the age of 85 (American Association of Retired Persons & The Administration on Aging, 1988). Gross and Capuzzi (1991) point out that approximately two thirds of adults over age 65 are women; half of these women are widows, while 25% of men over age 65 are widowers.

Medical progress over the last century has resulted in steady increases in life expectancy for older adults in general, although life expectancy varies within subgroups. For example, the average life expectancy of Native Americans is eight years less than that of non-Native Americans (National Indian Council on Aging, 1981). As a result of longer lifespans, older adults will be caring for their elders in greater numbers than ever before. Waters and Goodman (1990) note a Census Bureau prediction that by the year 2050, 33% of all Americans over the age of 65 will have a living parent. Thus, another important characteristic of older adults is that many are caretakers. Patrick's personal statement below articulates one older adult's experience of life after retirement.

> Prior to retirement, I sometimes wondered what my life would then be like. I knew there would be changes in my life and major adjustments to make. While working, I was gone from home about 55 hours per week. Additionally, I spent two to four hours per week reading trade journals and technical reports in the evenings, and was periodically required to respond to emergencies at any hour. For over 30 years, this job filled my daytime hours.
>
> As I reached retirement, two of my four children were single, living on their own in the next state, and two were married. One of the married children lived within a few miles and the other was almost 2,000 miles away. I always felt we were a close family, and we still were, but the

children had their own life-styles, and didn't need or rely on our involvement in their lives. Now this is entirely normal, and I went through the same process, but it was just another adjustment to adapt to.

When I retired, I had plans for the next five months. My wife and I went to my hometown and were involved in the construction of a cottage. A contractor did the major work while I was the "gofer" and the "sweeper upper." I helped with the wiring, the plumbing, and with the help of my wife and visiting family members, we installed the insulation. The construction spread over three years. The work was enjoyable to my wife and I; it never seemed tedious or boring.

During the first winter, we stayed home and cleared out the attic, etc. We also were looking at various types of volunteer work. We wanted to do something meaningful, challenging, and rewarding that would not tie us down to a schedule that had to be strictly adhered to. After decades of living with work schedules we both wanted some freedom in our volunteer work.

After looking at possible organizations, we decided to get involved with literacy training. After a training course, we began tutoring two mornings a week at a literacy center. Each tutor works individually with their assigned students. This work has met all of our desires. The students are there because they really want to learn to read; unfortunately, a few have such learning disabilities they are unable to learn to read the alphabet. Tutoring has been rewarding, challenging, and certainly meaningful.

I also volunteered to drive for an interfaith group that provides transportation for shut-ins for medical appointments and shopping, etc. Most clients are elderly widows who have never driven, while others, male and female, can no longer drive for medical reasons. The exposure to these people reminds me of the possible future.

In the past year I lost a very close friend of 45 years to a sudden heart attack. Another friend—I have known him since I was four years old, went to grade and high school with him, we even joined the army together and have remained in frequent contact since—has been suffering from cancer of the spine. The prognosis is not promising. These bring out an increasing awareness of my own mortality, and the need to enjoy life to the fullest.

All in all, we have had a most enjoyable retirement. Most importantly, we have had good health, and my wife and I have found things and projects to do, some jointly, some separately. When I retired, I wondered what my wife and I would have to talk about, whether we would get on each other's nerves, and what we would have in common. After four years of retirement I can state that these have been four of our best years.

As I look to the future, I now have a relationship with my children as adult to adult and I am proud of what they have accomplished. I like being a grandfather and enjoy watching young minds and bodies grow. Their curiosity and wonder about things is a joy to observe. I don't know what the future will bring, but with the strong family I am fortunate to have, it will be interesting, to say the least.

BARRIERS

Ageism

Ageism represents a significant barrier to empowerment for older adults. Whitbourne and Hulicka (1990) describe ageism as "a prejudiced attitude toward aging and elderly persons characterized by a combination of myths, negative attitudes, stereotypes, attempts to avoid contact, and various forms of outright discrimination" (p. 1127). They suggest that ageism is manifested in such behaviors as the omission of the later adult years from discussions of human development, the portrayal of aging as a process of inevitable decay or decline, and the portrayal of older adults as physically and mentally disabled. Patrick's personal statement attests to the potential vitality and activity of older adulthood.

Schaie (1993) contends that ageism is embedded in assumptions that older people are exclusively care *recipients* and not care *providers*; that disease is caused by age itself rather than other factors that co-occur with aging; and that the combined influences of gender, culture, and age are of little importance.

The pervasiveness of ageism is evidenced in many domains. For example, in a review of 139 undergraduate psychology texts, Whitbourne and Hulicka (1990) found condescending discussions of older adults as well as assumptions of multiple deficits, personal rigidity, and inevitable physical and psychological decline. More recent textbooks were less likely to perpetuate ageist biases, although some were still in evidence. The researchers argue that such biases are retained in students' attitudes and conceptual frameworks long after the details of the textbooks are forgotten. Ageist biases in textbooks are particularly disturbing because they are passed on in the guise of truth and knowledge and can have long-term consequences on attitudes and behavior.

Ageism is more clearly evident in a variety of other contexts. In the work force, older adult job applicants may be passed over in favor of younger applicants with equivalent or fewer qualifications. Company policies of mandatory, age-based retirement force some older adults to relinquish their worker roles in spite of continuing competence, contribution, vitality, and desire to continue working. Even when other avenues of fulfillment are accessible, a lack of choice about retirement may elicit frustration, lower self-esteem, and generate a sense of powerlessness. Such hiring and retirement policies may be based on perceived economic expediency. However, Waters and Goodman's (1990) review of older adults in the work force indicates otherwise. Myths that older workers are less productive, do not get along well with others, are unwilling to learn new jobs, are inflexible about work hours, cost more in benefits than they are worth, and are frequently ill and absent are all without basis in fact. On the contrary, numerous studies have indicated that hiring older workers can be very beneficial from economic and quality control perspectives.

Another manifestation of ageism may be found in the patterns of interaction between older adults and those close to them, such as family members, partners, or caretakers. Specifically, in a desire to be helpful, people often take responsibility for doing what older adults can do for themselves. This may occur in the arena of physical work or with respect to mental activities such as planning a dinner or discussing the problems of a teenage family member. Being told, "It's nothing, don't you worry about it" or "Sit down, I'll get that for you" sends a message of incompetence and frailty to the older adult. Consistent messages to this effect may contribute to declining vitality by eliminating physical and cognitive challenges from the environment.

Wahl's (1991) findings support these contentions. In a study of older adults and their caregivers, Wahl found that caregivers attributed the successful performance of self-care behaviors by older adults to their own (the caregivers') efforts. At the same time, caregivers attributed the *failure* to perform self-care behaviors to the older adults. While caregivers reported that they were supporting independence in the older adults they served, their actual behavior appeared to foster dependency instead. In contrast, the older adults attributed successful self-care behaviors to their own efforts and attributed nonuse of existing self-care skills to their caregivers. The values and goals of the older adults consistently reflected independence. To illustrate the findings, 82-year-old Addie might say she did not wash her face because her caretaker hadn't yet brought a clean towel; her caregiver might say that Addie was simply being stubborn. Although this study examined the behavior of professional caregivers, it seems likely that familial caregivers might perceive their actions similarly as supporting independence when, in fact, they are fostering dependency.

These manifestations of ageism are compounded and nourished by the nearly complete absence of strong, competent older adults in the mass media. Commercials often reflect stereotypes of older adults as doddering, silly people. In prime-time television they are often interfering or burdensome; seldom are older adults portrayed as a resource of wisdom and experience. There are some notable prime-time and silver screen roles in which older women are portrayed as intelligent, active, courageous, sexual, and humorous. Similar roles are in evidence for older men; hopefully, far greater numbers of affirmative roles for older adults will emerge in the years to come.

Poverty

Some data indicates that more than 20% of all older adults and 44% of African American older adults live below or just above the official poverty line (Waters & Goodman, 1990). Kramer (1991) notes that despite similarities in labor force participation, urban Native Americans over the age of 65 consistently earn less income than Euro Americans in the same age group. Older adults living in the South and older people of color are more likely to be impoverished than other older adults (Damron-Rodriguez, 1991; Waters & Goodman, 1990). Similar to younger women, older women workers earn less than older men. Mid-life lesbians, and presumably older lesbians, have low incomes relative to their education and experience (Bradford & Ryan, 1991; Hayes, 1991). Retirement and fixed incomes may combine with expensive medical problems, restricted mobility, or other related factors to compound the stress of poverty for older adults.

Impoverished people rarely have access to the quality of health care enjoyed by the wealthy. Older adults were raised during a time when questioning a doctor or being assertive with medical health professionals was more likely to be considered disrespectful. Thus, they may be less likely to be aware of their medical alternatives and available services. Kramer (1991) notes that one common misperception about urban Native American older adults is that they eventually retire to reservations. This is not true; in fact, the longer they have lived in urban areas, the less likely they are to move back to a reservation. Further, drawing from National Indian Council on Aging (NICOA) reports, Kramer (1991) points out that many Native Americans do not live long enough to qualify for older adult services, and age-related impairments typically occur 20 years earlier among Native Americans than among the non-Native Americans. Thus, Native American elders may have great difficulty accessing older adult health care services.

Actual Physical Decline

In and of itself age does not *cause* physical problems. Nevertheless, there is a pervasive belief that older people face inevitable physical decline. The word "actual" in the title of this section is intended to convey the message that decline does *not* inevitably accompany the aging process. On the contrary, similar to Patrick, older adults often enjoy excellent physical and mental health. For example, Harris and Associates (1981) found that 80% of their sample of older adults reported their health to be "excellent" or "good." Thus, assumptions of inevitable decline are unwarranted among older adults with a history of good health and adequate medical care. Nevertheless, physical and cognitive decline does occur among many older adults and may be a source of stress. The loss of physical and cognitive functioning may be accompanied by a declining sense of personal power, lowered self-esteem, and discouragement (Miller & Oertel, 1992).

Older adults in nursing homes and other institutional settings are surrounded by other older people with a wide range of physical, cognitive, and emotional competencies and limitations. Daily exposure to others with physical and cognitive impairments may result in fear and anxiety about the future, even when such impairments do not seem imminent. Miriam, a 78-year-old woman residing in a nursing home, alluded to her fear of the loss of autonomy and functioning as follows:

> See that? They even tell you how to lie down here. Sometimes I think I'll cry for the rest of my life. I can feed myself, you know, I just can't walk. Maybe, I think I'll be out of this chair in a few weeks.... I see some of these people, their mouths gaping open and all stiff—totally dependent—I don't want to be like that. I just hope I go before I get like them.
>
> And say, I know you can catch me when my thinking gets funny; I *do know* that [smiles]. You might think I don't.

For older adults confronted with failing health and decreasing capacities, awareness of their situation may be painful. Issues discussed in Chapter Eight may be applicable to many older adults with chronic illnesses or disabilities.

Loss

The presumption that old age is a time of continual losses is a mischaracterization for many older adults, and as such has been noted as an ageist assumption (Whitbourne & Hulicka, 1990). Nevertheless, older adults are more likely to lose parents, siblings, spouses and partners, and longtime friends than are younger adults. In addition, role transitions such as from worker to retiree incorporate loss just as they incorporate an opportunity for new pursuits and activities. Patrick's positive reflection on his experience of retirement also contains a hint of uneasiness as he acknowledges possible losses to come: "exposure to these people reminds me of the possible future"; "these bring out an increasing awareness of my own mortality."

Older adults who have had positive role models for retirement and coping with disability and death have an advantage. In the words of one woman, "My mother taught me how to die. She faced her death with such courage and grace—it was an incredible gift she gave me—lessons I could never have learned without her example." Those without role models, and who have not developed healthy coping skills, may need support beyond their usual network to deal with the sometimes multiple losses of older adulthood. Withdrawal, depression, and apathy among older adults is sometimes a response to the painful experience of loss and an attempt to prevent or diminish additional hurt.

SUGGESTIONS FOR EMPOWERMENT

Counselor Knowledge

Counselors must be knowledgeable about the implications of ageism and other barriers to empowerment for older adults. Ongoing self-exploration of ageist beliefs as well as constructive feedback from others, for example, will help minimize such beliefs. Ideally, counselors view older adults as capable of living satisfying and active lives. The transition from mid-life to later years is viewed as a time with the potential for richly rewarding experiences rather than as a prescription for a series of difficult losses. Many older adults experience a greater degree of personal fulfillment than at any other time in their lives; coping skills, happiness, and creativity may be at their peak. Sexual activity may continue to provide satisfaction and intimacy indefinitely, in spite of the popular myth that older adults are asexual.

One specific area for counselor self-exploration is communication—that is, an analysis of how one's communication patterns change when talking with older adults may reveal modifications based on assumed, rather than actual, limitations. Wood and Ryan (1991) suggest, "In speech toward frail older adults, modifications may involve slower speech rate, exaggerated intonation, high pitch, increased loudness, greater repetition, simpler vocabulary, and reduced grammatical complexity" (p. 169). When these modifications are unnecessary, they may do more than irritate or frustrate older adults. Wood and Ryan (1991) continue: "Over-accommodation for presumed communication difficulties can undermine the social identity, self-esteem and eventually the communication skills of older people who are concerned about possible age-related declines" (p. 169). Other inappropriate communication includes talking about the older adult in the third person rather than directly ("Has Mr. Ofstead finished his breakfast?"), using "we" instead of "you" ("How are we feeling today?"), or simply not naming or referring to the individual at all (Wood & Ryan, 1991). The way we speak with and address older adults will convey our attitudes about aging; patronizing communication gives people the impression that they are perceived as feeble, incapable, and helpless. On the other hand, addressing older adults in language that reflects respect, awareness of their resources and capacities, appreciation for their perspectives, and the expectation that they are competent will be empowering.

Counselor attitudes and knowledge regarding life transitions will be an important resource in empowering older adults. Life transitions may be difficult and painful, yet they also offer the opportunity to grow, to try new behaviors and attitudes, and to discover new strengths and qualities. Older adults may be faced with losses related to the death of a life partner, other family members, or friends; loss of the worker role due to retirement or layoff; loss of physical or mental abilities, and a host of other possibilities. The counselor's ability to identify transitions and growth opportunities and to honor the client's grieving process will be important.

Counselors and other professionals working with older adults would do well to investigate rituals associated with aging in various cultures. The performance of culturally prescribed rituals can ease transitions, mark losses, provide recognition, foster self-esteem, and provide a means of celebrating successes and accomplishments. Damron-Rodriguez (1991) comments that ethnic elders in senior centers or residential facilities may derive little benefit from the celebration of majority-accepted holidays, noting, "A life stripped of meaningful cultural rituals and ceremonies, substituted with Valentine parties or Bingo, may add a sense of despair rather than integrity" (p. 137). The *Journal of Cross-Cultural Gerontology* special issue entitled, "Ethnic Diversity in Aging and Aging Services in the U.S.," and Bass, Kutza, and Torres-Gil's (1990) *Diversity in Aging* are two sources of information on rituals associated with aging among ethnic minority cultures.

When there are no known rituals associated with important transitional events in the life of an older adult, the counselor and client can construct an appropriate ritual. For example, when Carolina's granddaughter graduated from college, she was unable to attend the graduation and the family party. The event was of great importance to Carolina. She had "failed" to convince her own daughter to go to college, but had provided continuous encouragement, as well as financial and emotional support, to her granddaughter Betina. Although neither her daughter nor Betina appeared to perceive her role as crucial, Carolina was convinced that without her support, Betina would have "gotten married and pregnant right out of high school like the rest of us." Unable to participate in the family rituals associated with the graduation, and unwilling to "ask for attention or glory," Carolina felt upset and ignored.

In response to Carolina's distress, she and her counselor devised an honorary, private ceremony in which Carolina received a "diploma of recognition" from the counselor that detailed her contribution to her granddaughter's education. Another part of the ceremony involved

Carolina describing, as if speaking to her granddaughter, what Betina's life would have been like without a college education, and what possibilities her life now held. They taped this portion of the ceremony as a gift to her granddaughter. Finally, to recognize the ending of a stage of Betina's life—as well as Carolina's changing role in Betina's life— Carolina taught the counselor a children's goodbye song from her childhood, and she and the counselor sang it together.

The ritual created by Carolina and her counselor was a product of the unique interaction among Carolina, her situation, and the counselor. The ritual honored Carolina's role in her granddaughter's accomplishment in a way that did not violate Carolina's value of modesty. The portion of the ritual shared with her granddaughter—the tape—reinforced Carolina's most important message to Betina. And the ritual also acknowledged the natural ending of one facet of Carolina's role in her granddaughter's life. This example clearly illustrates the importance of collaboration in creating a personally meaningful ritual.

Finally, awareness of community resources for older adults and their caregivers is important. Waters and Goodman (1990) refer to the "aging network" as the partnership of public and private organizations that provide care to older adults at local, state, and federal levels (p. 78). Examples from their comprehensive list of resources are included in the resource section of this chapter.

Power Analysis

Family members, professional caregivers, and institutional policies contribute importantly to the power dynamics at work in the lives of older adults. In addition, cultural views of aging, community resources for older adults, and social policies effecting older adults form part of the context in which older adults live. Specific issues that might be addressed with an older adult seen in counseling include: How is the problem defined and who is defining the problem? How does the client view the aging process and the role of older adults in the family? How do family members such as spouse or partner, children, siblings, and parents view the individual? What does the individual perceive his or her strengths and capacities to be? How do significant others view the person's strengths and capacities? Who makes decisions affecting the older adult, how are these decisions arrived at, and how satisfied is the older adult with the process and outcome of these decisions? Is the person experiencing decline in any area? If so, how is the person coping with perceived decline, and how are significant others responding? In what way do surroundings (including significant others) support healthy behaviors, and in what ways are learned helplessness, passivity, or dependency reinforced? What are the individual's expectations of decline, and what are the expectations of significant others? How do these expectations influence health and behavior? How does the individual exercise control over his or her environment? What capacities are underused or downplayed in the individual's environment? To what extent are hopefulness and competency nourished by the environment? What role models are available (or have been available in the past) for aging or coping with loss, and to what extent are these role models proactive and healthy? These questions represent potential avenues for identifying the power dynamics that influence the client's physical, cognitive, and emotional functioning.

Skill Application: Decision Making

Hopelessness among older adults has been linked with a lack of control over their environment (Miller & Oertel, 1992). Independence and autonomy are dominant cultural values, and older adults who are excluded or withdraw from making decisions about their health care, living arrangements, and daily schedule may feel a keen sense of displacement and loss. McDermott (1989) notes that "decision-free" environments, such as nursing homes, may promote apathy and depression in older adults by reducing their sense of personal power and eliminating reinforcement for identifying and expressing opinions and needs. Older clients may be unaware of their diminishing role as a decision maker, or they may be acutely aware but unsure of how or whether this can be altered. Even when physical and cognitive capacities have been reduced because of disease or disability, older adults can influence their environment through active decision making. Counselors and other mental health professionals can support the client's right to be involved in decisions, encourage interest and participation in decision making, help broaden the client's awareness of all the arenas in which decisions are still possible, and support the implementation of client decisions.

Lawton's (1990) work illustrates these issues. He notes that researchers have made significant advances in determining how nursing homes and other institutional environments for older adults can be designed to maximize comfort, efficiency, and independence. He goes on to note, however, that similar progress has not been made in learning how to promote proactive modification of the environment by those living in the environment. In other words, we know how to modify environments for other people, but we don't know how to help people modify their own environments. Lawton proposes that even in highly restrictive environments, people can actively make decisions that shape their surroundings. For example, in the movie *Fried Green Tomatoes*, the character played by

Jessica Tandy decorates the walls of her nursing home room with hundreds of roses. She personalizes and transforms her limited, institutional living space. Her efforts were preceded by a decision to change her surroundings. Lawton (1990) provides the example of an older man living at home who is unable to walk. Given the assistance of a caregiver to get from his bed to a living room chair in the morning, this man might establish a centralized *control center,* modifying his living room so that (a) his chair faces the front window, sidewalk, trees, etc., at the best possible angle; (b) the phone, television, and radio are within reach; (c) pictures of his family are visible; and (d) other items of importance such as reading materials, medicines, and letters are within reach. He himself chooses which items to keep on display or nearby and determines the optimal view and chair angle, thereby proactively influencing—rather than being a "captive" of—his environment. Lawton argues that individuals can create for themselves a large psychological space via observation of street life through the window, talking on the phone, writing letters, reading, and using the radio and television, even within the confines of a small physical space. Exercising control over the malleable aspects of their environment can increase their quality of life (Lawton, 1990).

Williams and Lair (1988) describe geroconsultation as a potential model for decision making. Geroconsultation is described as "a professional service offered to an elderly individual or other involved parties for the purpose of addressing the changing situation of the elderly person" (p. 198). Their description includes assessment of the capacities, resources, and needs of the older adult as well as the caregivers, partners, and family members. Careful exploration of options, including the potential consequences of various decisions, takes place in relation to the older adult and each member of his or her family/care network. For example, in the case of an older adult who wishes to continue living independently, options may be generated for environmental modifications (grab bars, ramps), medication (pills in envelopes labeled with days of the week), communication (phone calling network of family and friends), and a schedule of support availability (niece can come every other Tuesday evening; son can stop by after work each day during the week for 10 minutes; daughter-in-law can take shopping on Saturday mornings; etc.). The case of Ernie illustrates the integration of decision-making skills in working with an older adult:

Ernie was a 73-year-old second-generation German American who lived with his son, daughter-in-law, and their 17-year-old daughter in a modest three-bedroom home. Ernie's seven children all lived in the city, as well as two of his three living siblings. He had lived alone after his wife died of cancer six years earlier, but after a second mild heart attack, his children decided that he should no longer live by himself. Ernie was moved to his eldest son's home under protest.

Ernie spent his afternoons at a local senior center, and spent a good portion of his time there complaining about his children. His complaints became louder with time, and other center participants were reluctant to engage him in conversation or even to sit near him. An observant staff member noticed that Ernie became most vociferous when staff members and center participants tried to pacify him with statements such as "At least they care about you" and "They only want to help." This staff member began talking with Ernie several times a week. Through their conversations, she learned that Ernie's children had decided far more than where Ernie would reside. He was currently on a schedule in his son's home with respect to bathing, eating, going for walks, and even reading the paper and watching television. Apparently his son and daughter-in-law were so fearful that he would have another heart attack that they rigidly enforced their notion of a "healthy" schedule. Not surprisingly, this rigidity seemed to reflect Ernie's own child-rearing practices.

Ernie felt totally stifled and controlled. While at home he was morose and quiet, but at the senior center he expressed his unhappiness through anger. He kept people away with constant cynical complaints, thereby preventing anyone from detecting his falling self-esteem and sense of powerlessness. He was very fearful that people would pity him or see him as weak.

The staff member established a trusting relationship with Ernie by listening to his complaints and taking them seriously rather than pacifying him. She reviewed the different aspects of Ernie's schedule and identified the sources of greatest dissatisfaction. As they discussed his schedule step by step, Ernie became more aware of the specific sources of irritation and began to articulate his preferences. This represented a change, because initially he only made general statements about his awful children and his consequently awful life.

Once Ernie began voicing the changes he wanted, the staff member began framing these preferences in a decision-making context. For example, when Ernie stated that his walks to and from the senior center provided "more than enough exercise," the staff member helped him identify several alternatives beyond a) walking the set route indicated by his son—which conformed to his doctor's recommended amount of walking—and b) walking only between home and the center. They discussed the potential consequences of each of these options, which meant that Ernie had to call his doctor for more information about his health. The doctor had gotten into the habit of addressing his recommendations to Ernie's son instead of Ernie, and direct communication with the doctor helped reestablish Ernie as capable and proactive in the doctor's eyes. Treated as competent, Ernie decided to walk the recommended distance, but to alter the route he chose according to his own whims rather than his son's preference. Ernie and the staff member followed a similar procedure with respect to exploring his diet and leisure activities. Finally, the staff member proposed a consultative meeting with Ernie and his son and daughter-in-law to discuss Ernie's dissatisfaction and the changes he wanted to make, and to enlist the support of his family in carrying out *these changes. This meeting also provided an opportunity for Ernie's son and daughter-in-law to express their fears regarding Ernie's health and their sincere desire to "keep him around for a long time."*

As a result of Ernie's meetings with the staff member, his complaints decreased and he began to show more interest in other senior center participants. In one of their last meetings, the staff member teased him about his "admirers," and Ernie responded, "Well you can hardly blame them—we've got some smart ladies around here." This response seemed to sum up Ernie's increased confidence and self-esteem.

Remarks by Clark (1989), who describes empowerment as a state of balance, offer an important consideration when focusing on decision-making skills with older adult clients:

> Just as every elderly person's life represents a dialectic between frailty and strength, so too does it exist as a balance between a need for support and the requirement for individual freedom to determine the course and content of one's life. Empowerment as balance includes both the procedural right of the individual to decide precisely where this balance between dependence and independence is struck, and the actual outcome of this decision-making process—the optimal level of interdependence. (p. 277)

Group Participation

Numerous authors have advocated the use of group work with older adults (Brody, 1990; Capuzzi, Gross, & Friel, 1990; Waters & Goodman, 1990). Groups may provide a source of support for older adults around issues of identity, roles, resolution of past issues, and asserting rights as well as many other issues.

Identity. Just as counselors must not assume older adults are asexual, they cannot assume they are heterosexual either. Prejudice against gay, lesbian, and bisexual people was even greater in the past without the benefit of visible activist groups working for gay and lesbian rights. Literature on the lives of older gay men and lesbians indicates that their friends and family members are less likely to know of their lesbian or gay identity (Bradford & Ryan, 1991); maintaining a secret identity may deprive them of some opportunities for intimacy and social support. Research findings indicate that the myth of pervasive loneliness among older lesbians and gay men is not actually valid (Adelman, 1990; Friend, 1987, 1990); nevertheless, group participation may be a source of intimacy, learning, growth, and support. The devastating toll of HIV disease on young gay men means that in the future, we may see far fewer numbers of older gay men and a greater need for networking and support.

Older adults of color are less likely to be acculturated to the dominant society and may derive particular satisfaction from socializing with older adults with similar values and life experiences. Since they are more likely to be cared for by family members or to live on their own than to reside in institutional settings, gathering groups of ethnic elders may be difficult. Community religious leaders can be an invaluable resource for mental health professionals in establishing social, support, and other types of groups for older adults of color.

Roles. Support for older adults in their role as caretakers of grandchildren, parents, spouses or partners, and siblings may be extremely helpful to some older adults. The stresses and strains of caretaking are often unrecognized when the caretaker is an older adult, because of the ageist presumption that older adults are exclusively the recipients of care. Many older adults are caretakers. Here are two examples:

Catherine, age 69, was the primary caretaker of her four-year-old great-granddaughter, Rose. The little girl's mother was addicted to heroin and had been physically and emotionally abusive; Rose's grandmother had died, and because Rose was physically destructive, Catherine was the only member of the family willing to take care of her. She worked hard to offset Rose's early abuse, but when Catherine was diagnosed with diabetes, she became very anxious about what would happen to Rose if she became incapacitated.

Morris, a 65-year-old retiree, was the sole family member living in the same city as his 84-year-old mother. He lived two blocks from her nursing home and visited her every day. A fall on the ice left him unable to visit his mother for two weeks, and she refused to speak with him on the telephone, insisting that he was "purposely avoiding" her. Morris felt acutely anxious about not being able to visit his mother and about the future—what if he developed an illness or was incapacitated for a longer period of time? Who would visit his mother, listen to her stories, read to her from her favorite magazines, and rub her hands the way he did?

Morris and Catherine are not isolated cases. Sharing the fears and stresses related to caretaking, as well as the physical and emotional difficulties of caretaking itself, can help older adult caretakers step back from their situation, develop ways of regenerating energy, plan for the future, and connect with others experiencing similar struggles.

Older adults are an often untapped but excellent community resource. When the demands of worker and caretaker roles are lessened, the energy and talent of older adults may be used through volunteer work and other forms of community participation. As Patrick notes in his personal statment, volunteer work can provide stimulation, challenge, and fulfillment, to say nothing of the benefits experienced by those to whom volunteers offer their services.

Life review. The life review process has been described as a natural and universally occurring activity among older adults (Butler, 1963; English, 1987). *Life review* refers to taking stock of one's past and attempting to make meaning out of one's life. It may include searching for answers to questions such as, What were the most significant events in my life? Was I a good person? Did I make the right decisions about relationships, goals, directions? A life review can evoke negative feelings related to unresolved conflicts, but it also provides an opportunity for growth, insight, integration of past experiences, and increased self-satisfaction and acceptance. In the words of Birren, "Life review is not a passive process: It is a constructive effort to achieve an active, purposeful form of reminiscence" (1964, p. 275).

Guided life reviews in the context of a group can foster a sense of connectedness among group members. In addition, guided life reviews can be a powerful way to identify the inner strengths and resources of group members and enlist these resources in the service of group members. Brody (1990) describes her three-year program of reminiscing-type groups for women residing in a nursing home, noting that participants increased their interactions with other nursing home residents and staff, developed greater self-awareness and self-esteem, and expressed heightened empathy for the other women in the group. Brody's groups met weekly, with duration ranging from six weeks to six months, and were designed to help participants review key experiences in their lifetimes.

The activities of a reminiscence or life review group may be primarily verbal. They may incorporate activities intended to stimulate memories (music, readings, copies of the newspaper from a particular time period) or to give voice to the meaning of certain memories (writing a play or autobiographical essay, singing, dancing, drawing, making a family tree, tape-recording stories for children and grandchildren).

English (1987) suggests counselors consult resources such as Hately (1985) and Friedlob and Kelley (1984) for suggestions related to conducting group life reviews for older adults. In addition, English notes Hemingway's *The Snows of Kilimanjaro* and Tolstoy's *The Death of Ivan Ilych* as examples of literature integrating the notion of life reviews.

Rights. The physical and psychological deterioration associated with a sense of dependency and a lack of personal control can be reversed when older adults experience a return to independence (McDermott, 1989). Enhancing freedom of choice in an institutional environment can lead to increased self-esteem, motivation, and level of activity and mental clarity, as well as decreasing rates of depression and mortality. For example, a "Resident Rights Campaign" for elderly nursing home residents (McDermott, 1989) incorporated many ideal characteristics: The campaign had full administrative endorsement; residents *and* staff members participated in educational activities to learn resident rights; and residents were rewarded for demonstrating initiative and independence. Furthermore, the campaign was highly visible. Participants were encouraged to connect personally with and support each other, and the weekly meetings of campaign participants were confidential, allowing them to express freely their frustrations with the staff and discuss openly ways to assert their rights. Recognition of rights also can be facilitated by joining organizations such as the American Association of Retired Persons (AARP).

Each of these examples of group participation portrays a different arena in which the group supports the varying needs of participants. But the common elements of companionship, support, and sharing run through each group.

RESOURCES

Waters and Goodman (1990) include the following resources in their comprehensive list: The American Association of Retired Persons (1909 K Street, N.W., Washington, DC 20049); American Society on Aging (833 Market Street, Suite 516, San Francisco, CA, 94103); National Caucus and Center on Black Aged (1424 K Street, N.W., Washington, DC 20005); National Indian Council on Aging, Inc. (P.O. Box 2088, Albuquerque, NM 87103); National Association for Spanish-Speaking Elderly (1801 K Street, N.W., Suite 1021, Washington, DC 20006); Older Women's League (730 11th Street, N.W., Suite 300, Washington, DC 20001); and the Urban Elderly Coalition (600 Maryland Avenue, S.W., West Wing 204, Washington, DC 20024). These national organizations can provide information regarding specific community resources.

Bass and Davis (1988) provide numerous literary resources for counselors and older clients alike, including Adelman's (1986) *Long Time Passing: Lives of Older Lesbians*; the Calyx Editorial Collective's (1986) *Women and Aging: An Anthology by Women*; Greenwood's (1985) *Menopause Naturally: Preparing for the Second Half of Life*; and Painter's (1985) *Gifts of Age*.

CONCLUSION

The notions advanced in this chapter can be summarized in the words of Clark (1989). Clark describes the empowerment of older adults as a combination of *political activism* (drawing attention to the rights of older adults to have at least a minimum quality of life and reasonable choices among life plans and goals), *effective deliberation and moral reflection* (considering both facts and values while supporting the proactive decision making of older adults), and *balance and interdependence* (assisting older adults to achieve the optimal balance of autonomy and dependence in their environments). Through the use of power analysis, skill building, life reviews, celebration of rituals, and other means discussed in this chapter, counselors and other mental health professionals can contribute to the empowerment of older adults.

The valuable role of older adults as teachers and guides for those with less experience often is overlooked in our society. The following essay by D. Parker reflects part of the rich treasure older adults offer the young: wisdom, tradition, and history. This piece seems a fitting close to a chapter on the empowerment of older adults, a testimony to the great power that older adults may have on the lives of those around them, if only we allow it.

> I miss my grandfather's eyes. One never realizes the specific attributes that will be missed when a loved one leaves this world. I realized this only moments after they had closed for the final time. I am not sure what his last visual image on Mother Earth was: It may have been the cold white walls of his government hospital room; it may have been my grandmother reaching for him to assist him in making the journey. I hope it was a young grandson beaming with respect and admiration. As my grandfather took the step from this world into the next, his hand in mine began to soften and eventually let go. As tightly as I squeezed and as much as I willed life back into his now limp hands and closed eyes, this man—who had in essence taught me how to be Native American—left me to walk on earth without him.
>
> My earliest memories of my teacher, my grandfather, are of the first day of the first summer I spent with him. I was trying to sleep on the living room floor of his one-bedroom house. I laid there angrily while he sang songs in Kiowa at the top of his lungs, tapping a spoon against the woodstove. *Can't he see me laying here trying to sleep? Isn't 5:45 a.m. just a little early to be awake?* These thoughts raced through my mind as I watched him put yet another layer of lard on his head, making an immovable helmet of his thinning, gray hair. A nudge on my hip by a size 13 foot and a "Hey, boy, you can't fly with the eagles if you're up hooting with the owls" told me that my night of slumber had ended. Two nudges later and a baking soda teeth cleaning and we were headed out the door.
>
> We began to back out of his dirty gravel driveway in a rusty, one-eyed pickup that had been on its last legs for five years. Just then another decrepit pickup with a large Kiowa elder at the wheel pulled next to us. We might as well have been next to a mirror. *Don't people sleep around here?* Without hesitation the two men got out of their pickups, pulled down a

tailgate, and sat down together. Their entire conversation was in Kiowa. *I got up for this! Not only did I get up too early, but now I have to sit and listen to a conversation I can't even understand!* Of course I did not say these things; that would show disrespect for the elders. I just laughed when they laughed and nodded when they nodded. I think Grandfather was bragging about me because he messed my hair with his hands a few times and smiled at his friend. I was glad he did that (except for the fact that he still had remnants of lard on his hands and my hair was now also slicked back). It made the wait worthwhile, knowing I made him proud.

After two hours of conversation, of which I understood about seven words, we once again headed down the driveway. After 10 miles of bumpy dirt roads, we stopped at a store held together by Elmer's Glue and old chewing gum. My grandfather asked me to wait in the car. He returned with a half pound of beef jerky and a gallon of Coke; the ideal breakfast for a ten-year-old boy. Then we headed to the lake deep in the forest to go fishing. There was no road to the lake and the pickup had to work hard to get us there; no wonder it was on its last legs. Grandfather was having a big ol' time, laughing hysterically every time he hit a large bump while I'd almost fly out of my seatbelt and out the window. This being my first real experience with my grandfather, I began to wonder, *Do I really want to be with this person in the middle of nowhere for the next three months?* My answer came much sooner than I expected.

When we arrived at the lake, Grandfather sat at the shore and prayed quietly in Kiowa. I sat reverently and wondered what he was saying. By the time he opened his eyes I realized that he was the most amazing man I would ever meet. His stories captured my attention for the rest of the day and the rest of that summer. He told me how he met Grandmother and all about my father as a boy. He answered every question I could think of. I found myself more interested in his stories than the fish circling my hook. His eyes danced just like the sun on the water when he spoke of his children and his wife, and he often leaned back and laughed loudly so all the animals in the forest could hear his jokes.

Not everything he told me was happy. His parents were stripped of most of their belongings and spared only a few acres of land to raise their family. He was beaten in boarding school for speaking Kiowa. He told me about treaties that had been broken, and how the government made promises to the Indian people with their fingers crossed behind their backs. So much of the history was sad, but this man telling the stories was the most proud person I had ever seen or will ever see.

As the summer went on, my grandfather told me about the Creator and how all things are related. "I am one with the things that surround me," he would say. "We humans are only part of the earth just as the trees, the animals, and the grass." Grandfather told me about powwows and celebrations and what they mean to our people. He taught me songs, words, the ways of different animals, and told me traditional stories of how the world came to be. He taught me to look toward the sky and smell things around me; to listen to the grass under my feet as I walk; to listen to the birds as they fly overhead; to feel the breeze and the heat. "You are related to all these things and should respect and appreciate them all."

For the next several years, I spent nine months in school getting a formal education and spent the summers being educated. I wish I had known the significance of what was happening to me; I wish I had thought to take notes or relish the moments even more. But as a young boy these things don't come to mind.

I learned from my grandfather about who I am. Intelligent people with many letters behind their names refer to this as an "oral tradition." I think Grandfather viewed it as sharing his knowledge with a grandson that he loved. As I attempt to become "formally educated," I realize there is no greater education than the basic lessons that he taught me: Respect myself, respect others, and respect Mother Earth. So many psychological theories seem shallow and suffer in comparison to the basic knowledge that he gave me.

I often recall sitting in his hospital room; a room not fitting for what my grandfather gave to the earth. I remember him staring at something beyond the walls of his hospital room as he made the final step from this world into the next. I remember his warm eyes looking out from the shell he had lived in for 70 years, and his eyelids slowly closing.

I miss my grandfather's eyes.

Chapter Eleven
ADOLESCENTS

I won't always be thirteen but for now I use the button
no one sees it like you can when Jean-Luc says, "Bridge"
no one hears me say "Shields up!"
no one knows about this power but me and you

when he says you cry like a baby
I'm only taking your brother
your brother never says that
shut up and go in the house
when he says who cares
when he says nothing as if I weren't even there
I touch the button near my shoulder
and his lasers bounce off and hit the walls

sometimes I see the smoke and sparks
sometimes I have to reset the dial so it's thicker
once he said what's wrong with your shoulder
I smiled inside

I won't always be thirteen
and I already know more than he does about love
I already know what I'm not going to do
and for now I use the button

E.H.M.

INTRODUCTION

Adolescents today face the challenge of growing into mature, responsible, and healthy adults in a context of economic, political, and social change; this has always been the case. However, never in human history has technological growth occurred at such a rapid pace or with such profound everyday consequences. Our increasingly specialized systems of production, service, communication, and transportation compound the complexity of the often difficult tasks of identity formation, emotional growth, and life-skills development. The uncertainties of peer relationships, marital stability, physical changes, and personal safety that often accompany adolescence are currently combining with larger contextual influences such as changes in family composition, worldwide environmental deterioration, the potential for nuclear war, the availability and temptation of drugs, and an increasing number of media models who are characterized by sexual permissiveness, irrational risk taking, and the use of violence to cope with even the simplest of problems. Thus, adolescents today face greater risks to their health than ever before (Takanishi, 1993). Because of these factors, empowerment is critical for adolescents.*

Empowered adolescents might have the following characteristics: a sense of hope regarding their future; sufficient social and coping skills to develop affiliation with and obtain support from others; the ability to achieve goals within their environments in ways that are not destructive of themselves or others; a sense of responsibility for their behavior; a developing sense of identity characterized by pride and confidence; a sense of community among their peers; participation and interest in their larger community; and the skills and motivation to support the empowerment of others.

WHO ARE ADOLESCENTS?

Similar to older adults, adolescents come in every size, shape, and color. Adolescents demonstrate the entire variety of human life, representing all ethnicities, sexual orientations, and variations in able-bodiedness. For the purpose of this chapter, adolescents are considered all people between the ages of 10 and 18.

All adults share in common the fact that they experienced adolescence. Of course, this period is one that may be fraught with difficulty and strife and/or a period characterized by fun and adventure. The experience of adolescence varies over time within and between indi-

---

* Further elaboration of much of the information in this chapter is available in *At-Risk Youth: A Comprehensive Response* by J. J. McWhirter, B. T. McWhirter, A. M. McWhirter, and E. H. McWhirter (1993). Interested readers are encouraged to consult this resource for an in-depth exploration of prevention and treatment issues.

viduals. Two young people may have such vastly different experiences that they literally exist in different realities. A single adolescent may experience periods of great satisfaction as well as times of anguish and difficulty during these transitional years. Self-discovery and identity formation are pervasive themes of adolescence. And as Alicia Sexton shares in her personal statement below, the period of adolescence offers numerous challenges and opportunities related to identity development.

For me, adolescence has been a time of testing. Testing myself, to see if I am strong enough, if my ideals and opinions will stand up against the norm of society. It has been a time of testing teachers and administrators and of testing personal relationships.

My mother has always been a believer in free thought, and during these years she has encouraged me to discover for myself the world and my views of it. A certain sense of self came when I realized my ideas were my own, independent from my parents. That sense of self flourished when I also realized that despite my different ideas, I would always have the love and support of my mother and father. It was then that I began truly to test society, knowing that if I could express my thoughts and back them up with facts and values, people would have to listen to me and respect me just as my parents did.

During my ninth-grade year I had to make choices in situations that I never dreamed I would face at only 14 years old. I was a member of the volleyball team; we were a close group, many of us had gone to school together since our elementary years. But the girls I'd had slumber parties with were now involved in sexual relationships and drinking hard liquor; the entire team would gather at one girl's house and get drunk before practice. Although I was welcome to join them I made the personal choice not to. This choice alienated me for a while. The other girls acted as if I was saying I was better than them. It hurt very deeply to know that the friends I'd grown up with resented me because of my personal choice. My parents have always taught me to make my own choice and not to judge others based on their choices, but to see them as the person they really are. It hurt that even though I didn't pass judgment on them, my friends passed judgment on me. I gained strength from the knowledge that even though my decision wasn't a popular one, I stuck with it. I stood virtually all alone in my peer group and didn't back down from my beliefs.

One day that same year a good friend came to school with a bruise on her stomach—her boyfriend had hit her. Despite my concern I agreed not to say anything. As time went on she had more and more bruises and one day she confided to me that they were having sex. Although it was consensual, she really didn't want to be involved in a sexual relationship with him—she felt threatened. It wasn't long before she was pregnant. Her mother and his parents decided she ought to have an abortion. Although I am strongly prolife, I chose to support her as she worked through the trauma of her pregnancy and its termination. There were days my friend would come to school with bruises and I would want to force her to leave her boyfriend, but I knew that was no different than his forcing her into things she didn't want to do. I felt very powerless to help her. I learned that there are times when no one else will help, and that when you try and help—even if you yell and scream—it might not do any good. Eventually I realized that I truly was helping her by merely listening, and that I had the capability to support a friend in a situation I was deeply, morally opposed to. I could listen to her and love her and know her actions and mistakes were what made her human.

My views regarding freedom of speech were tested when I was asked to write a letter to a soldier serving in Desert Storm. I was strongly opposed to the war and this English assignment offended me. I asked several times for an alternate assignment, only to be told I could either write the letter or receive a zero in the grade book. Almost everyone in my class supported the war and many students had close relatives and friends stationed in Saudi Arabia. Even though some students accused me of being anti-American and unpatriotic, I held firm to my belief, and the teacher later removed the credits allotted to the assignment. Had I not been so willing to go against public opinion, others who opposed the war would have had to write a letter or sacrifice their grade.

It seems that during my ninth-grade year, everything I'd been taught and everything I believed was tested. I realized a strong sense of self is the most powerful thing a person can possess. With the power that comes from truly knowing who I am and that my opinions are my own, I am able to stand against the ideas and choices of others.

BARRIERS

Education

Environmental mismatch. For many adolescents, entry into this period of life coincides with the emergence of problems such as decreases in academic motivation, a declining self-concept, increasing rates of truancy, and greater inattentiveness in class (Eccles et al., 1993; Eccles & Midgely, 1989; Eccles, Midgely, & Adler, 1984). For girls, this time period has been associated with a loss of vitality, resilience, immunity to depression, and sense of self (Brown & Gilligan, 1992). Eccles et al. (1993) argue that these difficulties arise, in part, as a response to a mismatch between school environments and adolescent developmental needs. Specifically, an adolescent's needs for increasing independence, autonomy, and responsibility often are met with decreasing opportunities to exercise such independence and autonomy. The transition to junior high school typically involves changes in task structure, grouping practices, evaluation techniques, motivational strategies, locus of responsibility for learning, and quality of teacher-student relationships in a direction that is inconsistent with the developmental needs of students. For example, in their study of junior high schools, Eccles and her colleagues (Eccles et al., 1993) found that there was an increasing use of social comparison techniques, a decrease in opportunities for autonomous behavior, a decrease in teacher perceptions of their own efficacy for teaching, and classwork requiring lower-level cognitive skills than in the years prior to junior high. Further, they noted that when levels of teacher efficacy and support did *not* decrease in the transition from the middle grades to junior high school, declines in student motivation did not occur. When developmental needs are not met within the school environment, this mismatch becomes a serious issue and represents a formidable barrier to adolescent empowerment.

The influence of gender role socialization also may contribute to environmental mismatch for girls. Research by Gilligan (1982) suggests that girls respond differently to classroom environments from boys—for example, tending to prefer cooperative over competitive learning situations. According to the American Association of University Women (AAUW) (1989, 1990), ample research attests to the fact that teachers tend to pay less attention to girls, hold lower academic expectations of them, and provide less effective feedback to them than to their male classmates. These discrepancies are even greater for girls of color. The effects of a curriculum tailored to the learning styles and socialization patterns of boys include lower self-esteem, decreased independence, declining ambition, and self-defeating career choices among girls (AAUW, 1989).

Dropout. Environmental mismatch and other school, family, economic, and personal factors contribute to the dropout rate. Carter and Wilson (1993) report 1991 high school completion rates for U.S. 18- to 24-year-olds, by ethnic group, as follows: Whites 81.7%; African Americans 75.1%; Hispanics 52.1%; Native Americans 52–70% (by region); Asian Americans 82%. Dropping out of high school has serious long-term educational, social, and economic consequences for young people (McWhirter et al., 1993) and often precludes numerous life options.

Violence in the schools. Another barrier for adolescents is the increase of violence in society, and in particular violence on school grounds. The National Association of School Security Directors estimates that each year 12,000 armed robberies, 270,000 burglaries, 204,000 aggravated assaults, and 9,000 rapes occur in primary and secondary schools. Teachers are seriously assaulted 70,000 times each year. School vandalism costs our nation more than $500 million each year in property damage (Patterson, De Baryshe, & Ramsey, 1989). Fighting and intimidation among students also are increasing, with estimates that one in seven children are either bullies or victims of bullies in grade schools, and that approximately 4.8 million school children in the United States are threatened by the violent or aggressive behavior of other students ("Students Threaten...," 1987).

Handgun violence is also an increasing problem in schools. For example, the U.S. Department of Justice reported that more than 27,000 adolescents between 12 and 15 years of age were handgun victims in 1985, up from an average of 16,500 in preceding years ("Violence...," 1988). In one major metropolitan area, 60% of 390 high school students knew someone who had been shot, threatened, or robbed at gunpoint in their school, and nearly 50% of the male respondents admitted to having carried a handgun at least once ("Violence...," 1988). These examples of in-school violence demonstrate the enormous challenge faced by teachers and counselors who strive to create an atmosphere conducive to learning and to the development of prosocial behaviors.

Allocation of resources. Widespread dropping out and rising violence in school reflect many characteristics of our society, including the value we place on education. Funding cuts in education throughout the 1980s suggest that education was not a national priority (McWhirter et al., 1993). Kozol's (1991) work (see Chapter Five) graphically illustrates the lack of school resources in urban areas and the destructive educational consequences of this financial neglect. Teacher salaries also attest to the value we place on education: The salaries of our schoolteachers, many of whom hold master's degrees, are actually lower than the national average annual family income (*The World Almanac and Book of Facts*, 1991).

Recall Cummins's (1986) argument that the power relations between majority and minority groups in society are reflected in our schools (see Chapter One). Recapitulating the inequalities of the greater society within the schools has negative consequences for students of color. Unfortunately, we have not yet transformed our schools into microcosms of a just, diverse, and egalitarian society.

Identity: Sexual Orientation and Ethnic Identity Development

Identity development is a demanding task. For many adolescents, this process is compounded by the need to integrate other identities that are not accepted, or that are derogated, by their peers.

Sexual orientation. Although secrecy and confusion make such estimates difficult, it has been estimated that 3 million adolescents in the U.S. are gay or lesbian (Gonsiorek, 1988). Gay and lesbian people often describe having had a feeling of "being different" that preceded awareness of their homosexual orientation (Troiden, 1989). As individuals begin to recognize feelings and behaviors consistent with a same-gender sexual orientation, Troiden suggests that they cope in one of four ways: denial of impulses and feelings; avoidance of situations that arouse these feelings; attempts to develop heterosexual feelings; and, often as a last resort, acceptance of homosexual feelings and behaviors as a part of the self. O'Connor (1992) notes that gay or lesbian adolescents are faced with the task of forming a stigmatized identity and recognizing basic personal differences just at a time when sameness and affiliation with peers are very important. Adolescents experiencing this dilemma may withdraw from their peers, become rigid and restrict their affect to "hide" their identity, or develop a false identity. All of these strategies create anxiety. Not surprisingly, drug use, running away, and family rejection are significant problems among this group of adolescents (Hetrick & Martin, 1987; Martin & Hetrick, 1988). The enormous difficulty of their situation is mirrored in suicide attempt and completion rates. Between 20% and 35% of gay and lesbian adolescents attempt suicide (Herdt, 1989) and they may comprise 30% of suicide completions among adolescents (Freiberg, 1990).

Acculturation and ethnic identity development. Adolescents who have arrived recently in the United States face identity development issues complicated by the acculturation process. Second-, third- and even fourth-generation adolescents often face similar acculturation issues as they pass through adolescence. The increasing reliance on majority culture peers for social interactions often causes conflict at home when adolescents participate in behaviors and activities that are considered inappropriate by their elders. Adolescents wishing to maintain strong ties with their ethnic origins may be discouraged from doing so by strong messages within their social and educational environments that assimilation is optimal, or that "American" values and practices are superior. Exposure to conflicting cultural rules and expectations can produce emotional distress. For example, in Vietnamese culture, adolescents establish identity and self-worth through family relationships and their extended family system, allowing parents and other adults to assume a major role in career and other decisions (Matsuoka, 1990). By sharp contrast, Euro-American adolescents develop identity through identification with peers and increasingly autonomous decision making. Adolescent Vietnamese refugees have experienced great disruption in their family systems, disturbing their normal identity formation while being thrust into a context in which their normal development may be viewed as inappropriate, inferior, or repressive by peers (Matsuoka, 1990). Their parents, who are less likely to interact with Euro Americans, who are more thoroughly established in their Vietnamese identities, and who are going through the trauma of refugee status along with their children, may have difficulty understanding the dilemmas faced by their adolescent children. They may indeed feel threatened by their unfamiliar requests, desires, and behaviors.

Risky Behaviors

Parents, teachers, and mental health professionals have voiced a growing concern about adolescent behaviors that develop in response to social, emotional, and environmental problems and that place their mental and physical health at risk. Three such behaviors are discussed here as barriers to adolescent empowerment: drug use, gang membership, and unprotected sexual activity.

Drug use. The National Household Survey of drug abuse shows that smoking (45%) and drinking (56%) are common activities among early adolescents, age 12–15 (National Institute on Drug Abuse, 1987). The U.S. Public Health Service reports that about two-thirds of all high school seniors have used illegal drugs and 90% have used alcohol (McWhirter et al., 1993). Of the 1 million youth who regularly use illicit drugs, Euro Americans are most likely to use alcohol or marijuana, while young people of color are most likely to use alcohol or drugs other than marijuana (Dembo, Blount, Schmeider, & Burgos, 1985).

The often euphoric effects of drugs provide a strong physiological reinforcement for continued use. Peers provide another source of reinforcement by granting attention and status to adolescents who talk about their experiences with various types of substances. The commercial media inundate our culture with the message that substances are an appropriate solution to any physical complaint. Similarly, drug use may be reinforced at home and in the surrounding community. In many inner-city communities, for example, drugs are seen as a viable alternative to inadequate educational and employment opportunities.

The physiological consequences of drug use range from impaired judgment and altered perceptions of reality to impairment of the nervous system and internal organs. Psychosocial consequences are also significant; drug use during childhood and adolescence leads to more serious problems in early adulthood. Newcomb and Bentler (1988) found that early sexual involvement, early marriage, lack of pursuit in educational endeavors, and early entrance into the work force or early unemployment were all associated with high levels of teenage drug use. Young adults who were poly-drug users assumed roles for which they were unprepared, leading to failed marriages and job instability.

Newcomb and Bentler (1988) also found differential effects for different substances. Although moderate use of alcohol in later teen years—without other drugs—tended to increase a sense of connectedness, positive feelings about self, and positive affect, and to reduce loneliness and feelings of self-derogation in early adulthood, heavy use of "hard" drugs increased loneliness, depression, and suicide ideation and decreased social support in early adulthood.

Gang membership. The number of gangs in the United States is difficult to identify, in part because of the varying definitions of gangs. Morales (1992) points out that while lower-class, minority adolescents are identified quickly as gang members, middle-class White adolescents engaged in similar activities are unlikely to be considered a gang. Further, many youth may adopt gang culture—complete with complex hand signals, codes, and clothing—without ever participating in criminal activity. Morales (1978) proposes that engagement in destructive activity with peers serve as a criterion for gang membership.

Antisocial, aggressive behavior learned in the home, compounded by academic failure and rejection by normal peers, contributes to membership in deviant peer groups (Patterson et al., 1989). Morales (1992) suggests that gang membership may fulfill familial needs when the home environment is chaotic or lacks nurturance. Gang members become a surrogate family, hence inspiring the intense loyalty and protectiveness accorded to fellow members.

In one study, African American adolescent males who were rejected by peers were more likely to affiliate with deviant subgroups and engaged more frequently in violent behavior than nonrejected peers, and hence were more at risk for delinquency and substance use (Coie, Dodge, Terry, & Wright, 1991). Rejected youth usually are deficient in social and cognitive skills. They experience difficulty joining peer groups and accurately perceiving peer group norms, and they inappropriately interpret the reactions of their peers (Asarnow & Calan, 1985). Delinquent peers reinforce deviant behavior and punish behavior that is socially conforming (Patterson et al., 1989). Delinquent adolescents often do not see a need to change, because by adopting more positive social behavior they may alienate themselves from their major source of companionship and acceptance.

Gang membership may seem to incorporate aspects of empowerment if members learn life-survival skills, establish a sense of community, and commit to ensuring each others' welfare. However, if gang membership includes engagement in destructive activity, or ensuring each others' welfare at the expense of the welfare of others, it cannot be considered empowering.

Unprotected sexual activity. By all reports, teenage pregnancies are on the rise, and more teen mothers are keeping their babies than ever before. Adolescents are unlikely to use contraception the first time they have intercourse, and teenage girls often do not use contraceptives until six to nine months after becoming sexually active, by which time approximately one-half are already pregnant (Alan Guttmacher Institute, 1981). Of those who do use contraceptive methods, condoms and withdrawal are the two cited most frequently (Zelnick & Shah, 1983); withdrawal does not prevent HIV infection, nor is it an effective means of birth control.

Teen mothers are much less likely to receive prenatal care than are older mothers, and their children often are born underweight or with other health problems. Fifteen-year-old mothers are twice as likely to have low birth weight babies than mothers 20–24 years old (Alan Guttmacher Institute, 1981). Low birth weight has been related to a number of developmental difficulties and learning disabilities in children. For mothers 15–19 years of age, the infant death rate is 13% higher than the national average; for mothers 15 and younger, the rate is 60% higher (Levering, 1983). The African American infant mortality rate is about twice that of Euro Americans (Davis, 1988).

The demands of parenthood frequently influence adolescents to drop out of school, find a job, confront new problems of social isolation and loneliness, and become dependent on public aid for survival. Families headed by young mothers are seven times more likely to be impoverished than families with married mothers in their 20s (Miller & Miller, 1983). Thus, teen pregnancy often severely reduces a young woman's life options. However, because many teenagers already feel hopelessly restricted in their future options, bearing and keeping children may not be perceived as a barrier to the future. In one study, for example, girls with higher career maturity and greater career and life options were significantly less likely to engage in intercourse and more likely to use contraceptives when they did (Hambright, 1988). In another, teen pregnancy was associated with lower achievement scores and low vocational aspirations (Hayes & Cryer, 1988).

The increasing sexual activity of teenagers, and at younger ages (Hofferth & Hayes, 1987; Melchert & Burnett, 1990), contributes to the fact that 2.5 million teenagers contract sexually transmitted diseases annually, with chlamydia the most prevalent (Office of Population Affairs, 1988). More than 700 adolescents had been diagnosed with full-blown AIDS by 1988, and this number is doubling every year (Centers for Disease Control, 1988). The number of adolescents with HIV disease is unknown. Alarmingly, Reuben, Hein, and Drucker (1988) reported that in New York City, adolescents engaging in the highest risk sexual behavior did not use precautionary measures during sexual contact and perceived themselves to be at low risk of contracting HIV disease.

Educational barriers such as environmental mismatch and in-school violence, barriers to identity formation, and risky behaviors such as drug use, gang membership, and unprotected sexual activity are all barriers to adolescent empowerment. In the following section, recommendations are provided to empower adolescents confronting these barriers.

SUGGESTIONS FOR EMPOWERMENT

Power Analysis

Adolescents often are quite willing to explore how their behavior is shaped by peers, by the school, and by their community. In fact, many adolescents have a great deal to say about social problems such as violence and poverty, but lack a forum in which to explore the personal ramifications of these issues. When they understand *how* they are influenced and can explore this in a nonjudgmental atmosphere, they have a basis for choosing different attitudes and behaviors. Thus, power analysis can focus on family dynamics, school and community factors, and local and national governmental policy issues; it also can be applied to social problems such as racism, sexism, or ecological deterioration. The key is to help adolescents understand how these issues affect them as individuals and as a group. A better understanding of power dynamics helps them to decide what elements of their lives they may want to change and provides insight into resistance they may encounter in their efforts to do so.

Through power analysis, the counselor helps adolescents to appraise realistically the impact of relevant influences on their lives. Growing awareness of power dynamics, however, must be accompanied by the development of concrete alternative behaviors and choices. For example, a school counselor may work with 15-year-old Jimmy, who was suspended for taking money from a teacher's wallet. Noting that Jimmy has never been in any trouble at school before, and that he recently began associating with a new peer group, the counselor can facilitate exploration of how his new friends might have influenced this new behavior. If his new peer group embraces a norm of thrill seeking that includes stealing, the school counselor can help Jimmy separate his interests and desires from those of the group. A judgmental attitude is unlikely to be useful, and probably will lead only to resentment or guilt. Instead, exploring alternatives and consequences and assistance in enacting new skills and behaviors will be more effective. Providing students with opportunities to practice new behaviors and to pursue their choices actively is critical. As indicated in her personal statement, Alicia experienced a number of strong external pressures and used these experiences to test her ability to set boundaries and choose behaviors. In so doing, she translated her awareness of power dynamics into assertive action.

Family Involvement

Schneiderman (1979) argues that when we blame families for individual problems, we divert attention away from the fact that our society lacks a coherent national family policy and that the structural supports required for family life are grossly inadequate. Thus, when addressing adolescent empowerment via family interventions, it is important to blame neither the adolescent "victim" nor the family "victim" for the structural problems with which they are contending.

In some circumstances, parent training may benefit the family of an adolescent. For example, Connie was a 16-year-old whose parents had "caught her in the act"—they came downstairs and found her having sex on their living room floor with a young man they didn't know. Connie's parents had never discussed sex with her beyond a technical explanation when she was 13. They approached Connie's sexual education as their own parents had, but in a vastly different social context. Thus one component of working with Connie and her family included a parent training workshop on teen sexuality. The workshop addressed such issues as communication with adolescent children and up-to-date information about birth control, incidence of sexual intercourse, teen pregnancy, and sexually transmitted diseases. The workshop also provided Connie's parents with a forum for discussing their fears, concerns, and (in this case) shock with other parents and the professional facilitator. The workshop supported her parents' efforts in and out of counseling sessions to set realistic limits with Connie. The training increased their confidence and comfort with discussing sexual issues, and provided them with information they previously lacked. After initially responding to her parents' new, assertive approach with anger and withdrawal, Connie acknowledged that she preferred her parents' willingness to discuss sexuality issues.

Parent training may be used as a prevention measure as well as a treatment approach. Parent Effectiveness Training and Family Effectiveness Training are two models of parent training that have proven to be very effective.

Parent Effectiveness Training. Parent Effectiveness Training (PET) (Gordon, 1975, 1977) is a method of parent training based on the Rogerian principles of positive regard and empathy. PET combines lectures, role-playing, readings, and homework exercises to train parents in confrontation skills, conflict resolution, active listening, and giving "I" messages. Parents have the opportunity to practice and refine each of these skills throughout the sessions, and ultimately problems in the family are handled more constructively and with more open and healthy communication.

Family Effectiveness Training. Szapocznik and his colleagues (Szapocznik et al., 1986a; 1989) developed a preventive training model for Hispanic families of preadolescents at risk for future drug abuse. FET is designed to address three problems that often serve as antecedents to adolescent behavior problems: maladaptive family interactions; intergenerational conflict; and intercultural conflict. It is one of few empirically tested programs that directly address cultural differences. The model has three components.

The first component, *Family Development*, helps the family to negotiate the childhood-to-adolescence transition. All family members learn constructive communication skills and take increased responsibility for their own behaviors. Parents become educated about drugs so that they can teach their children; they also learn the skills to become democratic rather than authoritarian leaders.

The second component, *Bicultural Effectiveness Training* (BET) (Szapocznik et. al., 1984; 1986b), is designed to bring about family change by (a) temporarily placing the blame for the family's problems on the cultural conflict within the family and (b) establishing alliances between family members through the development of bicultural skills and mutual appreciation of the values of both cultures. The family learns to handle cultural conflicts more effectively and reduces the likelihood that such conflicts will occur. BET represents an excellent parent training program in and of itself.

The third component of FET is the implementation of *Brief Strategic Family Therapy*. Based on the work of Minuchin (1974), this component involves a series of family therapy sessions and is the most experiential aspect of this didactic/experiential model. The entire training consists of 13 sessions that last from $1\frac{1}{2}$ to two hours; the entire family is present for each session. Finally, FET can be modified to deal specifically with other adolescent behavior problems.

These sample programs are two of a multitude of potentially effective parent programs. For a review of family-oriented programs for the prevention of chemical dependency, see DeMarsh and Kumpfer (1986). Additional parent training topics of interest to many families include behavioral management and discipline, sex education, nutrition, and family budgeting.

Prevention, early intervention, and treatment programs for families exist along a continuum (McWhirter et al., 1993). This continuum begins with family-strengthening tactics that encourage interaction, communication, stability, support, and prosocial values, as well as prenatal and health care programs. With greater dysfunction, social and emotional support programs and training in parenting skills are appropriate, and counseling services also may be critical. Therapeutic programs attending to child abuse and neglect, parental dysfunction, and family violence also may be extremely beneficial.

Schools

Adolescents spend a majority of their week in classrooms. Decreasing or eliminating the mismatch between their classroom experiences and their developmental needs can reduce the likelihood of student boredom, academic failure, antagonistic attitudes toward schooling, and misconduct (Eccles et al., 1993). Student empowerment is facilitated by changes in the classroom structure that enable a sense of control (Bialo & Sivin, 1989; Conrath, 1988). This includes flexibility regarding course requirements and grading systems, school climate and culture, teacher and administrator support, teacher-student contact strategies, and instructional approaches. Counselors can work with other school personnel to identify school conditions that are alterable and work to modify those conditions. The work of Eccles and her colleagues suggests that opportunities for self-determination, participation in rule making, emotionally supportive relationships with teachers, and private versus public evaluation are critical features of a good student-environment fit (Eccles et al., 1993; Eccles & Midgely, 1989; Eccles, Midgely, & Adler, 1984). Girls may need extra encouragement to continue taking math courses, to value their academic achievement, and to maintain their educational and career aspirations (Betz & Fitzgerald, 1987).

A curriculum that hinders or ignores moral education, social-skill development, student dialogue, and critical thinking invites boredom and dependence, limits student goals and decision-making capabilities, and does little to help adolescents negotiate their developmental tasks. Counselors and education professionals can serve an important advocacy role for students by working to make these issues a part of the curriculum (McWhirter et al., 1993). Counselors as well as teachers must be free to discuss current issues pertinent to adolescents, including sexuality, relationships, pregnancy and STDs, AIDS education, drug use, and violence.

When students are treated as unique individuals who contribute to the group, the resulting environment may be characterized by acceptance and appreciation of differences, an increase in creativity, an enhancement of personal autonomy, and an improvement in mental health and the ultimate overall quality of learning (Wassermann, 1985). Students learn to approach their work, their interactions with others, and their lives with tolerance and democracy. However, they must see themselves as active makers-of-knowledge rather than passive containers to be filled with facts.

Casas (1990) suggests that when the responsibility for school problems is shared by students, parents, teachers, counselors, the school system, and the larger society, all those involved (individuals and organizations) are empowered. Rather than assigning blame at the individual level, this process distributes responsibility for the problem *and* the solution among all participants. Such an approach acknowledges the systemic dynamics that so often engender and maintain school problems. At the same time, this approach recognizes and engages the proactive and creative problem-solving skills of everyone involved.

Skill Application: Leadership Training

Students provided with leadership opportunities exercise decision-making skills and learn the importance of self-control ("What schools can..." 1987). Some researchers have found that improving students' problem-solving and decision-making skills has a positive effect on adolescents (Beyth-Marom, Fischhoff, Jacobs, Furby, 1989). Specifically, schools have reported marked reduction in disruptive behaviors after teaching students to mediate disputes on their own. The ability of students to solve their own problems and peacefully settle disputes directly and positively affects student climate and reduces the likelihood of violence. The development of school mediation programs has been especially helpful in this regard (Lane & McWhirter, 1993).

School peer mediation (Lane & McWhirter, 1993; Schrumpf, Crawford, & Usadel, 1992) is a mode of student conflict management students use to resolve conflicts. Trained peer mediators work in pairs to facilitate problem solving between disputants. Student involvement in the mediation process insures practice with critical thinking, problem solving, and self-discipline. The element of student participation in self- and peer-behavior change is directly related to the developmental construct of self-regulation. Further, awareness of socially approved behaviors is a critical feature of the concept.

In a similar way, peer counseling (sometimes referred to as peer leadership or peer helping) provides a very helpful tool for increasing the impact and efficiency of professional counseling. Peer counseling is a process in which trained and supervised students perform interpersonal helping tasks—listening, support, alternatives, and other verbal and nonverbal interactions—that qualify as counseling functions with similar-aged clients who either have referred themselves or have been referred by others. Peer-mediation and peer-counseling programs help diminish the negative effects of peer pressure, and promote more positive norms for adolescent behaviors.

A final example of developing leadership skills is Teencourt (see resource section for an address). Teencourt is an innovative program used in Gila County, Arizona, for first-time juvenile offenders between the ages of eight and 17 who have committed a misdemeanor or status offense or a minor traffic violation. Youth referred to Teencourt have a choice of 1) pleading guilty, participating in the program, and keeping their record clean, or 2) going through the traditional juvenile court system. Teencourt sentencing is designed to fit the offense and usually includes community service, tutoring, attending workshops, or traffic survival school.

Each session of Teencourt lasts four months and involves six attorneys, 20 jurists, one court clerk, and three bailiffs, all of whom are trained high school students. Thus, offenders passing through Teencourt are tried by their peers; the judge is the only representative of the legal system. All defendants are required to serve a term of jury duty after their own sentencing. This is consistent with the goals of Teencourt, which include prevention of repeat offenses among those who are tried; prevention of first-time offenses among the many students who voluntarily participate as attorneys, bailiffs, etc.; educating adolescents about the legal system; and using peer pressure to evoke conformity to positive behaviors.

Teencourt has been in operation for more than five years, and has developed cooperative relationships with numerous agencies in the local community. During the program's first three years, the average recidivism rate was 12.5%, compared to the state and national average of 40–45%. This program models an empowerment philosophy in a variety of ways: by increasing adolescents' awareness of the legal system; providing specific skills training as well as the broader experience of leadership; using peers—of equal power status—rather than adults; involving adolescents with community organizations; tailoring sentences to individual offenses; and emphasizing responsibility for behavior. Those students trained to perform roles such as defending or prosecuting attorneys obtain a unique and valuable exposure to a specific career.

Group Participation: Life-Skills Training

Life skills are those that involve behaviors and attitudes necessary for coping with academic challenges, communicating with others, forming healthy, stable relationships, and making good decisions. Life-skills training programs emphasize the acquisition of generic, social, and cognitive skills. The theoretical foundation of life-skills training includes Bandura's (1977b) social learning theory and Jessor and Jessor's (1977) problem behavior theory. In accord with these perspectives, risky or deviant behaviors are viewed as socially learned, functional behaviors that emerge from an interplay of personal and environmental factors. As such, adolescents are not blamed for causing their problems, but are viewed as capable of learning new ways to behave that reduce the likelihood of future problems.

Counselors and other mental health professionals can be involved in teaching life skills. Procedures for teaching life skills resemble those used in the teaching of any other skill. Overall tasks are broken down into smaller stages or component parts and taught systematically, moving from simple to more complex skills. Each life-skills session follows a five-step model: (a) instruction (teach); (b) modeling (show); (c) role-play (practice); (d) feedback (reinforce); and (e) homework (apply). Within this general framework, steps may be modified in accord with the needs of the group. Three broad skill categories are usually included in basic life-skills programs: *interpersonal communication skills*, including assertiveness and refusal skills; *cognitive change strategies*, including problem-solving, decision-making, self-management and self-control skills, and cognitive-behavioral restructuring approaches; and, *anxiety-coping approaches*, including relaxation and imagery training.

One example of a very comprehensive life-skills program is STAR (Skills, Tenacity, Attitude, Readiness; see resource section for an address). STAR is a Phoenix-based program for young women in high school. Critical components of this program include skills training, mentoring, and group and individual activities. Members of the STAR program participate in a wide variety of activities designed to prevent dropout, expand career awareness, support educational and occupational aspirations, and provide a strong, supportive peer group. Participants receive training in enhancing self-esteem, communication, leadership, and job skills such as preparing a resume and interviewing for jobs. Each member is paired with a mentor in the community, who provides personal support and encouragement and serves as a role model. Parents are encouraged to be involved in all facets of the program. STAR partnerships with organizations such as Junior Achievement provide young women with training in community awareness and public speaking; after this training, the young women return to their own elementary schools and conduct presentations for second-, third-, and sixth-grade students on community awareness and participation. Thus, the young women serve as role models for their own communities. Tutoring, team building, cross-cultural understanding, and apprenticeships are additional components of the STAR program. Since STAR's inception in 1989, its members have taken an increasingly active role in leading the organization, including planning community events, fund raising, designing a new brochure, and making a video on child abuse. The young women designed their own STAR slogan: *Don't be afraid of the dark, because that's when STARS shine their brightest.* At the time of this writing, more than 400 young women have been involved in the STAR program. STAR clearly embodies not only life-skills training, but a philosophy of empowerment as well.

RESOURCES

For those interested in existing models of drug abuse prevention programs, a free copy of "Adolescent Drug Use Prevention: Common Features of Promising Community Programs" (GAO/PEMD-92-2) can be obtained by writing or calling the U.S. General Accounting Office (P.O. Box 6015, Gaithersburg, MD 20877, 202-275-6241). The GAO surveyed 226 programs and visited 10 in person.

Resources for counseling interventions and prevention include *At-Risk Youth: A Comprehensive Response* by McWhirter, McWhirter, McWhirter, & McWhirter (1993); Capuzzi & Gross's (1989) *Youth at Risk: A Resource for Counselors, Teachers and Parents*; and Vargas and Koss-Chioino's (1992) *Working with Culture: Psychotherapeutic Interventions with Ethnic Minority Children and Adolescents.*

The STAR program was founded by Yvette Fernandez and Virgie Estrada, and can be contacted at P.O. Box 34411, Phoenix, AZ 85067, 602-264-7827). TEENCOURT is spearheaded by the Gila County Juvenile Probation Department. For information or materials contact TEENCOURT, Gila County Probation Department, 1400 E. Ash Street, Globe, AZ 85501, 602-425-3231.

CONCLUSION

Empowerment of adolescents is an investment in our future. When we provide adolescents with an environment more conducive to healthy development; encourage critical awareness, personal responsibility, and action; and nourish their creativity, their hopes, and their investment in their future, we provide a better future for everyone. Adolescent empowerment can be accomplished by involving the community, schools, and families, and by encouraging youth to develop and exercise their individual strengths. The combined efforts of educational and mental health professionals is essential.

Chapter Twelve
THE NON-BEAUTIFUL

---

we fall in line
to do the right things, please, attract
we don't have to think about it anymore
it's part of our makeup
matching purse and heel
matching breast to ideal
implanted in our desires

my tv
my self
when will

we draw the line
fight to do the right things, hey, sit back:
we have to think about it some more
what is our makeup
what is so wrong that
our smell, curves, hair
must be blamed, tamed, retrained
cream, powder, razor, needle
knife are required
to meet our desire

E.H.M.

INTRODUCTION

One of the most disheartening and frightening phenomena in our society is the relentless and all-consuming desire for physical beauty. This is not new, of course. We have chased after physical beauty for centuries, exchanging one view of ideal beauty for another. Some "beauty practices" such as footbinding and wearing corsets appear to have had other functions as well. Women certainly could not run away or protect themselves from danger in such trappings. Fortunately, these practices are no longer popular. Unfortunately, they have been replaced with increasingly sophisticated methods, moving us into a more dangerous phase of the ostensible pursuit of beauty.

In this chapter, the nature of empowerment will be explored in relation to contemporary notions of beauty and acceptability. Empowerment in this context might include acceptance and valuing of one's physical characteristics; consideration of physical appearance as a single aspect of a multidimensional self; valuing family and friends for internal rather than external qualities; the ability to recognize and critically analyze the consequences of society's obsession with physical appearance, as well as the power dynamics that contribute to this obsession; possession of the skills and competencies to deal in a healthy manner with others who place great value on physical appearance; and the ability to provide support for others with similar goals.

WHO ARE THE NON-BEAUTIFUL?

The non-beautiful, quite simply, are all those who perceive themselves as having *failed to achieve* societal standards of beauty. For women, the decades-long progression toward a thinner body ideal has been accompanied by the recent idealization of full lips, large breasts (but not *too* large), and a deep tan. It goes without saying that they also have to be White (unless they are really *quite* stunning, and then they are "exotic") and free of any kind of irregularity or visible disability. Men must be tall, tan, bulging with muscles, and have a full head of hair; they, too, must be free of visible disability. Through cosmetic surgery and a range of other cosmetic endeavors, some of these characteristics can be accomplished—for a price. Apparently balding scalps can now even be "revitalized," *à la* the men in countless commercials whose formerly receding hairlines were some kind of horror to anyone (and especially *beautiful* women) who encountered them.

Both women and men are oppressed by society's obsession with appearance. Pressure on men in this particular arena is a relatively recent phenomenon, however, and more attention will be given to the implications of this pressure on women. How is the body ideal communicated? What are the consequences of the pursuit of beauty to those running the race? And finally, how do we help facilitate the empowerment of women and men who are oppressed by this phenomenon? The first personal statement below is drawn from a larger statement by Blair (1992).

But there is always something not quite right. There aren't enough curves here and too many there; my waist is too high and too large; my nose isn't absolutely straight. And, of course, I want to take off some weight. I'm not fat, but I'm never the size I would like to be. *If only, if only.*

How could so many be eating their hearts out because they don't look like Madonna or Cher? With those ideals, no one measures up, including the stars themselves. Most celebrities have had major body makeovers—not just the usual nips and tucks, but implants here and excess stuffing sucked out there. They undoubtedly have personal trainers—probably squads of them, 'round the clock—and all have made lucrative careers out of their appearance. They're professionals; it's their *job* to look, quite literally, unbelievably good.... The embarrassing fact is that for way too long I have thought this is my job, too.... Even though I know it's not true, a part of me still believes that if I could look right, I'd be right....

Yes, yes, I know I've had some help in obsessing about how I look. All day, every day, movies, television, magazines and billboards show me those flat stomachs, perfect breasts, flawless teeth, glowing complexions and long, long legs. And all day, every day, advertisements suggest that I should invest my money, my time, my hopes and dreams into trying to get as close as I can to that platonic ideal. But as much as I'd like to stick it to the media, I think they reflect what too many women—myself included—are all too ready to hear (Blair, 1992, p. 138-139).

The second personal statement is from an autobiographical piece by Alice Walker (1983):

...it is really how I look that terrifies me most. Where the BB pellet struck there is a glob of whitish scar tissue, a hideous cataract, on my eye. Now when I stare at people—a favorite pastime, up to now—they will stare back. Not at the "cute" little girl, but at her scar. For six years I do not stare at anyone, because I do not raise my head. (p. 387)

BARRIERS

Factors contributing to feelings of failure to achieve the body beautiful—barriers to feeling satisfied and content with one's physical appearance—are considered below.

Social Pressures on Women: Thin Is In

The pressure to conform is multifaceted. The mass media have certainly been a strong factor in promoting the thinness ideal for women. A content analysis of television shows, general magazines, and women's magazines revealed many more thin women than men (69% versus 17%) and far fewer heavy women than heavy men (5% versus 25%)

were depicted (Silverstein, Perdue, Peterson, & Kelly, 1986). In addition, these researchers identified distinct trends in fashion models and movie stars toward increasing thinness over the past 50 years. A study of two decades of *Playboy* centerfolds and Miss America contestants (Garner, Garfinkel, Schwartz, & Thompson, 1980) found similar trends toward thinness. Thus, the "ideal women" to whom we are exposed are steadily becoming thinner and more difficult to emulate. The paradoxical nature of media messages is highlighted in studies by Silverstein et al. (1986) and Kaufman (1980). Silverstein et al.'s (1986) review of 96 women's and men's magazines found discrepancies such as 63 diet food advertisements and 1,179 total food advertisements in the women's magazines, compared to one diet food and 10 total food advertisements in the men's magazines. In Kaufman's (1980) study of television commercials and programming, 95% of the 537 characters viewed in 600 minutes of television were depicted in situations involving food, but the food was rarely part of a balanced meal or eaten explicitly to satisfy hunger. Kaufman notes that while TV viewers witness people eating in ways "almost guaranteed" to make people fat (p. 45), the characters are and remain unrealistically thin. In their review of the literature on eating disorders among women of color, Osvold and Sodowsky (1993) note that the few women of color with prominent media roles tend to have features that conform to Euro American beauty standards.

Other researchers have noted the intense preoccupation of women with thinness and argue that women are more stigmatized for being overweight than are men (Cook, 1990; Rodin, Silberstein, & Striegel-Moore, 1985). Dieting and preoccupation with weight have become normative concerns for women in contemporary mainstream society.

Current societal emphasis on weight is accompanied by the prevalent myth that weight loss is a simple matter of willpower and discipline. In spite of increasing medical evidence that safe and permanent weight loss is not possible for most obese people (Rothblum, Brand, Miller, & Oetjen, 1990), the message that "You can and *should* lose weight!" is promulgated on a daily basis. For lower socioeconomic status (SES) women of color, who have higher proportions of obesity than other segments of the population, this myth adds to their experience of oppression. In their review of the literature on gender, class, and race differences in weight, Bowen, Tomoyasu, and Cauce (1991) point out that while eating disorders associated with being underweight are largely a phenomenon of White upper- and middle-class women, lower SES women of color are far more likely to experience problems with obesity. Another study reported that 30% of lower SES, 16% of middle SES, and 5% of upper SES women were obese (Furnham & Alibhai, 1983). Nonetheless, a great deal of money is poured into weight-reduction programs for middle-class White women, with very few such programs targeted at lower-income women or men of color. Bowen and her colleagues point out that the attribution of obesity to laziness and lack of self-restraint overlooks the critical role of issues such as lack of nutritional information, the expense of special low-fat foods versus cheaper, high-calorie fast foods, the economic and geographic inaccessibility of exercise clubs, the real danger of exercising outside (walking, jogging) in violence-ridden neighborhoods, and the influence of biological factors on weight.

The mass media portray women as constantly worried about "their weight, their muscle tone, their lifeless hair, their chipped nails, their facial wrinkles, and their visible panty lines" (Cash & Brown, 1989, p. 369). Cash and Brown (1989) found that in reality, women were not as worried about and dissatisfied with their own bodies as believed. They found that males *and* females negatively distorted how typical women feel about their bodies and positively distorted how typical men feel about their bodies. Perhaps the media influence what we believe about *others* more than what we believe about *ourselves*.

The "thin is happy" ideal is not embraced uniformly across cultures. Some evidence suggests that Mexican Americans view Euro Americans as overly concerned with weight and body image (Stern, Pugh, Gaskill, & Hazuda, 1982). A series of studies reviewed in Bowen et al. (1991) identifies similar attitudes among African American women and adolescents; African Americans were less concerned with weight, less likely to perceive themselves as fat, and less likely to go on diets than their Euro American counterparts (Desmond et al., 1989; Fetzer, Solt, & McKinney, 1985; Hsu, 1987; Huenemann et al., 1966). However, more acculturated Mexican American (Hazuda, Haffner, Stern, & Eifler, 1988), African American (Anderson & Hay, 1985), and Native American (Osvold & Sodowsky, in press) women appear more likely to succumb to the pressure to be thin. In response to the question, "How do you feel when you see slender White women on TV and in magazines exhibited as the traditional symbol of beauty?" 66% of Native American and 80% of African American women responded negatively—for example: "Jealous, that is the way I feel" and "I feel angry—like they don't care about Blacks" (Osvold & Sodowsky, in press).

Social Pressures on Men: Muscles Are Mandatory

Women are not alone in the pressure to conform to an ideal; men also express significant discontent with their bodies. Specifically, men are most likely to be dissatisfied with their chest, weight, and waist, and frequently indicate arms, nose, stomach, hips, shoulders, and height as areas of dissatisfaction as well (Mishkind, Rodin, Silberstein, & Striegel-

Moore, 1986). The ideal body type for men is typically characterized as a muscular mesomorphic body or the muscleman physique. Mishkind and his associates reviewed research suggesting that this physique corresponds with cultural views of masculinity and the male gender role, concluding, "The embodiment of masculinity, the muscular mesomorph, is seen as more efficacious, experiencing greater mastery and control over the environment and feeling more invulnerable" (p. 550). These researchers argue that correlations between men's body image and their self-esteem suggest that there may be a similar relationship between their body image and their self-perceptions of masculinity.

In the past several years, hair loss commercials for men have become commonplace. Suddenly men with receding hairlines have been targeted; they are apparently as great an affront as women with uneven complexions. Perhaps the belief that older men are dignified and even sexy, while older women are just worn out, is being replaced by the notion that *all* older adults are unattractive. We are told that balding men look old and, therefore, feel badly about themselves and are unattractive. They are an embarrassment to their companions.

Research reviewed by Shim, Kotsiopulos, and Knoll (1990) suggests that short men are less positive about their bodies than their average-height or tall peers (Martel, 1985) and that short men are much more dissatisfied with their height, more likely to compensate through hypermasculinity, and evidence more psychological distress than average-height or tall men (Klebanoff, 1987). Shim et al. (1990) found that short men are significantly less satisfied with their bodies than average, tall, and big men, and are especially dissatisfied with their height in relation to the other three groups. Certainly being larger and having a full head of hair would correspond with the cultural image of mastery and masculinity.

Skin Color

The skin color aspect of body image satisfaction has been addressed only recently. Bond and Cash (1992) found that 70% of their sample of African American women assumed that lighter skin tones were more attractive to African American men; they noted, however, that in another study only 14% of the African American men sampled had actual preferences for lighter-than-average skin tones in women (Robinson & Cash, 1992). In addition, both light- and dark-skinned participants reported ideal skin shades congruent with their own, and only women with medium skin shades preferred lighter shades of skin. The majority of women in the study reported satisfaction with their skin color (Bond

& Cash, 1992). Bond and Cash (1992) suggest that African Americans with more positive ethnic identities will be more satisfied with their physical attributes and have a better body image.

It is rather ironic that, in the midst of historic and ongoing discrimination against dark-skinned people, Euro Americans should be so preoccupied with obtaining a year-round "perfect tan." Skin tanned by sunlight, presumably a sign of a healthy, active life, is purchased now in the form of artificial light, injections, and skin creams. In spite of warnings about health risks, tanning salons and lotions are a booming business across the country.

Gender Role Socialization

The physically "ideal" characteristics of women and men, and the pressure to conform to these ideals, cannot be understood apart from the sociocultural influences on gender role socialization. The way people feel about their bodies is shaped by cultural and personal factors. Franzoi (1992) argues that women are socialized early on to view their bodies as the objects of other people's attention, while men are socialized to view their bodies as instruments of action in the world. This societal perspective probably is rooted in women's historical status as the "possessions" of their fathers and husbands; more aesthetically pleasing women were of greater value. In accord with Synnott's (1989) analysis, "The beautiful woman is a status symbol; she not only does not work, but cannot work; long hair, corsets, high heels, long dresses, and so on are intended to indicate this: they too are status symbols; and the decoration of the women with jewelry, making her an expensive ornament, reinforces this process...." (p. 629).

Franzoi (1992) contends further that while males are not actually expected to attain the lofty standards of physical competence set by models such as Michael Jordan, females are judged by unrealistic standards of beauty. He proposed that women who are more traditionally "feminine" (expressive) as opposed to androgynous or "masculine" (instrumental) in their orientations would be more likely to view their bodies as objects of other people's attention, and consequently feel more pressure to achieve society's standards of beauty. Consistent with his hypothesis, Franzoi found that females with a higher expressive orientation were less satisfied with their weight and more desirous of changing their bodies than women with androgynous or instrumental orientations. Similarly, Kelson, Kearney-Cooke, and Lansky (1990) found that feminists associated having a competent body with awareness of internal sensations, while nonfeminists associated having a competent body with their appearance. Basow (1991) found that feminists and lesbians were least likely to remove body hair, a practice reflective of the fundamental belief that women's bodies are unattractive and unacceptable in their natural state.

Kaschak's (1992) analysis of this issue contends that women are trained from childhood onward to evaluate their bodies through the eyes of men. At puberty, girls are told, "Don't wear that nightgown around your father anymore," as if their developing bodies are a problem they caused. Girls are not to sit with their legs apart, because this means they are lustful. Girls and women in public are subjected constantly to male reactions to their bodies, from wolf whistles and comments from passing cars, to silent grabs on a crowded bus, to jocular comments in the lunchroom. Discussions of women frequently include references to their physical characteristics, even when appearance is unrelated to the topic: "She's not very attractive, but she really does a good job with the accounts." Fashion-conscious practices such as wearing high heels may contribute to a woman's attractiveness (from a male perspective), vulnerability (from the perspective of a potential attacker), and physical pain (from the perspective of the woman wearing them) (Kaschak, 1992). Based on her analysis of the role of these experiences in women's development, Kaschak (1992) contends:

> The important components here are central in the development of the self-concept in women: (1) the physicalness of woman's identity; (2) that the physicalness is always evaluated; (3) that this physicalness is evaluated first and primarily by individual men or by the masculinist context as mediated by significant others; (4) that what is deemed pleasurable to men is often not pleasurable to women, but harmful, dangerous, or diminishing; (5) that these evaluations can change situationally with the presence or absence of different men and temporally with the inevitable change in fashion; and (6) that women's own internal experience, hurting feet in this case, is secondary and often kept invisible from others and eventually, as a result, from herself. (p. 98)

Thus, the culmination of the multifaceted influences of gender role socialization establish an intimate link between women's identity and their physical appearance.

CONSEQUENCES

What are the ramifications of having an identity that is tied to appearance, and the overwhelming pressure to conform to unrealistic body ideals? Many would argue that disordered eating and the growing demand for cosmetic surgery are consequences of this pressure. While the health benefits of regular exercise and low-fat diets are clear, the following incident illustrates how the obsession with food and fitness has been used to humiliate and oppress.

Sunday night was ice cream night at the dining hall of a major private university. One Sunday evening, women approaching the dessert area were dismayed to find themselves confronted by a row of men. They were physically blocking the ice cream containers and told every approaching woman, "You're too fat, you can't have any" or "Go on a diet—no ice cream for you tonight." All of the young men were wearing T shirts proclaiming "NO FAT CHICKS," with a red circle and bar over the figure of a large woman.

In reaction to the furor that erupted over this and a string of similar incidents, one of the students involved wrote an editorial to the school paper defending his actions. He argued that he and his companions were concerned about the health of all the overweight women on campus, and that it was their "Christian duty" to do something to help them.

Eating disorders and cosmetic surgery can be understood only in the context of a society in which incidents such as the one above are commonplace.

Eating Disorders

Laidlaw (1990) argues that women's disordered eating behavior is clearly related to women's oppression via gender role socialization and the pressure to be thin. Disordered eating may be viewed as a continuum (Striegel-More, Silberstein, & Rodin, 1986) that includes occasional dieting, chronic dieting, binging, purging, and specific disorders such as bulimia and anorexia nervosa. The prevalence of bulimia has been estimated at between 8% and 10% of females (Mitchell, 1992). The incidence of anorexia nervosa has been estimated to be approximately 11% of young females (Herzog & Copeland, 1985). Although 90–95% of anorectics are Euro American adolescent females of middle- and upper-middle socioeconomic status (Herzog & Copeland, 1985), the incidence of anorexia appears to be increasing among girls and women of color as well (Anderson & Hay, 1985; Hooper & Garner, 1986; Root, 1990). Andersen and Hay (1985) and Hsu (1987) suggest that increases in SES may increase vulnerability to eating disorders.

Sociocultural factors are considered increasingly to be part of the etiology of eating disorders (Laidlaw, 1990; Mintz & Wright, 1993). A few studies have linked eating disorders among women of color with levels of acculturation, with greater acculturation being associated with a higher incidence of eating problems (Garb, Garb, & Stunkard, 1975; Osvold & Sodowsky, 1993; Rosen et al., 1988). As discussed in the section on gender role socialization, women are socialized to view themselves as sexual objects, to value themselves based on their appearance, and to devote time and energy to their appearance so as to win the approval of a particular man and men in general (Laidlaw, 1990). Orbach (1979) characterizes compulsive overeating and fat as a rejection of these socialization messages and gender role stereotypes.

Some researchers argue that the growing pressure on men to conform to physical ideals also places them at increasing risk for the development of eating disorders (Mishkind, Rodin, Silberstein, & Striegel-Moore, 1986; Striegel-Moore, Silberstein, & Rodin, 1986). Regardless of the many other factors involved in the development of eating disorders among individuals, sociocultural pressures are an irrefutable part of the context in which they occur.

The seriousness of eating disorders cannot be underestimated. The counseling and medical literature is replete with evidence of the negative effects of eating disorders. At the more severe end of the continuum, they pose a serious threat to health, with physical complications that include tooth decay, sterility, heart failure, and ulcers. For some, these complications result in death.

Cosmetic Surgery

Cosmetic surgery has become a $3 billion industry in the United States, with almost half of the world's cosmetic surgeons living in this country ("Cosmetic surgery," 1992). Dull and West (1991) report that in 1988 more than half a million people in the United States underwent cosmetic surgery; only 90,000 were men. They note that this figure is conservative, because it only includes surgery performed by members of the American Society of Plastic and Reconstructive Surgeons. In fact, any licensed medical doctor can perform plastic surgery. In their interviews with recipients of cosmetic surgery and cosmetic surgeons, Dull and West (1991) found that their sample viewed cosmetic surgery as a normal and natural pursuit for women, but not for men. Surgeons often described what women "needed," with respect to surgery, in terms of their race and ethnicity. Further, they noted:

> Throughout these interviews, surgeons and patients alike alluded to technically normal features as "flaws," "defects," "deformities," and "correctable problems" of appearance. Surgeons referred to patients as "needing" facelifts and breast augmentations, while patients referred to the specific part (or parts of parts) that they had "fixed"...surgeons were united in their view that women's concerns for their appearance are essential to their nature as women. (Dull & West, 1991, pp. 63-64)

Breast enlargement, collagen injections (to get rid of facial lines), and eyelid surgery are among the most popular operations. Among ethnic minority group members, operations changing "racial characteristics" are most popular ("Cosmetic surgery," 1992). Cosmetic surgery is not limited to the wealthy, either; one survey found that one in three individuals who underwent cosmetic surgery earned less than $25,000 per year ("Cosmetic surgery," 1992).

The popularization of cosmetic surgery was captured in a question posed on the Maury Povich show (aired on CBS May 5, 1992): "What's a small-busted woman to do?" The question was asked in relation to the expense of breast implants. Obviously a small-busted woman has to do *something*, she can't just go around with her insultingly small breasts as if life is worth living. On this particular program, Michael Stivers of the National Hypnosis Center claimed that for a $1,000 fee he could make women's breasts grow using hypnosis. After his initial treatment, all they had to do was follow up with three months of listening, morning and evening, to his (apparently breast-inspiring) audiotapes.

Although many people engaged in the pursuit of beauty likely would justify their efforts on the grounds of raising self-esteem, there is evidence that members of stigmatized groups such as women, African Americans, and people who are obese do not in fact have lower self-esteem than others (Crocker & Major, 1989). Body image is correlated only moderately with self-esteem (Jackson, 1992). Further, a meta-analysis of the literature on physical attractiveness found no relationship between physical attractiveness and self-esteem (Feingold, 1992). That is, attractive people were no more likely to have high self-esteem than unattractive people. While people who lose weight, change their makeup, or obtain breast implants may feel better about how they look, it is quite likely—given our cultural context—that eventually they will shift their focus to another "flawed" feature. Indeed, many cosmetic surgery patients return repeatedly, in search, perhaps, of that one last detail, that final alteration, that will make them perfect.

SUGGESTIONS FOR EMPOWERMENT

Power Analysis

Power analysis is an important component of working with clients who are troubled by their appearance. In the context of this concern, power analysis should include exploration and discussion of societal messages regarding appearance, the influence of these messages, and the implications of succumbing to these messages. In addition, women may benefit from consideration of the pressure to conform to standards that they may experience within their personal relationships. For example, one young woman seen in counseling had become "inexplicably" obsessed with her appearance. Prior to seeking counseling, she had considered herself attractive and had not paid much attention to her looks. She soon made a connection between her "diminishing" looks and the beginning of her relationship with a bodybuilder who hoped to "improve her."

Power analysis can spring from diverse activities: directed readings, scholarly or popular; fact-based discussions; assignments to watch TV or review magazine pictures; values-clarification exercises; or attending a workshop, lecture, or support group on a topic related to the pressure to conform to body ideals. Readings that might be useful include *The Beauty Trap* by Nancy Baker (1984), *Face Value: The Politics of Beauty* by Robin Lakoff and Raquel Scherr (1984), and *The Obsession: Reflections on the Tyranny of Slenderness* by Kim Chernin (1981). Marcia Hutchinson's (1985) *Transforming Body Image* provides helpful suggestions for women wanting to enhance their self-acceptance. The film, *Still Killing Us Softly*, by Cambridge Documentary Films (1987) also can serve as a valuable discussion starter.

Simple facts also can be used to initiate a power analysis. For example, the weight-loss industry is estimated to have made $33 billion in 1990 and was expected to near $50 billion in 1992 (Cannella, 1992). Such information can launch a concrete discussion of who benefits from promotion of the thinness ideal, and who pays for—and benefits from— the pursuit of this ideal.

A power analysis of physical standards cannot be complete without specific exploration of gender role socialization. The pressure for men to conform to the mesomorphic physique is bound inextricably to traditional gender role expectations that, for example, men should restrict their affect by hiding feelings of insecurity and hurt. Gender aware therapy (GAT) (Good, Gilbert, & Scher, 1990), which integrates awareness of how women and men are affected negatively by gender role socialization and expectations, is consistent with the notion of empowerment. The principles of GAT include (a) regard conceptions of gender as integral aspects of counseling and mental health; (b) consider problems within their societal context; (c) actively seek to change gender injustices experienced by women and men; (d) emphasize development of collaborative therapeutic relationships; and (e) respect clients' freedom to choose (Good, Gilbert, & Scher, 1990, p. 377). Ultimately, reducing societal constraints on male and female behavior will decrease the potency and popularity of narrowly defined physical standards and behavioral expectations. In the short term, counselors can assist male and female clients to express a fuller range of human emotions and behaviors and help them to identify how socially constructed expectations of behavior may be contributing to their psychological and physical distress (Cook, 1990; Good, Gilbert, & Scher, 1990; Scher & Good, 1990).

Group Participation

Men's, women's, and mixed-gender groups all can be effective contexts for exploring the power dynamics involved in the pressure to meet physical ideals. Groups also can provide a supportive atmosphere for trying out new beliefs and behaviors, which may be especially valuable when the new attitudes and behaviors are countercultural. In addition, group work incorporates a natural intervention for individuals with a narcissistic obsession with their appearance. All-male groups have been noted as particularly beneficial in addressing the influences of stereotypical male gender roles and in overcoming traditional restrictions to intimacy (Cochran & Rabinowitz, 1983; Scher, Stevens, Good, & Eichenfeld, 1987; Rabinowitz, 1991).

Where available, women's studies classes may provide an excellent group format for critical analysis of the role of beauty standards in women's socialization. There appears to be a slow but steady move toward incorporating the history and perspectives of women of color into women's studies classes, which often have focused only on the history of Euro American women. The emerging focus on men's studies offers another arena for group exploration of gender role socialization and the pressure to conform to certain standards.

Jordan's (1992) group for African American women (discussed in Chapter Five) devotes an entire meeting to physical and spiritual beauty. Participants identify their perceptions of physical beauty and share ways that they have attempted to alter their natural appearances. Euro American and African standards of beauty are contrasted, with information regarding the latter standards provided by the facilitator. The group also explores the meaning of spirituality and spiritual beauty and attempts to integrate notions of spiritual and physical beauty. Thus, the group addresses power dynamics, provides support, integrates the important cultural value of spirituality, and enhances ethnic pride.

There are many possibilities for group involvement beyond those provided here. Groups provide the contribution of many opinions, experiences, and viewpoints to the construction of a new understanding of the function—and the effects—of the pursuit of beauty. As with other empowering group experiences, group members have the opportunity to support each other, challenge existing gender role attitudes and construct new ones, learn from each other, and make self-discoveries that evolve uniquely from the group process.

Skill Application: Creative Self-Expression

There are limitless ways to engage clients' creativity in confronting their negative views of their physical selves. With a few magazines, newspapers, scissors, and glue, clients can represent their perceptions powerfully by making a series of collages representing "who I am," "who I'm told I should be," and "who I want to be." In a group context, participants could share collages as a means of demonstrating their changing self-perceptions. Participants can exchange insights and feedback about each member's use of images or words in the collages.

Storytelling is another vehicle for creative self-expression. Counselors and clients can construct stories reflecting various aspects of the pursuit of beauty, such as the following.

Once there was a caterpillar who was very concerned with all the wrinkles on her body. She tried creams and powders, medicines and therapies, but nothing helped her hide or reduce those wrinkles. She was so concerned with how ugly those wrinkles were, she didn't notice the wrinkles that covered the bodies of her friends. In fact, she became so consumed with hiding or reducing her "ugliness" that she didn't even notice when all her friends started spinning cocoons. When her friends disappeared, she was convinced that her ugliness had driven them away. And when they appeared again months later, fanning themselves and sailing across gardens, she again blamed her ugliness for her own inability to do more than crawl slowly from leaf to leaf.

As a group or in individual work, clients might be asked to take this or a similar story and rewrite it. Rewriting or retelling a story can facilitate empowerment; it supports the notion that change is possible and that we are all capable of being active rather than passive participants in constructing our lives. Hill (1992) describes the use of fairy tales in the treatment of eating disorders and integrates the notion of active participation in the fairy tale drama as a means of developing a stronger sense of self, developing control over eating behaviors, and engaging in more active self-direction.

Literary resources for counselors and clients include Brant's (1984) *A Gathering of Spirit: Writing and Art by North American Indian Women*, Rico's (1986) *Writing the Natural Way*, and Olsen's (1978) *Silences*. Each of these works deals with creativity, and Olsen's book discusses how race, gender, class, and other factors influence creativity.

Cognitive Compensation Strategies

Miller and Rothblum (1992) suggest that members of stigmatized groups develop means of compensating for the negative attitudes and behaviors directed at them by others. They reviewed two theories regarding the nature of this compensation. According to self-verification theory, people try to verify their self-concepts in their social interactions. Specifically, as they interact with others, they reject or challenge information that is inconsistent with their self-concepts. For example, if I perceive myself to be socially skilled, I might dismiss a friend's comment that I appeared to be insecure at the party last night, attributing it to my friend's inability to read me. I might say this to myself or I might choose to confront my friend.

Self-enhancement theory suggests that people work hard to maintain positive self-images, and will compensate for any negative traits or behaviors by emphasizing their positive traits and behaviors. In accord with self-enhancement theory, if I agree that my social skills are somewhat inadequate, I might convey to my concerned friend above that I *do* have good *written* communication skills, or that in spite of my poor social skills I'm a very *friendly* person overall. Given the evidence that both self-verification theory and self-enhancement theory appear to be used effectively by people in marginalized groups, counselors might teach clients to employ these as conscious strategies.

Positive self-statements or affirmations constitute another effective cognitive strategy. One young man developed his own set of affirmations in response to intense negative feelings about his body. His negativity centered on his legs, which had been affected by cerebral palsy. In his words, "I finally realized that my legs took me everywhere I wanted to go—maybe not at the same speed as everyone else, or in the same way, but they carried me. I became grateful to my legs and would silently thank them for being strong, for helping me get places, and for supporting me. I really changed my attitude." A more extensive case example is provided below. This case illustrates the use of positive self-statements, in conjunction with assertiveness training and strategies to enhance ethnic identity, with a client who perceived herself as "non-beautiful."

Barbara was a 35-year-old Japanese American accountant who came in for individual counseling regarding her upcoming marriage to a 28-year-old Euro American. Her fiance had threatened to call off their wedding, which was nine months away, unless she agreed to have breast augmentation surgery. She reported that he had told her he would "never think of her as a woman" as long as she was small-breasted, that he could not become sexually aroused because of her "little girl looks." Barbara stated that she was very much in love with him and would do anything to hold on to the relationship, yet she was afraid to have surgery. She said that several of her female relatives in Japan had already had the surgery to "look more American." Her parents were against the idea and disapproved of her fiance, but they were "old fashioned." Barbara wanted the opinion of "an American" and requested a male counselor.

The counselor explained that before he could be of assistance in her decision process, he would have to learn more about the relationship and about Barbara herself. Barbara lived with her parents and, until meeting her fiance, had socialized only with her extended family and one female friend who was married and also Japanese American. She was intelligent, sensitive, and extremely shy. This was Barbara's first serious relationship. She had met her fiance two years earlier at work. He invited her out on a date, but then did not call her for a second date for three months. Barbara reported that although previous to this date she had been content with her life-style, afterward she began to question whether she would ever marry and wondered if something was wrong with her. When he called her for a second date, she agonized over how to dress and what to say. This time, he called her back within two weeks. They dated regularly then, going to movies or watching TV in his apartment. When asked what they had in common, Barbara replied, "We really complement each other because our interests are so diverse." After dating for three months he insisted that it was not normal to refrain from sex any longer, and they began having intercourse. At this point, he let Barbara know that her breast size was a problem and would be "for any man," but he always reassured her that her eyes "didn't bother him." It wasn't until after their engagement that he became more insistent that she have surgery performed on her breasts. The counselor made it clear to Barbara that breast size was a matter of individual preference, and that small breasts were not a "problem" for many men. He noted that Barbara consistently approved of things she associated with "American" culture. Barbara reacted with surprise when he asked about Japanese culture; she did not think an "American man" would be interested in such things. They decided to spend a few minutes of each therapy session enjoying a Japanese art object, family story, or aspect of Japanese culture that Barbara picked out in advance. They also decided to identify other traits, besides "interest in Japanese culture," that Barbara enjoyed in other people. After a level of trust had developed, they developed a series of self-statements that Barbara used when she felt inadequate about her breast size and her sexual attractiveness, such as "My breasts are exquisite" and "Sexuality comes from the inside, not the outside." (She would not rehearse the former statement in front of the counselor, but reported that it was very effective.) Finally, Barbara and her counselor used assertiveness training techniques to support Barbara's expression of her feelings about surgery and her decision not to have surgery.

These processes occurred over a nine-week period, at which time Barbara told her fiance that she would not marry him if he insisted she have surgery. He subsequently broke off the relationship. Barbara remained in counseling for several more months working on issues related to self-esteem, enhancing her sense of ethnic identification and pride, identifying how her values differed from those of her parents, and enhancing her social skills. On termination, Barbara expressed profound satisfaction with her decision not to have surgery, stating, "I am a Japanese woman; I look just fine, that's who I am!"

Skill Application: Self-Esteem

In Chapter Three, Walz and Bleur's (in press) three-dimensional framework for enhancing self-esteem was described. Recall that the *personal initiatives* (appreciate your uniqueness, connect with others, be goal driven, strive to achieve, act courageously, respond with resilience, live your values, value your spirituality, and release your creativity) represent behaviors contributing to increased self-esteem. Clients concerned with their physical appearance might consider the *life arena* of physical self in relation to each personal initiative, asking, for example, "Do I value my physical uniqueness?" "Do I allow my physical appearance to mediate how I connect with others, and with whom I connect?" "Do I strive to achieve a physical ideal in a manner consistent with my values, or do I [for example] violate my value of physical health with the use of diet pills and laxatives?" Walz and Bleur's model is applicable to these issues.

Feedback specifically addressing physical appearance may be appropriate when clients dress and groom themselves in a manner that is obviously unflattering. This may be related to a rejection of a parental message that fashionable clothes and the "right" haircut are reasonable conditions of worth. Such behavior may also reflect hopelessness, low self-esteem, unawareness that their manner of dress is unflattering or their lack of hygiene potentially offensive, or a reflection of their economic situation. Counselors should moderate their approach depending on which of these factors is at play. An individual in the process of actively rejecting early negative messages may be healing and growing through this rejection, while another client might be trying to call attention to inner discouragement. A sloppily dressed client having difficulty getting beyond initial job interviews might benefit from a frank discussion of first impressions and physical appearance. Discussion of the effect of physical appearance on first impressions can serve a pragmatic function and is not necessarily an endorsement of such norms.

CONCLUSION

The objective of this chapter is not to advocate for an end to all beauty enhancement for all people. But the incredible pressure to meet physical ideals, and the consequences of that pressure, must be recognized. Blair (1992) writes, "constantly fretting about how I look gives me an excuse not to put my all into what really *is* my job: Earning a living, being in charge of my own life and home, taking on new challenges...." (p. 139). In the words of Synnott, "The feminist critique of the beauty mystique...emphasiz[ed] that beautification was unnecessary, time-consuming, expensive, unhealthy, ecologically disastrous, degrading, unauthentic and ultimately futile and contributing to self-hatred" (1990, p. 66). As counselors we are called on to be aware of the dynamics that create and nourish our society's obsession with physical appearance. We facilitate client empowerment when we name this pressure and support client efforts to extricate themselves from its grasp, when we help clients access social networks in which physical appearance is not a crucial focus, and when we reflect an attitude of respect and appreciation of clients' inner qualities. Finally, a vital question underlies this issue that counselors and other mental health professionals, and indeed our entire society, cannot afford to overlook: What might we see, and what might we have the time and energy to do, if we turned away from our mirrors and looked out at the world?

PART IV

CONCLUSION

Chapter Thirteen

EMPOWERMENT AND THE FUTURE OF COUNSELING

gather all your tears, gather all your failures
wear them as a badge of your integrity
they are simply wrinkles on an old beloved face
they make you who you are

you are not alone; you are one small candle
in a burning chain that circles 'round the world
you are one voice, but your song is mighty
love will find a way

From "One Small Candle," E.H.M.

INTRODUCTION

Adopting empowerment as a goal of counseling has many implications for practice and training. Following a brief synopsis of the book, the practice implications of counseling for empowerment are summarized in relation to the definition of empowerment. Next, several implications for the training of counselors, psychologists, and other helping professionals are discussed. Finally, some specific reflections on the empowerment of counselors and other mental health professionals are offered.

SYNOPSIS

Throughout this book, I have attempted to address how the notion of empowerment can be practically applied to counseling. In Part I, the respective natures of empowerment and counseling were examined, resulting in a definition of empowerment in the context of counseling. The skills component of counseling for empowerment was illustrated in Part II. In Part III, counseling for empowerment was applied to a variety of groups. Discussing clients in terms of general categories—people of color, people who are disabled, adolescents—creates artificial boundaries and oversimplifies the reality of human lives. All people are simultaneously members of multiple categories, with distinct sociopolitical, cultural, and economic histories and realities as well. Nevertheless, members of each of the groups discussed in the preceding chapters have important commonalities. These commonalities are integral to the analysis of power dynamics and represent potential sources of identity affirmation and channels for community involvement. The skills described in Part II and the groups discussed in Part III are but a fraction of those that could have been included. I hope that these illustrations of the application of empowerment to counseling provide a solid basis for generalizing beyond the specific barriers, power dynamics, skills, and issues addressed in Chapters Five through Twelve. The responsibility of counselors and other mental health professionals to take part in larger social change processes has been emphasized throughout these pages.

IMPLICATIONS FOR PRACTICE

The practice implications of counseling for empowerment echo what multicultural and feminist voices have been articulating for years (Enns, 1993; Lee, 1991a; Sue & Sue, 1991). Indeed, the definition of empowerment offered herein was derived from many sources, including multicultural and feminist writers. After a restatement of the definition of empowerment, each component of the definition is reviewed. Relevant aspects of the ethical standards of the American Counseling Association (ACA) (American Association of Counseling and Development, 1988) and the first draft of the revised ACA ethical standards (American Counseling Association Ethics Committee [ACAEC]) (ACAEC, 1993) are noted. (The projected publication date of the revised ethical standards is 1995–1996; the revised standards could differ significantly from the first draft).

> Empowerment is the process by which people, organizations, or groups who are powerless or marginalized: (a) become aware of the power dynamics at work in their life context, (b) develop the skills and capacity for gaining some reasonable control over their lives, (c) which they exercise, (d) without infringing upon the rights of others, and (e) which coincides with supporting the empowerment of others in their community.

In a society marred by inequality and injustice, racism and sexism, economic stratification and violence, and numerous other sources of oppression, the counseling relationship can reflect society all too easily. Band-Aid solutions, pacification, and redirection of the client's energy may serve to maintain the status quo rather than to inspire fundamental change. The goal of empowerment requires a professional and personal commitment to challenge rather than to reflect the dynamics of oppression.

Become aware of the power dynamics at work in their life context refers to identifying systemic and structural influences on clients' lives at personal, interpersonal, and societal levels. The barriers to empowerment discussed in each chapter provide some insights into particular power dynamics. For example, racism (Chapter Five), homophobia (Chapter Six), inaccessible environments (Chapter Eight), and drug use (Chapter Eleven) all contribute to oppressive power dynamics for specific groups. The counselor's awareness of the potential effects of these barriers lays a foundation for exploring these effects with individual clients. Specifically, the counselor working with a client who uses a wheelchair might explore the personal repercussions of society's adherence to economic, medical, or sociopolitical models of disability (see Chapter Eight). Exploration of these contrasting models with the client may illuminate a variety of dynamics at work in the client's life. But when the counselor is unaware of how the public's views of disability relate to the treatment of people with disabilities (from interpersonal experiences to accessibility issues to legislative efforts), this aspect of power analysis is precluded. There are, of course, many barriers and power dynamics at work beyond those discussed in each chapter.

ACA's ethical standards (AACD, 1988) state that professional counselors must be aware of the negative effects of racial and sexual stereotyping within the counseling relationship. The first draft of the revised standards (ACAEC, 1993) prohibits engaging in or condoning discrimination based on age, color, culture, disability, ethnic group, gender, race, religion, sexual orientation, or socioeconomic status; thus, discrimination is defined more broadly. Further, in accord with this draft of the revised standards, counselors working with clients different from themselves in any of these categories are ethically bound to gain knowledge, awareness, and sensitivity relevant to their clients and to provide culturally relevant services. Thus, awareness of power dynamics is likely to be a growing concern of all counseling professionals.

Developing the skills and capacity for gaining some reasonable control over their lives refers to what some practitioners consider the primary role of the counselor, psychoeducation and skills training. Indeed, these are very important to the empowerment process. Sue and Sue (1990) point out that many culturally different clients will expect, and be best served by, the provision of information from an active, expert, and directive counselor, in contrast to a reflective, insight-oriented counselor. However, counselors often are trained in skill-building exercises rooted in Euro American values, worldviews, and norms. Thus the nature of each skill, as well as the manner and context in which the skill is practiced, must be shaped in accord with the client's concerns as well as other salient client characteristics such as personal and sociopolitical history, culture, interpersonal style, level of acculturation, and preferences. The perception-feeling-want triad (see Chapter Four) may be a completely inappropriate skill for a Chinese American man consulting a counselor about a family difficulty. Even if he is highly acculturated, the traditional Chinese values of preventing others' shame or loss of face, and the practice of deliberate indirectness as one means of doing so, may mean that this skill is useless for family situations. Further, the client may wish to save face for the counselor by agreeing to learn this particular communication skill, knowing all the while he will not be able to use it to resolve his primary concern. Counselor sensitivity is important in the consideration of skills, but sensitivity cannot compensate for lack of counselor knowledge of cultural values and practices.

The series of intrapersonal (Chapter Three) and interpersonal (Chapter Four) skills described in Part II must be modified for use with each client if they are to facilitate empowerment. Current ethical standards require that all professional counselors recognize their need for continuing education (AACD, 1988); counselors without formal training in diversity issues are ethically bound to obtain the information necessary to effect appropriate skills training with clients. The skills training component of counseling for empowerment is consistent with the explicit statement, in the draft of the new ethical standards, that professional counselors must avoid fostering dependent relationships with clients. The draft further emphasizes that counselors must work jointly with clients to establish a plan for counseling that is consistent with the client's abilities and circumstances (ACAEC, 1993).

Which they exercise without infringing upon the rights of others is an important component of empowerment that is addressed implicitly in this book. The examples of skill application reflect the fundamental nature of empowerment as integrative power or "power *with* others" (Hagberg, 1984) rather than power over others, or power "to do to" others (see Chapter One). For example, while setting boundaries might upset or offend those people in a client's life who were violating those boundaries, setting boundaries is not a case of using power over another. Setting boundaries often creates, in fact, the opportunity for interactions that are more satisfying, mutual, and healthy. Developing and using interpersonal skills to facilitate one's own and another's empowerment is well articulated by Surrey (1991):

> This process creates a relational context in which there is increasing awareness and knowledge of self and other.... Both participants gain new energy and new awareness since each has risked change and growth through the encounter. Neither person is in control; instead, each is enlarged and feels empowered, energized, and more real. (p. 168)

As noted in the discussion of gang membership (see Chapter Eleven), the exercise of skills that violate the human rights of others is incompatible with empowerment.

Coinciding with support for the empowerment of others in their community can range from adopting particular interpersonal behaviors and attitudes (see the preceding quote from Surrey's work) to community consciousness-raising efforts such as participating in a Take-Back-the-Night march (see Chapter Nine) or helping to organize cultural and educational events. The role of the counselor or other mental health professional is to increase the client's awareness of such options as appropriate. Given that empowerment is a long-term process, many clients will not be ready for or interested in the empowerment of others—in the form of interpersonal relationships or community participation—when they terminate the counseling relationship. This must not be considered a failure on the part of the client or the counselor to "achieve" the goal of empowerment. The counselor's overt value of empowerment as a goal of counseling does not mean this value is shared by the client; needless to say, imposing this value on clients would be quite hypocritical.

The practice implications discussed to this point have focused on in-session behaviors. A final implication of counseling for empowerment pertains to the mental health professional's behavior outside the session. Counseling for empowerment can only be authentic when the counselor is committed to larger social transformation processes that challenge structural and systemic oppression. While we need not and cannot follow all issues and causes with the same intensity, activism of some kind is the logical concomitant to personal and professional goals of empowerment. In many respects, mental health professionals possess a more intimate, collective knowledge of society's ills than do others. We have an obligation to "name the devil" publicly and to take a stand against the injustices that plague our society and disempower our clients.

IMPLICATIONS FOR TRAINING

What does the adoption of the goal of empowerment mean for training? First, it means that we must pay more attention to the *person of the counselor*. Research has indicated consistently that the person of the counselor has far more influence on counseling outcome than the techniques employed or the counselor's theoretical orientation (Mahoney, 1991). Mahoney notes, for example, that the counselor's capacity to "invite and co-maintain a highly specialized human relationship involving mutual trust and genuine caring" is a skill not all will master (p. 355). The counselor's personal history of trusting relationships will interact with factors such as motivation for being a counselor and worldview, yielding the primary "tool" of the trade—the self. Training our students to conduct ongoing self-analysis of potential personal barriers to providing effective counseling relationships is essential.

A second, related implication for training is this: Counselors and other mental health professionals must be aware of how counseling can be a vehicle of oppression. This notion is fundamental; without such awareness counselors are unlikely to be able to critique themselves and their work. Counseling is oppressive when counselors perpetuate systemic biases in working with clients—for example, when counselors use Eurocentric interventions with clients of color; work in inaccessible facilities; cling to the notion that they are unbiased, nonracist, nonheterosexist; and so forth. Counseling can be oppressive when counselors are not trained in the kind of critical self-analysis that enables insight into one's prejudices, limitations, blind spots, and other forms of bias. Sue and Sue (1990) note that while many training programs give lip service to such self-analysis, the reality is that most counselors-in-training do not experience such rigorous self-exploration.

The goal of learning to identify areas of weakness is that, consistent with ACA ethical standards, counselors and other mental health professionals make such self-analysis an ongoing part of their work. We have to assume that even as we grow by minimizing one particular form of bias, another blind spot awaits our attention. Our society is so permeated by biases and "isms" that we cannot hope to "remove every shred" from within; we can only hope to reduce them greatly. We will be in a better position to do so if we operate from the premise that we are continuously racist, sexist, heterosexist, ageist, and hold able-bodied assumptions. Since human nature seems inclined to confirm, rather than disconfirm, hypotheses, we are more likely to discover and minimize our biases by holding such presumptions.

Sue, Arredondo, and McDavis (1992) point out that two political realities of which counseling professionals must be aware are that (a) counselor and client worldviews are always linked to past and present racism and oppression in society, and (b) counseling does not occur in a vacuum but in the context of larger social, economic, and political events in society. To the extent that counselors-in-training are not provided with a means for exploring the development of worldviews and linking the larger societal context with the specific counseling session, we fail to prepare counselors for the realities of their client's lives. The larger society influences not only the nature of the client's life experience, but the nature of counseling itself. In other words, the counselor's role, definitions of "successful" outcomes, the counselor's expectations of the client, etc., are shaped by the larger context. Awareness of the realities of oppression is a necessary but insufficient condition of counseling for empowerment.

The reality of oppression is not merely to be "known" but acted on as well. Returning to the notion of counselor participation in the community, D'Andrea's (1992) comments highlight the fundamental issue:

> I am surprised and disappointed that some of my colleagues have expressed disagreement, discomfort—even anger—at the notion that counselors should be ethically bound to play a more active role as agents of social change. I argue that every time counselors refrain from opposing racism, they are indeed being unethical and are in conflict with the spirit of the counseling profession (p. 31).

In essence, the role of social change agent is intrinsic to the professional identity of the counselor. The illusion of "value-free" counseling and "neutrality" on issues such as violence, poverty, and discrimination is no longer tenable. Counseling for empowerment leaves no protective, ambivalent veil about the person of the counselor. If we simultaneously identify barriers and "accept" them all as an immutable part of reality, we are not participating in empowerment; we are merely another facet of the problem.

A third implication of the goal of empowerment is that coursework in multicultural and feminist perspectives must be an integral component of training programs. Traditional theories of counseling have been based on research conducted by Euro American middle-class males using samples of Euro American middle-class males. Every aspect of the research, from the questions posed, to the methods of investigating these questions, to the conclusions drawn from the data, is rooted in the masculinist perspective (e.g., Unger, 1983). While we learned a great deal about this population, we learned quite a bit less about women, people of color, and people of lower SES. Nevertheless, these theories have been used in working with all clients, leading to conclusions such as "minorities aren't suited for counseling" or "people without a formal education don't do well in therapy." Multicultural, feminist, and other perspectives have offered a wealth of information for helping professionals over the past several decades. However, integration of these perspectives into training programs has been inconsistent, at least partly because these perspectives have implications for *how* we teach and train as well as the content of our teaching and training.

Abandoning traditional theories and methods is not advocated here. But we can no longer afford to train counselors in traditional theories and methods without also training them in critical analyses of these theories, and drastically expanding our methods to include those successful with the diverse range of clients we actually serve. Training must incorporate a comprehensive critique of each theory and present emerging theoretical work that addresses the counseling and development processes of women; people of color; gay, lesbian and bisexual people; and other groups not recognized in traditional theories. Further, multicultural and feminist perspectives (for example) should not be voiced in single courses only. Every class in contemporary training programs should integrate these and other perspectives, from career counseling, assessment, and human relations training to courses in psychopathology and family therapy. To exclude these perspectives would be to continue to risk labeling the behaviors of women and people of color as "less than," "unhealthy," or "inappropriate." Inclusion of consciousness-raising components in all such coursework, in addition to affective, cognitive, and skills components, is critical (Sue & Sue, 1990).

Excellent sources of information on increasing multicultural awareness (e.g., Pedersen, 1988), multicultural training (e.g., Part 2 of the *Journal of Counseling and Development* special issue on multiculturalism, 1991; Sue & Sue, 1990) as well as information on multicultural counseling competencies and standards (Sue & Sue, 1990; Sue, Arredondo, & McDavis, 1992) are available. Numerous sources of feminist perspectives on counseling women (e.g., Cook, 1993), the psychology of women (e.g., Jordan, Kaplan, Miller, Stiver, & Surrey, 1991; Kaschak, 1992), and feminist therapy (e.g., Enns, 1993) are also available. Our training must incorporate models of the development of sexual orientation and positive sexual identity—models based on the premise that gay, lesbian, and bisexual orientations are normal and healthy. Many more specific resources are provided at the end of each chapter in Part III.

While integration of numerous perspectives is essential in our work, it is important to recognize that we will always filter such perspectives through our own subjective experiences and understandings. We will always be plagued by one "ism" or another. For example, to adopt a feminist approach to therapy (recognizing that there is no single feminist approach) (Enns, 1993; Kaschak, 1981) may be to ignore the perspectives and concerns of women of color, since feminist approaches have emphasized the experiences of Euro American middle-class women (Espin, 1993). At the same time, adoption of a multicultural perspective (recognizing there is no single multicultural approach) risks perpetuating the sexism that permeates many cultural groups. The point of this "warning" is not to paint our endeavors as hopeless, but to emphasize that our need for critical self-examination is never-ending.

We can expect resistance to these training issues. The critical self-examination and reconceptualization of ourselves, our counseling, and our training will be painful for some, embarrassing for others, and complicated for everyone. One form of that resistance is articulated in reflections by Ahlquist (1991) and Tatum (1992) of their respective experiences teaching multicultural and race-relations courses. Each encountered resistance, anger, discouragement, and dismay en route to raising student awareness of the realities of racism and oppression in U.S. society. Other forms of resistance are epitomized in responses such as: "They already get that in their multicultural class"; "Why should we say Michelangelo was gay and Gertrude Stein was lesbian—we don't announce that everyone else is heterosexual"; "But we don't have an expert in that area"; or "They can take that as an elective if they are interested." In the most positive light, this resistance might be understood as a parallel to the "reintegration" phase of Helms's (1984; 1990) model of White identity development (see Chapter Two).

A final implication of counseling for empowerment bears on the research component of counselor training. Students should be able to identify the philosophical premises on which studies are based and to recognize the relationship among paradigms, the type of questions considered important, funding, and the conclusions drawn from particular studies. Responsibility to research participants should be emphasized, with participation yielding more than, "Thanks, you've contributed to the scientific enterprise, you ought to be really proud of yourself." Students should be able to identify biased or discriminatory research studies. An analysis of the power dynamics influencing research activity, such as paradigm shifting (Kuhn, 1970) and the psychology of science (Mahoney, 1979), would provide an excellent basis for critique. Finally, students should recognize the potential for research to support and facilitate the empowerment of participants; an excellent example of empowering research participation is offered by Morrow and Smith (in press).

EMPOWERING COUNSELORS AND OTHER MENTAL HEALTH PROFESSIONALS

Counselors and other mental health professionals are not an oppressed group in our society. Our training alone reflects the privilege of higher education. And yet, application of the empowerment framework to the mental health profession as a whole helps identify some important issues for consideration. For example, an analysis of power dynamics could illuminate the dual possiblilities of our professional role in society: as sanctioned oppressors who serve to maintain the status quo, or as active facilitators of personal and societal transformation. Our historic struggle for professional recognition and the ethnic and social class composition of mental health professionals form a part of the power dynamics that make the role of social change agent a radical—rather than a commonsensical or central—aspect of our current identity. National policy issues such as health care reform also shape aspects of our role in society. For example, if *all people* have access to mental health care, we will be hard put to convice anyone that our clients, rather than our methods, are unsuitable. These influences are joined by all those power dynamics influencing our personal lives and those of our clients. We might benefit from developing skills and strategies to initiate and support mental health legislation consistent with a philosophy of empowerment. Developing and exercising our collective voices at the national level will be an important part of keeping mental health care consistent with the needs of clients amidst reforms and funding shortages.

Membership in state, regional, and national professional organizations can provide a source of solidarity, support, and continued learning opportunities. For example, members of a national counseling organization participated in a cultural awareness tour to West Africa ("Reflections...," 1992). Ongoing contact with other mental health professionals also offers a rich source of encouragement and challenge, can help offset the stresses inherent in the work of counseling, and can be considered a form of self-care (Mahoney, 1991). Nonetheless, even our own organizations tend to reflect the hierarchies of our "ism"-bound society. Thus, the voices of counseling professionals of color may be ignored; consciousness-raising efforts of gay, lesbian, and bisexual counselors may be sidelined; and the inaccessibility or expense of professional conferences may prevent many otherwise interested professionals from attending. We have much work to do to bring our professional organizations in sync with an empowerment philosophy.

CONCLUSION

In the words of Chicana artist Gloria Anzaldua:

> *Nepantla* is the Nahuatl* word for an in-between state, that uncertain terrain one crosses when moving from one place to another, when

---

* Nahuatl is the language of the Aztec.

changing from one class, race or gender position to another, when traveling from the present identity into a new identity. The Mexican immigrant at the moment of crossing the barbed-wire fence into the hostile "paradise" of *el Norte*, the United States, is caught in a state of *nepantla*. Others who find themselves in this bewildering transitional space may be those people caught in the midst of denying their projected/assumed heterosexual identity and coming out, presenting and voicing their lesbian, gay, bi or transsexual selves. Crossing class lines—especially from working class to middle classness and privilege—can be just as disorienting. The marginalized, starving Chicana artist who suddenly finds her work exhibited in mainstream museums...for a time inhabits *nepantla*. (Anzaldua, 1993, p. 39)

Perhaps our work can be described as that of fellow travelers, companions, through the *nepantla* of our clients' lives. Sometimes we are called on to be guides, describing possible routes and their terrain, sometimes scouts, forewarning about dangers and difficulties ahead. Sometimes we are lost alongside our fellow travelers, and often we are led into new places, insights, and experiences by their wisdom. Even as we "teach" new skills, our fellow travelers shape and transform these skills into tools fit for their own life contexts, for crossing their personal *nepantla*. While we do not deny our own expertise and training, we recognize that these resources are not guaranteed to be helpful, and may indeed get in the way of accompanying our clients. Further, it is the blend of our expertise with that of our clients that supports empowerment. We have never traveled their roads.

While our accompaniment provides a source of encouragement and challenge, counseling for empowerment requires that we traverse our own *nepantla*, challenging those structures that oppress, and constructing and reconstructing our personal and professional roles within our particular societal context. Counseling for empowerment is a way of being and thinking as much as it is a way of "doing counseling." It is a commitment leading to endless challenges and frustrations. It is a commitment that demands the unlikely partnership of realism and hopefulness. But it is also a commitment that privileges us to witness and participate in the profoundest acts of human courage, and a commitment honoring all that humanity can become.

REFERENCES

Acquired Immunodeficiency Syndrome (AIDS) Weekly Surveillance Report, United States AIDS Activity. (1988, July 4). Atlanta, GA: Centers for Disease Control, Center for Infectious Disease.

Adelman, M. (Ed.) (1986). *Long time passing: Lives of older lesbians.* Boston: Alyson Publications.

Adelman, M. (1990). Stigma, gay lifestyles, and adjustment to aging: A study of later life gay men and lesbians. *Journal of Homosexuality, 20*(3/4), 7–32.

Agosta, C., & Loring, M. (1988). Understanding and treating the adult retrospective victim of child sexual abuse. In S. M. Sgroi (Ed.), *Vulnerable populations,* Vol. I, *Evaluation and treatment of sexually abused children and survivors* (pp. 114–135). Lexington, MA: Lexington Books.

Ahlquist, R. (1991). Position and imposition: Power relations in a multicultural foundations class. *Journal of Negro Education, 60*(2), 158–169.

Alan Guttmacher Institute. (1981). *Teenage pregnancy: The problem that hasn't gone away.* New York: Author.

American Association of Counseling and Development. (1988). *Ethical Standards.* Alexandria, VA: Author.

American Association of Retired Persons and the Administration on Aging. (1988). *A profile of older Americans.* Washington DC: Author.

American Association of University Women. (1989, June). *Equitable treatment of girls and boys in the classroom.* Washington, DC: Author.

American Association of University Women. (1990, August). *Restructuring education: Getting girls into America's goals.* Washington, DC: Author.

American Association of University Women. (1991). *Shortchanging girls, shortchanging America.* Washington, DC: Author.

American Counseling Association Ethics Committee. (1993). ACA proposed standards of practice and ethical standards. *Guidepost, 36*(4), 15–22.

American Psychiatric Association. (1987). *Diagnostic and statistical manual of mental disorders* (3rd ed., rev.). Washington, DC: Author.

American Psychological Association. (1993). Guidelines for providers of psychological services to ethnic, linguistic, and culturally diverse populations. *American Psychologist, 48*(1), 45–48.

Anderson, A. E., & Hay, A. (1985). Racial and socioeconomic influences in anorexia nervosa and bulimia. *International Journal of Eating Disorders, 4,* 479–487.

Angelou, M. (1980). *I know why the caged bird sings.* New York: Bantam Books.

Anzaldua, G. (1993). Chicana artists: Exploring nepantla, el lugar de la frontera. *NACLA Report on the Americas, 27*(1), 37–42.

Arbona, C. (1990). Career counseling research and Hispanics: A review of the literature. *The Counseling Psychologist, 18*(2), 300–323.

Asarnow, J. R., & Calan, J. R. (1985). Boys with peer adjustment problems: Social cognitive processes. *Journal of Consulting and Clinical Psychology, 53,* 80–87.

Astin, H. S. (1989, November). *Women and power: Collective and empowering leadership.* Paper presented at the annual meeting of the American Educational Research Association, San Diego, CA.

Atkinson, D. R., Morten, G., & Sue, D. W. (1979). *Counseling American minorities.* Dubuque, IA: W. C. Brown.

Baker, N. C. (1984). *The beauty trap.* London: Piatkus.

Balcazar, F. E., Seekins, T., Fawcett, S. B., & Hopkins, B. L. (1990). Empowering people with physical disabilities through advocacy skills training. *American Journal of Community Psychology, 18*(2), 281–296.

Bandura, A. (1977a). Self-efficacy: Toward a unifying theory of behavioral change. *Psychological Review, 84,* 191–215.

Bandura, A. (1977b). *Social learning theory.* Englewood Cliffs, NJ: Prentice-Hall.

Bandura, A. (1982). Self-efficacy mechanism in human agency. *American Psychologist, 37*(2), 122–147.

Banzhaf, M. D. (1993, Spring). Doin' it for themselves: How women deal with physicians. *Positively Aware,* 20.

Basow, S. A. (1991). The hairless ideal: Women and their body hair. *Psychology of Women Quarterly, 15,* 83–96.

Bass, E., & Davis, L. (1988). *The courage to heal: A guide for women survivors of child sexual abuse.* New York: Harper & Row.

Bass, S. A., Kutza, E. A., & Torres-Gil, F. M. (1990). *Diversity in aging.* Glenville, IL: Scott Foresman and Company.

Baum, A., & Nesselhof, S. E. A. (1988). Psychological research and the prevention, etiology, and treatment of AIDS. *American Psychologist, 43*(11), 900–906.

Bayer, R. (1981). *Homosexuality and American psychiatry.* New York: Basic Books.

Bear, E., with Dimock, P. (1988). *Adults molested as children: A survivor's manual for women and men.* Orwell, VT: Safer Society Press.

Beattie, M. (1989). *Beyond codependency and getting better all the time.* New York: HarperCollins.

Beit-Hallahmi, B. (1974). Salvation and its vicissitudes; clinical psychology and political values. *American Psychologist, 29,* 124–134.

Bersoff, D. N., & Ogden, D. W. (1991). APA amicus curiae briefs: Furthering lesbian and gay male civil rights. *American Psychologist, 46*(9), 950–956.

Betz, N. E., & Fitzgerald, L. (1987). *The career psychology of women.* San Francisco: Academic Press.

Beyth-Marom, R., Fischhoff, B., Jacobs, M., & Furby, L. (1989). *Teaching decision making to adolescents: A critical review.* Washington, DC: Carnegie Council on Adolescent Development.

Bialo, E. R., & Sivin, J. P. (1989). Computers and at-risk youth: A partial solution to a complex probelm. *Classroom Computer Learning, 9*(4), 34–39.

Birle, R. (1993, March). *Gay, lesbian and bisexual curriculum inclusion.* Paper presented at the Personal Growth Through Diversity conference of the Teachers College Equity Committee, University of Nebraska-Lincoln, Lincoln, NE.

Birren, J. E. (1964). *The psychology of aging*. Englewood Cliffs, NJ: Prentice-Hall.

Blair, G. (1992, April). Eat your heart out, Madonna: I may not have your perfect hard body, but I'm learning to love the way I look. *Self*, 138–139.

Bloom, L. Z., Coburn, K., & Pearlman, J. (1975). *The new assertive woman*. New York: Dell.

Boden, R. (1992). Psychotherapy with physically disabled lesbians. In S. H. Dworkin & F. J. Gutierrez (Eds.), *Counseling gay men and lesbians: Journey to the end of the rainbow* (pp. 157–174). Alexandria, VA: American Counseling Association.

Boland, M. L. (1992). "Mainstream" hatred. *The Police Chief, 59*, 30–32.

Bond, S., & Cash, T. F. (1992). Black beauty: Skin color and body images among African American college women. *Journal of Applied Social Psychology, 22*(11), 874–888.

Bowen, D. J., Tomoyasu, N., & Cauce, A. M. (1991). The triple threat: A discussion of gender, class, and race differences in weight. *Women & Health, 17*(4), 123–143.

Bowman, J. (1992, March). Empowering Black males through positive self-esteem. Paper presented at the annual convention of the American Association for Counseling and Development, Baltimore, MD.

Bradford, J., & Ryan, C. (1991). Who we are: Health concerns of middle-aged lesbians. In B. Sang, J. Warshow, & A. Smith (Eds.), *Lesbians at midlife: The creative transition* (pp. 147–163). San Francisco: Spinster.

Brant, B. (Ed.). (1984). *A Gathering of spirit: Writing and art by North American Indian women*. Rockland: Sinister Wisdom Books.

Brody, C. M. (1990). Women in a nursing home: Living with hope and meaning. *Psychology of Women Quarterly, 14*, 579–592.

Brown, L. M., & Gilligan, C. (1992). *Meeting at the crossroads: Women's psychology and girls' development*. Cambridge: Harvard University Press.

Brownmiller, S. (1975). *Against our will: Men, women, and rape*. New York: Bantam.

Buckley, W. F., Jr. (1986, March 18). Crucial steps in combating the AIDS epidemic: Identify all the carriers. *New York Times*, p. A27.

Buhrke, R. A. (1989). Incorporating lesbian and gay issues into counselor training: A resource guide. *Journal of Counseling and Development, 70*(1), 77–80.

Buriel, R. (1983). Teacher-student interactions and their relationship to student achievement: A comparison of Mexican-American and Anglo-American children. *Journal of Educational Psychology, 75*(6), 889–897.

Burrell, L. F. (1981). Is there a future for Black students on predominantly White campuses? *Integrateducation, 18*, 23–27.

Butler, R. N. (1963). The life review: An interpretation of reminiscence in the aged. *Psychiatry, 26*, 65–76.

Caldwell, J. (1988, August). *Organized hate crimes and anti-gay violence*. Paper presented at the annual convention of the American Psychological Association, Atlanta, GA.

Calyx Editorial Collective. (1986). *Women and aging: An anthology by women*. Corvallis: Calyx Books (P.O. Box B, Corvallis, OR 97339).

Cambridge Documentary Films. (1987). *Still killing us softly* [Film]. Cambridge, MA.

Cannella, D. (1992, January 12). Weighty obsession: Desire to be lean fattens industry coffers. *Arizona Republic,* A1.

Capuzzi, D., & Gross, D. (Eds.). (1989). *Youth at risk: A resource for counselors, teachers and parents.* Alexandria, VA: American Association of Counseling and Development.

Capuzzi, D., Gross, D., & Friel, S. E. (1990). Recent trends in group work with elders. *Generations, 14*(1), 43–48.

Carter, D. J., & Wilson, R. (1993). *Minorities in higher education.* Washington, DC: American Council on Education, Office of Minorities in Higher Education.

Casas, M. (1990, January). Respondent. In D. Brown (Co-chair), *Work in America: Report of the Gallup survey.* Symposium conducted at the annual meeting of the National Career Development Association, Scottsdale, AZ.

Cash, T. F., & Brown, T. A. (1989). Gender and body images: Stereotypes and realities. *Sex Roles, 5/6,* 361–373.

Cass, V. C. (1979). Homosexual identity formation: A theoretical model. *Journal of Homosexuality, 4,* 219–235.

Centers for Disease Control. (1988). Guidelines for effective school health education to prevent the spread of AIDS. *Morbidity and Mortality Weekly Report Supplement, 37,* 1–13.

Centers for Disease Control. (1992). *HIV/AIDS surveillance-United States. AIDS cases reported through December 1991.* Washington, DC: U.S. Department of Health and Human Services.

Chan, C. S. (1989). Issues of identity development among Asian-American lesbians and gay men. *Journal of Counseling and Development, 70*(1), 16–20.

Chan, C. S. (1992). Cultural considerations in counseling Asian-American lesbians and gay men. In S. H. Dworkin & F. J. Gutierrez (Eds.). *Counseling gay men and lesbians: Journey to the end of the rainbow* (pp. 115–124). Alexandria, VA: American Association of Counseling and Development.

Chan, F., Lam, C. S., Wong, D., Leung, P., & Fang, X. (1988). Counseling Chinese Americans with disabilities. *Journal of Applied Rehabilitation Counseling, 19*(4), 21–25.

Chavez, C. (1993, Spring). Starting off on the right foot: How to choose a physician. *Positively Aware,* 5.

Chernin, K. (1981). *The obsession: Reflections on the tyranny of slenderness.* New York: Harper & Row.

Chesler, M. A., & Chesney, B. K. (1988). Self-help groups: Empowerment attitudes and behaviors of disabled or chronically ill persons. In H. E. Yuker (Ed.). *Attitudes toward persons and disabilities* (pp. 230–271). New York: Springer.

Clark, D. (1977). *Loving someone gay.* New York: Signet.

Clark, P. G. (1989). The philosophical foundation of empowerment: Implications for geriatric health care programs and practice. *Journal of Aging and Health, 1*(2), 267–285.

Cochran, S. D., & Mays, V. M. (1991). Psychosocial HIV interventions in the second decade: A note on social support and social networks. *The Counseling Psychologist, 19*(4), 551–557.

Cochran, S. V., & Rabinowitz, F. E. (1983). An experiential men's group for the university community. *Journal of College Student Personnel, 24,* 163–164.

Cohen, C. J., & Stein, T. S. (1986). Reconceptualizing individual psychotherapy with gay men and lesbians. In T. S. Stein & C. J. Cohen (Eds.). *Contemporary perspectives on psychotherapy with lesbians and gay men* (pp. 27–54). New York: Plenum.

Coie, J., Dodge, K., Terry, R., & Wright, V. (1991). The role of aggression in peer relations: An analysis of aggression episodes in boys' play groups. *Child Development, 62,* 812–826.

Coll, R. (1986). Power, powerlessness and empowerment. *Religious Education, 81*(3), 412–423.

Comstock, G., & Strasburger, V. C. (1990). Deceptive appearances: Television violence and aggressive behavior. *Journal of Adolescent Health Care, 11*(1), 31–44.

Conrath, J. (1988). A new deal for at-risk students. *National Association of Secondary School Principals Bulletin, 72*(495), 36–40.

Cook, E. P. (Ed.). (1990). *Women, relationships, and power: Implications for counseling.* Alexandria, VA: American Counseling Association Press.

Corey, G., & Corey, M. S. (1991). Are your values showing? *Guidepost, 34*(7), 24.

Cosmetic surgery: The price of beauty. (1992). *The Economist, 322,* 25–26.

Crocker, J., & Major, B. (1989). Social stigma and self-esteem: The self-protective properties of stigma. *Psychological Review, 96,* 608–630.

Cross, W. E., Jr. (1971). The Negro-to-Black conversion experience: Towards a psychology of Black liberation. *Black World, 20,* 13–27.

Croteau, J. M., & Morgan, S. (1989). Combating homophobia in AIDS education. *Journal of Counseling and Development, 68*(1), 86–91.

Cummins, J. (1986). Empowering minority students: A framework for intervention. *Harvard Educational Review, 56*(1), 19–36.

Damron-Rodriguez, J. (1991). Commentary: Multicultural aspects of aging in the U.S.: Implications for health and human services. *Journal of Cross Cultural Gerontology, 6*(3), 135–143.

D'Andrea, M. (1992). The violence of our silence: Some thoughts about racism, counseling and development. *Guidepost, 35*(4), 31.

D'Andrea, M., & Daniels, J. (1991). Exploring the different levels of multicultural counseling training in counselor education. *Journal of Counseling and Development, 70*(1), 78–85.

Daniel, S. P. (1991). Letter to the editor. *Monitor, 22*(12), 4.

Davenport, D. S., & Yurich, J. M. (1991). Multicultural gender issues. *Journal of Counseling and Development, 70*(1), 64–71.

Davis, L. (1990). *The courage to heal workbook: For women and men survivors of child sexual abuse.* New York: Harper & Row.

Davis, R. A. (1988). Adolescent pregnancy and infant mortality: Isolating the effects of race. *Adolescence, 23*(92), 899–908.

DeAngelis, T. (1992). Kentucky high court repeals sodomy law. *Monitor, 23*(12), 1.

DeCecco, J. P. (1981). Definition and meaning of sexual orientation. *Journal of Homosexuality, 6,* 51–69.

DeMarsh, J., & Kumpfer, K. L. (1986). Family-oriented interventions for the prevention of chemical dependency in children and adolescents. *Childhood and Chemical Abuse, 18*(1-2), 117–151.

Dembo, R., Blount, W. R., Schmeider, J., & Burgos, W. (1985). Methodological and substantive issues involved in using the concept of risk in research into the etiology of drug use among adolescents. *Journal of Drug Issues, 15*, 537–553.

Desmond et al. (1989). Black and white adolescents' perceptions of their weight. *Journal of School Health, 59*, 353–358.

Douglas, M. A. (1985). The role of power in feminist therapy: A reformulation. In L. B. Rosewater & L. E. A. Walker (Eds.). *Handbook of feminist therapy* (pp. 241–249). New York: Springer.

Downing, N. E., & Roush, K. L. (1985). From passive acceptance to active commitment: A model of feminist identity development for women. *The Counseling Psychologist, 13*(4), 695–709.

Duffy, Y. (1981). *All things are possible*. Ann Arbor: A. J. Garvin and Associates.

Dull, D., & West, C. (1991). Accounting for cosmetic surgery: The accomplishment of gender. *Social Problems, 38*(1), 54–69.

Dworkin, S. H., & Gutiérrez, F. J. (Eds.). (1989). Special issue: Gay, lesbian, and bisexual issues in counseling. *Journal of Counseling and Development, 68*(1).

Dworkin, S. H., & Gutiérrez, F. J. (Eds.). (1992). *Counseling gay men and lesbians: Journey to the end of the rainbow*. Alexandria, VA: American Association of Counseling and Development.

Eccles, J. S., & Midgley, C. (1989). Stage/environment fit: Developmentally appropriate classrooms for early adolescents. In R. E. Ames & C. Ames (Eds.). *Research on motivation in education* (Vol. 3, pp. 139–186). San Diego, CA: Academic Press.

Eccles, J. S., & Midgley, C., & Adler, T. (1984). Grade-related changes in the school environment: Effects on achievement motivation. In J. G. Nicholls (Ed.). *The development of achievement motivation* (pp. 283–331). Greenwich, CT: JAI Press.

Eccles, J. S., Midgley, C., Wigfield, A., Buchanan, C. M., Reuman, D., Flanagan, C., & MacIver, D. (1993). Development during adolescence: The impact of stage environment fit on young adolescents' experiences in schools and in families. *American Psychologist, 48*(2), 90–101.

Ellis, A. (1973). *Humanistic psychotherapy*. New York: McGraw-Hill Book Company.

English, M. D. (1987). Life review and its utilization with the elderly. Unpublished master's thesis, Arizona State University, Tempe, AZ.

Enns, C. Z. (1993). Twenty years of feminist counseling and therapy: From naming biases to implementing multifaceted practice. *The Counseling Psychologist, 21*(1), 3–87.

Erickson, V. L. (1978). The development of women: An issue of justice. In P. Scarf (Ed.). *Readings in moral education* (pp. 110–122). Minneapolis: Winston Press.

Espin, O. (1987). Issues of identity in the psychology of Latina lesbians. In Boston Lesbian Psychologies Collective (Ed.). *Lesbian psychologies: Explanations and challenges*. Urbana, IL: University of Illinois Press.

Espin, O. (1993). Feminist therapy: Not for or by White women only. *The Counseling Psychologist, 21*(1), 103–108.

Evert, K., & Bijkerk, I. (1988). *When you're ready: A woman's healing from childhood physical and sexual abuse by her mother*. Walnut Creek, CA: Launch Press.

Family Research Newsletter. (1987, September/October). (Available from Family Research, P.O. Box 6725, Lincoln NE 68506.)

Feingold, A. (1992). Good-looking people are not what we think. *Psychological Bulletin, 111*, 304–341.

Fertman, C. I., & Long, J. A. (1990). All students are leaders. *The School Counselor, 37*, 391–396.

Fetzer, J. N., Solt, P. F., & McKinney, S. (1985). Typology of food preferences identified by Nutri-Food sort. *Journal of the American Dietetic Association, 85*(8), 961–965.

Figley, C. R. (1985). Introduction. In C. R. Figley (Ed.). *Trauma and its wake: The study and treatment of post-traumatic stress disorder* (pp. xvii–xxvi). New York: Brunner/Mazel.

Fine, M., & Asch, A. (1988). Disability beyond stigma: Social interaction, discrimination, and activism. *Journal of Social Issues, 44*(1), 3–21.

Fingerhut, L., Ingram, D., & Feldman, J. (1992). Firearm and nonfirearm homicide among persons 15 through 19 years of age. *Journal of the American Medical Association, 267*, 3048–3053.

Finn, P., & McNeil, T. (1987, October 7). *The response of the criminal justice system to bias crime: An exploratory review.* Contract report submitted to the National Institute of Justice, U.S. Department of Justice. (Available from Abt Associates, Inc., 55 Wheeler Street, Cambridge, MA 02138-1168.)

Fisher, J. D. (1988). Possible effects of reference group-based social influence on AIDS-risk behavior and AIDS prevention. *American Psychologist, 43*(11), 914–920.

Fowler, C. A. & Wadsworth, J. S. (1991). Individualism and equality: Critical values in North American culture and the impact on disability. *Journal of Applied Rehabilitation Counseling, 22*(4), 19–23.

Franzoi, S. L. (1992, August). Body esteem: Gender and gender role considerations. Paper presented at the annual convention of the American Psychological Association, Washington, DC.

Freiberg, P. (1990, July). Sullivan is criticized by APA over report. *Monitor,* 41.

Freire, P. (1971). *Pedagogy of the oppressed.* New York: Herder and Herder.

Friedlob, S. A., & Kelly, J. J. (1984). Reminiscing groups in board-and-care homes. In I. Burnside (Ed.). *Working with the elderly: Group process and techniques* (2nd ed.) (pp. 308–337). Monterey, CA: Wadsworth Health Sciences Division.

Friedrich-Cofer, L., & Huston, A. C. (1986). Television violence and aggression: The debate continues. *Psychological Bulletin, 100*(3), 364–371.

Friend, R. (1987). The individual and social psychology of aging: Clinical implications for lesbians and gay men. *Journal of Homosexuality, 14*, 307–331.

Friend, R. (1990). Lesbian and gay people: A theory of successful aging. *Journal of Homosexuality, 20*(3/4), 77–87.

Frigo, M. A., Zones, J. S., Beeson, D. R., Rutherford, G. W. Echenberg, D. F., & O'Malley, P. M. (1986). The impact of structured counseling in acute adverse psychiatric reactions associated with LAV/HTLV-III antibody testing (Abstract 284). *Proceedings of the 114th Annual Meeting of the American Public Health Association.* Las Vegas, NV.

Furnham, A., & Alibhai, N. (1983). Cross-cultural differences in the perception of female body shapes. *Psychological Medicine, 13*, 829–837.

Fusfeld, D., & Bates, T. (1984). *The political economy of the urban ghetto.* Carbondale: Southern Illinois University Press.

Gannon, L. (1982). The role of power in psychotherapy. *Women & Therapy, 1*(2), 3–11.

Garb, J. L., Garb, J. R., & Stunkard, A. J. (1975). Social factors and obesity in Navajo children. In A. Howard (Ed.). *Recent Advances in obesity research* (pp. 27–39). London: Newman.

Gardner, S. E. (1992). A feminist perspective on the psychology of shame. Unpublished doctoral dissertation, University of Denver Professional School of Psychology.

Garner, D. M., Garfinkel, P. E., Schwartz, D., & Thompson, M. (1980). Cultural expectations of thinness in women. *Psychological Reports, 47*, 483–491.

Garnets, L., Hancock, K. A., Cochran, S. D., Goodchilds, J., & Peplau, L. A. (1991). Issues in psychotherapy with lesbians and gay men: A survey of psychologists. *American Psychologist, 46*(9), 964–972.

Garnets, L., Herek, G. M., & Levy, B. (1990). Violence and victimization of lesbians and gay men: Mental health consequences. *Journal of Interpersonal Violence, 5*(3), 366–383.

Getzel, G. S. (1991). Survival modes for people with AIDS in groups. *Social Work, 36*(1), 7–10.

Giarusso, R., Johnson, P., Goodchilds, J., & Zellman, G., (1979, April). Adolescents' cues and signals: Sex and assault. Paper presented at the convention of the Western Psychological Association, San Diego, CA.

Gibson, C. H. (1991). A concept analysis of empowerment. *Journal of Advanced Nursing, 16*, 354–361.

Gilbert, L. A. (1980). Feminist therapy. In A. M. Brodsky & R. Hare-Mustin (Eds.). *Women and psychotherapy: An assessment of research and practice* (pp. 245–266). New York: Guilford Press.

Gilligan, C. (1982). *In a different voice.* Cambridge: Harvard University Press.

Glassgold, J. M. (1992). New directions in dynamic theories of lesbianism: From psychoanalysis to social constructionism. In J. C. Chrisler & D. Howard (Eds.). *New directions in feminist psychology: Practice, theory, and research* (pp. 154–164). New York: Springer.

Gleghorn, A. A., Kilbourn, K. M., Celentano, D. D., & Jemmott, J. B. (1993, August). "Magic" Johnson's HIV status: Impact on African American STD patients. Paper presented at the Annual Convention of the American Psychological Association, Toronto, Ontario, Canada.

Goldstein, A. P., Keller, H., & Erne, D. (1985). *Changing the abusive parent.* Champaign, IL: Research Press.

Gonsiorek, J. C. (1982). Results of psychological testing on homosexual populations. *American Behavioral Scientist, 25*, 385–396.

Gonsiorek, J. C. (1988). Mental health issues of gay and lesbian adolescents. *Journal of Adolescent Health Care, 9*, 114–122.

Gonsiorek, J. C., & Weinrich, J. D. (1991). *Homosexuality: Social psychological, and biological Issues* (2nd ed.). Newbury Park, CA: Sage.

Good, G. E., Gilbert, L. A., & Scher, M. (1990). Gender Aware Therapy: A synthesis of feminist therapy and knowledge about gender. *Journal of Counseling and Development, 68*(4), 376–380.

Goodman, L. V. (Ed.). (1987). *The education almanac, 1987–1988.* Alexandria, VA: National Association of Elementary School Principals.

Goodman, L. A., Koss, M. P., & Russo, N. F. (1993). Violence against women: Mental health effects. Part II. Conceptualizations of posttraumatic stress. *Applied & Preventive Psychology, 2*(3), 123–130.

Gordon, T. (1975). *P.E.T.: Parent effectiveness training.* New York: American Library.

Gordon, T. (1977). Parent effectiveness training: A preventive program and its delivery system. In G. W. Albee & J. M. Joffe (Eds.). *Primary prevention of psychopathology.* Hanover, NH: University Press of New England.

Grauman, C. F. (1970). Conflicting and convergent trends in psychological theory. *Journal of Phenomenological Psychology, 1,* 51–61.

Gray, R. E., & Doan, B. D. (1990). Empowerment and persons with cancer: Politics in cancer medicine. *Journal of Palliative Care, 6*(2), 33–45.

Green, R. (1989). AIDS and the duty to warn: Ethical and legal factors. In C. D. Kain (Ed.). *No longer immune: A counselor's guide to AIDS* (pp. 251–262). Alexandria, VA: American Association of Counseling and Development.

Greenwood, S. (1985). *Menopause naturally: Preparing for the second half of life.* San Francisco: Volcano Press (330 Ellis St., San Francisco, CA 94102).

Gross, D. (1988). Counseling and the elderly: Strategies, procedures and recommendations. *Counseling and Human Development.* Denver, CO: Love Publishing.

Gross, D. R., & Capuzzi, D. (1991). Counseling the older adult. In D. Capuzzi and D.R. Gross (Eds.). *Introduction to counseling: Persopectives for the 1990's* (pp. 299–319). Boston: Allyn and Bacon.

Gross, L., Aurand, S. K., & Addessa, R. (1988). *Violence and discrimination against lesbian and gay people in Philadelphia and the Commonwealth of Pennsylvania.* Philadelphia: Philadelphia Lesbian and Gay Task Force.

Gruber, J., & Trickett, E. J. (1987). Can we empower others? The paradox of empowerment in the governing of an alternative public school. *American Journal of Community Psychology, 15*(3), 353–371.

Guinan, M. E., & Hardy, A. (1987). Epidemiology of AIDS in women in the United States: 1981 through 1986. *Journal of the American Medical Association, 257,* 2039–2042.

Gutiérrez, L. (1988, August). *Culture and consciousness in the Chicano community: An empowerment perspective.* Paper presented at the annual convention of the American Psychological Association, Atlanta, GA.

Gutiérrez, L. (1990, August). *Empowerment in the Hispanic community: Does consciousness make a difference?.* Paper presented at the annual convention of the American Psychological Association, Boston, MA.

Gutiérrez, S. J., & Dworkin, S. H. (1992). Gay, lesbian, and African American: Managing the integration of identities. In S. H. Dworkin & F. J. Gutiérrez (Eds.). *Counseling gay men and lesbians: Journey to the end of the rainbow* (pp. 141–156). Alexandria, VA: American Association of Counseling and Development.

Hagberg, J. (1984). *Real Power*. Minneapolis: Winston.

Hahn, H. (1988). The politics of physical differences: Disability and discrimination. *Journal of Social Issues, 44*(1), 39–47.

Hall, M. (1985). *The lavender couch: A consumer's guide to psychotherapy for lesbians and gay men*. Boston: Alyson Publications.

Hall, M., & Allen, W. R. (1983). Race consciousness and achievement: Two issues on the study of Black graduate/professional students. *Integrateducation, 20*, 56–61.

Hambright, J. E. (1988). Effects of perceived life options on female adolescent sexual responsibility: A test of a conceptual model. Unpublished dissertation study, Arizona State University, Tempe.

Harris, L., and Associates. (1981). *Aging in the eighties: American in transition*. Washington, DC: National Council on Aging.

Harris, M. B. (1992). Television viewing, aggression, and ethnicity. *Psychological Reports, 70*(1), 137–138.

Hately, B. J. (1985). Telling your story, exploring your faith. St. Louis: CBP Press.

Hawxhurst, D. M., & Morrow, S. L. (1984). *Living our visions: Building feminist community*. Tempe, AZ: Fourth World.

Hayes, S. (1991). Financial planning for retirement. In B. Sang, J. Warshow, & A. Smith (Eds.). *Lesbians at midlife: The creative transition* (pp. 122–133). San Francisco: Spinster.

Hayes, R. L., & Cryer, N. (1988). When adolescents give birth to children: A developmental approach to the issue of teen preganancy. In J. Carlson & J. Lewis (Eds.). *Counseling the adolescent: Individual, family, and school interventions* (pp. 21–39). Denver: Love.

Hazuda, H. P., Haffner, S. M., Stern, M. P., & Eifler, C. W. (1988). Effects of acculturation and socioeconomic status on obesity and diabetes in Mexican Americans: The San Antonio Heart Study. *American Journal of Epidemiology, 128*(6), 1289–1301.

Helms, J. E. (1984). Toward a theoretical explanation of the effects of race on counseling: A Black and White model. *The Counseling Psychologist, 12*(4), 153–165.

Helms, J. E. (Ed.). (1990). *Black and White racial identity attitudes: Theory, research, and practice*. Westport, CT: Greenwood.

Helms, J. E. (1993, September). *Constructing scales for assessing racial identity stages*. Paper presented at the Multicultural Assessment Symposium of the Buros Institute of Mental Measurements, Lincoln, NE.

Herdt, G. (1989). Gay and lesbian youth: Emergent identities and cultural scenes at home and abroad. *Journal of Homosexuality, 17*(1/2), 1–42.

Herek, G. M. (1988). Hate crimes against lesbians and gay men: Issues for research and policy. *American Psychologist, 44*(6), 948–955.

Herek, G. M., & Glunt, E. K. (1988). An epidemic of stigma: Public reactions to AIDS. *American Psychologist, 43*(11), 886–891.

Herman, J. L. (1981). *Father-daughter incest*. Cambridge: Harvard University Press.

Herzog, D. B., & Copeland, P. M. (1985). Eating disorders. *New England Journal of Medicine, 313*, 295–303.

Hetherington, C., & Orzek, A. (1989). Career counseling and life planning with lesbian women. *Journal of Counseling and Development, 68*(1), 52–57.

Hetrick, E. S. (1988). The stigmatization of the gay and lesbian adolescent. *Journal of Homosexuality, 15*(1/2), 163–183.

Hetrick, E. S., & Martin, A. D. (1987). Developmental issues and their resolution for gay and lesbian adolescents. *Journal of Homosexuality, 14*(1/2), 25–43.

Hill, L. (1992). Fairy tales: Visions for problem resolution in eating disorders. *Journal of Counseling and Development, 70*(5), 584–587.

Hobus, R. (1992). Literature: A dimension of nursing therapeutics. In J. F. Miller (Ed.). *Coping with chronic illness: Overcoming powerlessness* (2nd ed.). Philadelphia: F.A. Davis Company.

Hofferth, S. L., & Hayes, C. D. (Eds.). (1987). *Risking the future* (Vol. 2). Washington, DC: National Academy Press.

Hooper, M. S. H., & Garner, D. M. (1986). Application of the Eating Disorders Inventory to a sample of Black, White and mixed-race school-girls in Zimbabwe. *International Journal of Eating Disorders, 5*, 161–168.

Horowitz, F. D., & O'Brien, M. (1989). In the interest of the nation: A reflective essay on the state of knowledge and the challenges before us. *American Psychologist, 44*(2), 441–445.

House, R. M., & Holloway, E. L. (1992). Empowering the counseling professional to work with gay and lesbian issues. In S. H. Dworkin & F. J. Gutiérrez (Eds.). *Counseling gay men and lesbians: Journey to the end of the rainbow* (pp. 307–324). Alexandria, VA: American Association of Counseling and Development.

Howard, G. S. (1985). Can research in the human sciences become more relevant to practice? *Journal of Counseling and Development, 63*(9), 539–544.

Hsu, L. K. G. (1987). Are the eating disorders becoming more common in blacks? *International Journal of Eating Disorders, 5*(1), 101–112.

Huang, L. N. (1989). Southeast Asian refugee children and adolescents. In J. T. Gibbs & L. N. Huang (Eds.). *Children of color: Psychological interventions with minority children*. San Francisco: Jossey-Bass.

Huenemann et al. (1966). A longitudinal study of gross body composition and body conformations and their association with food and activity in a teenage population: View of teenage subjects on body conformation, food, and activity. *American Journal of Clinical Nutrition, 18*, 325–338.

Hutchinson, M. G. (1985). *Transforming body image*. New York: Crossing Press.

Iasenza, S. (1989). Some challenges of integrating sexual orientations into counselor training and research. *Journal of Counseling and Development, 68*(1), 73–76.

Icard, L. (1986). Black gay men and conflicting social identities: Sexual orientation versus racial identity. In J. Gripton & M. Valentich (Eds.). [Special issue of the *Journal of Social Work & Human Sexuality, 4*(1/2)] *Social work practice in sexual problems* (pp. 83–93). New York, London: Haworth.

Jackson, L. A. (1992). *Physical appearance and gender: Sociobiological and sociocultural perspectives*. Albany, NY: State University of New York Press.

Jackson, M. L. (1991). Counseling Arab Americans. In C. C. Lee & B. L. Richardson (Eds.). *Multicultural issues in counseling: New approaches to diver-*

sity (pp. 197–208). Alexandria, VA: American Association of Counseling and Development Press.

Janoff-Bulman, R. (1985). The aftermath of victimization: Rebuilding shattered assumptions. In C. R. Figley (Ed.). *Trauma and its wake: The study and treatment of post-traumatic stress disorder*, (pp. 15–35). New York: Brunner/ Mazel.

Jennings, C. (1988). *Understanding and preventing AIDS: A book for everyone.* Cambridge, MA: Health Alert Pess.

Jessor, L. C., & Jessor, S. L. (1977). *Problem behavior and psychosocial development: A longitudinal study of youth.* New York: Academic Press.

Jones, P. S., & Meleis, A. I. (1993). Health is empowerment. *Advanced Nursing Science, 15*(3), 1–14.

Jordan, I. K. (1992, August). A place in the sun: Psychology, deafness, and Americans with disabilities. Paper presented at the annual convention of the American Psychological Association, Washington, DC.

Jordan, J. M. (1991). Counseling African American women: "Sister-friends." In C. C. Lee & B. L. Richardson (Eds.). *Multicultural issues in counseling: New approaches to diversity* (pp. 51–64). Alexandria, VA: American Association of Counseling and Development.

Jordan, J. V., Kaplan, A. G., Miller, J. B., Stiver, I. P., & Surrey, J. L. (Eds.). (1991). *Women's growth in connection: Writings from the Stone Center.* New York: Guilford Press.

Kahn, A., & Bender, E. I. (1985). Self-help groups as a crucible for people empowerment in the context of social development. *Social Development Issues, 9*(2), 4–13.

Kain, C. D. (1989). *No longer immune: A counselor's guide to AIDS.* Alexandria, VA: American Association of Counseling and Development.

Kaschak, E. (1981). Feminist psychotherapy: The first decade. In S. Cox (Ed.). *Female psychology: The emerging self* (pp. 387–401). New York: St. Martin's Press.

Kaschak, E. (1992). *Engendered lives.* New York: Basic Books.

Katz, A. H., & Bender, E. I. (1976). *The strength in us: Self-help groups in the modern world.* New York: New Viewpoints.

Katz, J. (1976). *Gay American history: Lesbians and gay men in the U.S.A.: A documentary.* New York: Avon.

Katz, J. (1983). *Gay/lesbian almanac.* New York: Harper & Row.

Katz, J. (1985). The sociopolitical nature of counseling. *The Counseling Psychologist, 13*(4), 615–623.

Katz, J., & Ivey, A. (1977). White awareness: The frontier of racism awareness training. *Personnel and Guidance Journal, 55*, 485–489.

Kaufman, L. (1980). Prime-time nutrition. *Journal of Communication, 30*(3), 37–46.

Keeling, R. K. (1993). HIV disease: Current concepts. *Journal of Counseling and Development, 71*(3), 261–274.

Kelson, T. R., Kearney-Cooke, A., & Lansky, L. M. (1990). Body-image and body-beautification among female college students. *Perceptual and Motor Skills, 71*, 281–289.

Kiecolt-Glaser, J. K., & Glaser, R. (1988). Psychological influences on immunity: Implications for AIDS. *American Psychologist, 43*(11), 892–898.

Kieffer, C. H. (1984). Citizen empowerment: A developmental perspective. *Prevention in Human Services, 3*(2/3), 9–30.

Kim, J. (1988, July 3). Are homosexuals facing an ever more hostile world? *The New York Times*, p. E16.

Kimmich, M. H. (1985). *America's children: Who cares? Growing need and declining assistance in the Reagan era.* Washington, DC: Urban Institute.

Klebanoff, S. J. (1987). Psychological correlates of height. Unpublished doctoral dissertation, New York University.

Klein, F. (1982, December). Are you sure you're heterosexual? Or homosexual? Or even bisexual? *Forum Magazine*, 41–45.

Klein, F., & Wolf, T. (Eds.). (1985). *Bisexualities: Theory and research.* New York: Haworth.

Knox, M. D. (1989). Community mental health's role in the AIDS crisis. *Community Mental Health Journal, 25*(3), 185–196.

Kopp, J. (1989). Self-observation: An empowerment strategy in assessment. *Social Casework: The Journal of Contemporary Social Work, 70*(5), 276–284.

Koss, M. P., & Dinero, T. E. (1989). A discriminant analysis of risk factors for rape among a national sample of college women. *Journal of Consulting and Clinical Psychology, 57*, 242–250.

Kozol, J. (1991). *Savage inequalities: Children in America's schools.* New York: Crown Publishers, Inc.

Kramer, B. J. (1991). Urban American Indian aging. *Journal of Cross Cultural Gerontology, 6*(3), 205–217.

Kristal, A. (1986). The impact of the Acquired Immunodeficiency Syndrome on patterns of premature death in New York City. *Journal of the American Medical Association, 255*, 2306–2310.

Kubler-Ross, E. (1969). *On death and dying.* New York: Macmillan.

Kuhn, T. S. (1970). *The structure of scientific revolutions* (2nd ed.). Chicago: The University of Chicago Press.

La Fromboise, T. D. (1988). American Indian mental health policy. *American Psychologist, 43*(5), 388–397.

Laidlaw, T. A. (1990). Dispelling the myths: A workshop on compulsive eating and body image. In T. A. Laidlaw & C. Malmo (Eds.). *Healing voices: Feminist approaches to therapy with women.* San Francisco: Jossey-Bass.

Lakoff, R. T., & Scherr, R. L. (1984). *Face value: The politics of beauty.* London: Routledge and Kegan Paul.

Lane, P. S., & McWhirter, J. J. (in press). A peer mediation model: Conflict resolution for elementary and middle school children. *Elementary School Guidance and Counseling.*

Lawton, M. P. (1990). Residential environment and self-directedness among older people. *American Psychologist, 45*(5), 638–640.

Lee, C. C. (1991a). Empowerment in counseling: A multicultural perspective. *Journal of Counseling and Development, 69*(3), 229–230.

Lee, C. C. (1991b). Cultural dynamics: Their importance in multicultural counseling. In C. C. Lee & B. L. Richardson (Eds.). *Multicultural issues in counseling: New approaches to diversity* (pp. 11–22). Alexandria, VA: American Association for Counseling and Development.

Lee, J. C., & Cynn, V. E. H. (1991). Issues in counseling 1.5 generation Korean Americans. In C. C. Lee & B. L. Richardson (Eds.). *Multicultural issues in counseling: New approaches to diversity*, (pp. 127–142). Alexandria, VA: American Association for Counseling and Development Press.

Lee, C. C., & Richardson, B. L. (Eds.). (1991). *Multicultural issues in counseling: New approaches to diversity*. Alexandria, VA: American Counseling Association Press.

Lerner, H. G. (1989). *The dance of intimacy*. New York: Harper & Row.

Levering, C. S. (1983, January/February). Teenage pregnancy and parenthood. *Childhood Education*, 182–185.

Lew, M. (1990). *Victims no longer: Men recovering from incest and other sexual child abuse*. New York: Harper & Row.

Lichtenberg, J. W. (1985). Free will and determinism: A story. *Journal of Counseling and Development*, 63(9), 583–584.

Lieberman, M. (1992). Preventing hate crime: New tools, new expectations for law enforcement. *The Police Chief*, 59, 33–35.

Loiacano, D. K. (1989). Gay identity issues among Black Americans: Racism, homophobia, and the need for validation. *Journal of Counseling and Development*, 68(1), 21–25.

Lombana, J. H. (1989). Counseling persons with disabilities: Summary and projections. *Journal of Counseling and Development*, 68(2), 177–179.

Lukesch, H. (1989). Video violence and aggression. *German Journal of Psychology*, 13(4), 293–300.

Mahoney, M. J. (1979). *Scientist as subject: The psychological imperative*. Cambridge, MA: Ballinger.

Mahoney, M. J. (1991). *Human change processes: The scientific foundations of psychotherapy*. New York: Basic Books.

Malamuth, N. M. (1981). Rape proclivity among men. *Journal of Social Issues*, 37(4), 138–157.

Marshall, C. A., Martin, W. E., Jr., Thomason, T. C., & Johnson, M. J. (1991). Multiculturalism and rehabilitation counselor training: Recommendations for providing culturally appropriate counseling services to American Indians with disabilities. *Journal of Counseling and Development*, 70(1), 225–234.

Martel, L. F. (1985). Short stature in Caucasian males: Personality correlates and social attribution. Unpublished doctoral dissertation, University of Rhode Island.

Martin, D. J. (1989). Human immunodeficiency virus infection and the gay community: Counseling and clinical issues. *Journal of Counseling and Development*, 68(1), 67–72.

Martin, A. D., & Hetrick, E. S. (1988). The stigmatization of the gay and lesbian adolescent. *Journal of Homosexuality*, 15(1/2), 163–183.

Matsuoka, J. K. (1990). Differential acculturation among Vietnamese refugees. *Social Work*, 35(4), 341–345.

May, R. (1972). *Power and innocence*. New York: W.W. Norton.

Mays, V. M., & Cochran, S. D. (1988). Issues in the perception of AIDS risk and risk reduction activities by Black and Hispanic/Latina women. *American Psychologist*, 43(11), 949–957.

McCann, I. L., & Pearlman, L. A. (1990). Vicarious traumatization: A framework for understanding the psychological effects of working with victims. *Journal of Traumatic Stress, 3*(1), 131–145.

McCann, I. L., Pearlman, L. A., & Abrahamson, D. J. (1988, August). Understanding variations in victim experiences: A framework for traumatic stress. Paper presented at the convention of the American Psychological Association, Atlanta, GA.

McCarty, T. L., Lynch, R. H., Wallace, S., & Benally, A. (1991). Classroom inquiry and Navajo learning styles: A call for reassessment. *Anthropology & Education Quarterly, 22,* 42–59.

McDermott, C. J. (1989). Empowering the elderly nursing home resident: The resident rights campaign. *Social Work, 35*(2), 155–157.

McKay, M., & Fanning, P. (1987). *Self-esteem.* New York: St. Martin's Press.

McWhirter, B. T., McWhirter, E. H., & McWhirter, J. J. (1988). Groups in Latin America: *Comunidades eclesial de base* as mutual support groups. *The Journal for Specialists in Group Work, 13*(2), 70–76.

McWhirter, E. H. (1991). Empowerment in counseling. *Journal of Counseling and Development, 69*(3), 222–227.

McWhirter, E. H. (1992). A test of a model of the career commitment and aspirations of Mexican American high school girls. Unpublished doctoral dissertation, Arizona State University, Tempe.

McWhirter, E. H., & Linzer, M. (in press). The provision of critical incident stress debriefing services by EAPs: A case study. *Journal of Mental Health Counseling.*

McWhirter, J. J., McWhirter, B. T., McWhirter, A. M., & McWhirter, E. H. (1993). *At-risk youth: A comprehensive response.* Pacific Grove, CA: Brooks/Cole.

Melchert, T., & Burnett, K. F. (1990). Attitudes, knowledge, and sexual behavior of high-risk adolescents: Implications for counseling and sexuality education. *Journal of Counseling and Development, 68*(3), 293–298.

Melton, G. B. (1991). Ethical judgements amid uncertainty: Dilemmas in the AIDS epidemic. *The Counseling Psychologist, 19*(4), 561–565.

Melton, G. B., & Gray, J. N. (1988). Ethical dilemmas in AIDS research: Individual privacy and public health. *American Psychologist, 43,* 60–64.

Messner, S. F. (1986). Television violence and violent crime: An aggregate analysis. *Social Problems, 33*(3), 218–235.

Miller, C. T., & Rothblum, E. D. (1992, August). Compensating for prejudice against fat people. Paper presented at the annual convention of the American Psychological Association, Washington, DC.

Miller, E. K., & Miller, K. A. (1983). Adolescent pregnancy: A model for intervention. *Personnel & Guidance Journal, 62*(1), 15–20.

Miller, J. F. (1992a). Patient power resources. In J. F. Miller (Ed.). *Coping with chronic illness: Overcoming powerlessness* (2nd ed.). (pp. 3–18). Philadelphia: F.A. Davis Company.

Miller, J. F. (Ed.). (1992b). *Coping with chronic illness: Overcoming powerlessness* (2nd ed.). Philadelphia: F.A. Davis Company.

Miller, J. F., & Oertel, C. B. (1992). Powerlessness in the elderly: Preventing hopelessness. In J. F. Miller (Ed.). *Coping with chronic illness: Overcoming powerlessness* (2nd ed.) (pp. 135–160). Philadelphia: F.A. Davis Company.

Miller, V. (Ed.). (1985). *Despite this flesh: The disabled in stories and poems*. Austin: The University of Texas Press.

Mintz, L. B. , & Wright, D. M. (1993). Women and their bodies: Eating disorders and addictions. In E. P. Cook (Ed.). *Women, relationships, and power: Implications for counseling*. Alexandria, VA: American Counseling Association Press.

Minuchin, S. (1974). *Families and family therapy*. Cambridge, MA: Harvard University Press.

Miranda, J., & Storms, M. (1989). Psychological adjustment of lesbians and gay men. *Journal of Counseling and Development, 68*(1), 41–45.

Mishkind, M. E., Rodin, J., Silberstein, L. R., & Striegel-Moore, R. H. (1986). The embodiment of masculinity: Cultural, psychological, and behavioral dimensions. *American Behavioral Scientist, 29*(5), 545–562.

Mitchell, W. E. (1992). Psychotherapy for bulimia from a feminist perspective. In J. C. Chrisler & D. Howard (Eds.). *New directions in feminist psychology: Practice, theory, and research*. New York: Springer.

Montagu, A. (1972). *Statement on race*. New York: Oxford Press.

Montagu, A. (1974). *Man's most dangerous myth: The fallacy of race* (5th ed.). New York: Columbia University Press.

Morales, A. T. (1978). The need for nontraditional mental health programs in the barrio. In J. M. Casas & S. E. Keefe (Eds.). *Family and mental health in the Mexican American community*. Monograph no. 7. Los Angeles: Spanish-Speaking Mental Health Research Center, University of California, Los Angeles.

Morales, A. T. (1992). Therapy with Latino gang members. In L. A. Vargas & J. D. Koss-Chioino (Eds.). *Working with culture: Psychotherapeutic interventions with ethnic minority children and adolescents* (pp. 129–156). San Francisco: Jossey-Bass.

Morales, E. S. (1983). *Third world gays and lesbians: A process of multiple identities*. Paper presented at the Annual Convention of the American Psychological Association, Anaheim, CA.

Morales, E. S. (1992). Counseling Latino gays and Latina lesbians. In S. H. Dworkin & F. J. Gutiérrez (Eds.). *Counseling gay men and lesbians: Journey to the end of the rainbow* (pp. 125–140). Alexandria, VA: American Association for Counseling and Development.

More minorities, men needed to teach. (1992, July). *The Arizona Republic*, p. A3.

Moreland, J. W. (1988, August). *Equal protection of American Indians' privacy rights: A psycholegal analysis*. Paper presented at the annual meeting of the American Psychological Association, Atlanta GA.

Morin, S. F. (1988). AIDS: The challenge to psychology. *American Psychologist, 43*(11), 838–842.

Morrow, S. L. (1992). Voices: Constructions of survival and coping by women survivors of child sexual abuse. Unpublished doctoral dissertation, Arizona State University, Tempe.

Morrow, S. L., & Smith, M. L. (in press). Constructions of survival and coping by women survivors of child sexual abuse. *Journal of Counseling Psychology*.

Moses, S. (1992). More clinicians needed to help a graying American. *Monitor, 23*(8), 34.

Nash, K. B. (1989). Self-help groups: An empowerment vehicle for sickle cell disease patients and their families. *Social Work with Groups, 12*(4), 81–97.

National Center for Health Statistics. (1992). Unpublished data tables from the NCHS Mortality Tapes, FBI-SHR. Atlanta, GA: Centers for Disease Control.

National Indian Council on Aging [NICOA]. (1981). *American Indian elderly: A national profile.* Albuquerque, NM: NICOA/Cordova.

National Institute on Drug Abuse. (1987). *National household survey of drug abuse: Population estimates, 1985.* Rockville, MD: Author.

National Research Council. (1991, June). *Doctorate records file.*

Newcomb, M. D., & Bentler, P. M. (1988). *Consequences of adolescent drug use: Impact on the lives of young adults.* Newbury Park, CA: Sage.

Nikelly, A. G. (1988, August). *Empowerment or "depowerment?": Confronting economic victimization.* Paper presented at the Annual Convention of the American Psychological Association at Atlanta, GA.

O'Connor, M. F. (1992). Psychotherapy with gay and lesbian adolescents. In S. H. Dworkin & F. J. Gutiérrez (Eds.). *Counseling gay men and lesbians: Journey to the end of the rainbow* (pp. 3–22). Alexandria, VA: American Association for Counseling and Development.

Office of Population affairs. (1988, November). Family life information exchange, U.S. Deparment of Health and Human Services, Public Health Service, Resource Memo.

Olsen, T. (1978). *Silences.* New York: Delacorte Press.

Orbach, S. (1979). *Fat is a feminist issue.* New York: Berkeley Books.

Orzek, A. M. (1989). The lesbian victim of sexual assault: Special considerations for the mental health profession. *Women & Therapy, 8,* 107–117.

Osvold, L. L., & Sodowsky, G. R. (1993, in press). Eating attitudes of Native American and African American women: A study of ethnicity/race and acculturation. *Journal of Multicultural Counseling and Development.*

Osvold, L. L., & Sodowsky, G. R. (1993). Eating disorders of White American, American racial and ethnic minority American, and international women: A descriptive review. *Journal of Multicultural Counseling and Development, 21*(3), 143–145.

Painter, C. (1985). *Gifts of age.* San Francisco: Chronicle Books.

Patterson, G. R., De Baryshe, B. D., & Ramsey, E. (1989). A developmental perspective on antisocial behavior. *American Psychologist, 44*(2), 329–335.

Payne, C. (1984). Multicultural education and racism in American schools. *Theory Into Practice, 23*(2), 124–131.

Pedersen, P. (1987). *Handbook of cross-cultural counseling and therapy.* New York: Praeger.

Pedersen, P. (1988). *A handbook for developing multicultural awareness.* Alexandria, VA: American Association for Counseling and Development.

Peterson, J. L., & Marin, G. (1988). Issues in the prevention of AIDS among Black and Hispanic men. *American Psychologist, 43*(11), 871–877.

Pharr, S. (1988). *Homophobia: A weapon of sexism.* Inverness, CA: Chardon Press.

Pinderhughes, E. B. (1983). Empowerment for our clients and for ourselves. *Social Casework, 64*(6), 331–338.

Powell, R., & Collier, M. J. (1990). Public speaking instruction and cultural bias. *American Behavioral Scientist, 34*(2), 240–250.

Rabinowitz, F. E. (1991). The male-to-male embrace: Breaking the touch taboo in a men's therapy group. *Journal of Counseling and Development, 69*(6), 574–576.

Rappaport, J. (1981). In praise of paradox: A social policy of empowerment over prevention. *American Journal of Community Psychology, 9*(1), 1–21.

Rappaport, J. (1987). Terms of empowerment/exemplars of prevention: Toward a theory for community psychology. *American Journal of Community Psychology, 15*(2), 121–145.

Ray, C., Fisher, J., & Wisniewski, T. K. M. (1986). Surgeons' attitudes toward breast cancer, its treatment, and their relationship with patients. *Journal of Psychosocial Oncology, 4*, 33–43.

Reese, J., & Thomas, D. (1993, Spring). HIV manifestations in women: Advocate awareness among patients *and* physicians. *Positively Aware, 21.*

Remer, P. (1986). Stages in coping with rape. Unpublished manuscript.

Reuben, N., Hein, K., & Drucker, E. (1988, March). Relationship of high-risk behaviors to AIDS knowledge in adolescent high school students. Paper presented at the Annual Meeting of the Society for Adolescent Medicine Research, New York.

Richardson, B. L. (1991). Utilizing the resources of the African American church: Strategies for counseling professionals. In C. C. Lee & B. L. Richardson (Eds.). *Multicultural issues in counseling: New approaches to diversity* (pp. 65–78). Alexandria, VA: American Association for Counseling and Development.

Rico, G. (1986). *Writing the natural way.* Los Angeles: J.P. Tarcher.

Riger, A. L. (1992). Disability issues stance tests our ethical integrity. *Monitor, 23*(11), 4.

Rindt-Wagner, J. (1992). Legal prosecution of perpetrators of sexual assault: Implications for counselors and clients. *Women & Therapy, 12*(1/2), 113–123.

Robinson, J. L., & Cash, T. F. (1992). *African-American body images: The roles of racial identity and physical attributes.* Unpublished manuscript, Old Dominion University, Norfolk, VA.

Rodin, J., Silberstein, L. R., & Striegel-Moore, R. (1985). Women and weight: A normative discontent. In T. B. Sonderegger (Ed.). *Nebraska Symposium on motivation, 1984: Psychology and gender.* Lincoln: University of Nebraska Press.

Root, M. P. P. (1990). Disordered eating in women of color. *Sex Roles, 22*(7/8), 525–536.

Rosen, L. W., Shafer, C. L., Dummer, G. M., Cross, L. K., Deuman, G. W., & Malmberg, S. R. (1988). Prevalence of pathogenic weight-control behaviors among Native American women and girls. *International Journal of Eating Disorders, 7*(6), 807–811.

Rothblum, E. D., Brand, P. A., Miller, C. T., & Oetjen, H. A. (1990). The relationship between obesity, employment discrimination, and employment-related victimization. *Journal of Vocational Behavior 37*, 251–266.

Rudolph, J. (1988). Counselors' attitudes toward homosexuality: A selective review of the literature. *Journal of Counseling and Development, 67*(3), 165–168.

Russell, D. (1986). *The secret trauma: Incest in the lives of girls and women.* New York: Basic Books.

Ryan, W. (1971). *Blaming the victim.* New York: Random House.

Sanday, P. R. (1981). *Female power and male dominance: On the origins of sexual inequality.* New York: Cambridge University Press.

Saxton, M., & Howe, F. (Eds.). (1987). *With wings: An anthology of literature by and about women with disabilities.* New York: The Feminist Press.

Schaie, K. W. (1993). Ageist language in psychological research. *American Psychologist, 48*(1), 49–51.

Scher, M., & Good, G.E. (1990). Gender and counseling in the twenty-first century: What does the future hold? *Journal of Counseling and Development, 68*(4), 388–391.

Scher, M., Stevens, M., Good, G., & Eichenfeld, G., (Eds.). (1987). *The handbook of counseling and psychotherapy with men.* Beverly Hills: Sage.

Schneiderman, L. (1979). Against the family. *Social Work, 24*(5), 386–389.

Schrumpf, F., Crawford, D. K., & Usadel, H. C. (1992). *Peer mediation: Conflict resolution in schools.* Champaign, IL: Research Press.

Schulenberg, J. (1985). *Gay parenting: A complete guide for gay men and lesbians with children.* Garden City: Anchor Press.

Shearer, C. (1990, January 17). Bankrupt: Educational reforms costly. *State Press* (Tempe, AZ).

Shilts, R. (1987). *And the band played on: Politics, people, and the AIDS epidemic.* New York: St. Martin's Press.

Shim, S., Kotsiopulos, A., & Knoll, D. S. (1990). Short, average-height, tall, and big men: Body-cathexis, clothing and retail satisfactions, and clothing behavior. *Perceptual and Motor Skills, 70,* 83–96.

Shorris, E. (1992). Latinos: The complexity of identity. *Report on the Americas, 26*(2), 19–26.

Silverstein, B., Perdue, L., Peterson, B., & Kelly, E. (1986). The role of the mass-media in promoting a thin standard of bodily attractiveness for women. *Sex Roles, 14*(9–10), 519–532.

Simms, M. (1987). How loss of manufacturing jobs is affecting blacks. *Focus: Monthly Newsletter of the Joint Center for Political Studies, 15,* 6–7.

Skillings, J. H., & Dobbins, J. E. (1991). Racism as a disease: Etiology and treatment implications. *Journal of Counseling and Development, 70*(1), 206–212.

Smart, J. F., & Smart, D. W. (1991). Acceptance of disability and the Mexican American culture. *Rehabilitation Counseling Bulletin, 34*(4), 357–366.

Smith, A. J., & Siegal, R. F. (1985). Feminist therapy: Redefining power for the powerless. In L. B. Rosewater & L. E. A. Walker (Eds.). *Handbook of feminist therapy* (pp. 241–249). New York: Springer.

Smith, E. J. (1981). Cultural and historical perspectives in counseling Blacks. In D. W. Sue (Ed.). *Counseling the culturally different* (pp. 141–185). New York: Wiley.

Smith, E. J. (1991). Ethnic identity development: Toward the development of a theory within the context of majority/minority status. *Journal of Counseling and Development, 70*(1), 181–188.

Solomon, B. B. (1976). *Black empowerment social work in oppressed communities.* New York: Columbia University Press.

Solomon, B. B. (1987). Empowerment: Social work in oppressed communities. *Journal of Social Work Practice, 2*(4), 79–91.

Spicuzza, F. J., & DeVoe, M. W. (1982). Burnout in the helping professions: Mutual aid groups as self-help. *The Personnel and Guidance Journal, 61*(2), 95–99.

Stall, R. D., Coates, T. J., & Hoff, C. (1988). Behavioral risk reduction for HIV infection among gay and bisexual men: A review of results from the United States. *American Psychologist, 43*(11), 878–885.

Steinbock, A. J. (1988). Helping and homogeneity: Therapeutic interactions as the challenge to power. *Quarterly Journal of Ideology, 12*(1), 31–46.

Stern, M. P., Pugh, J. A., Gaskill, S. P., & Hazuda, H. P. (1982). Knowledge, attitudes, and behavior related to obesity and dieting in Mexican Americans and Anglos: The San Antonio heart study. *American Journal of Epidemiology, 115,* 917–927.

Stiles, D. A. (1986). Leadership training for high school girls: An intervention at one school. *Journal of Counseling and Development, 65,* 211–212.

St. Louis, M. E., Hayman, C. R., Miller, C., Anderson, J. E., Petersen, L. R., & Dondero, T. J. (1989). HIV infection in disadvantaged adolescents in the U.S.: Findings from the Job Corps Screening Program. *Abstracts of the V International Conference on AIDS* (p. 711). Ottawa, Ontario, Canada: International Research Development Center.

Striegel-Moore, R. H., Silberstein, L. R., & Rodin, J. (1986). Toward an understanding of risk factors for bulimia. *American Psychologist, 41,* 246–263.

Stroebe, M., Gergen, M. M., Gergen, K. J., & Stroebe, W. (1992). Broken hearts or broken bonds: Love and death in historical perspective. *American Psychologist, 47*(10), 1205–1212.

Stuart, P. (1992). Murder on the job. *Personnel Journal, 72*–77.

Students threaten other students (1987, March 19). *USA Today,* p. 1.

Sue, D. W. (1981). *Counseling the culturally different, theory and practice.* New York: Wiley-Interscience Publications.

Sue, D. W., Arredondo, P., & McDavis, R. J. (1992). Multicultural counseling competencies and standards: A call to the profession. *Journal of Counseling and Development, 70*(4), 477–486.

Sue, D. W., & Sue, D. (1990). *Counseling the culturally different.* New York: John Wiley & Sons.

Sue, D., & Sue, D. W. (1991). Counseling strategies for Chinese Americans. In C. C. Lee & B. L. Richardson (Eds.). *Multicultural issues in counseling: New approaches to diversity,* (pp.79–90). Alexandria: American Association for Counseling and Development Press.

Surrey, J. L. (1991). Relationship and empowerment. In J. V. Jordan, A. G. Kaplan, J. B. Miller, I. P. Stiver, & J. L. Survey. (Eds.). *Women's growth in connection: writings from the Stone Center* (pp. 162–180). New York: The Guilford Press.

Synnott, A. (1989). Truth and goodness, mirrors and masks Part I: A sociology of beauty and the face. *British Journal of Sociology, 40*(4), 607–636.

Synnott, A. (1990). Truth and goodness, mirrors and masks Part II: A sociology of beauty and the face. *British Journal of Sociology, 41*(1), 55–76.

Szapocznik, J., Santisteban, D., Kurtines, W. M., Perez-Vidal, A., & Hervis, O. (1984). Bicultural effectiveness training: A treatment intervention for enhancing intercultural adjustment in Cuban-American families. *Hispanic Journal of Behavioral Sciences, 6,* 317–344.

Szapocznik, J., Santisteban, D., Rio, A., Perez-Vidal, A., & Kurtines, W. M. (1986). Bicultural effectiveness training (BET): An experimental test of an intervention modality for families expereincing intergenerational/intercultural conflict. *Hispanic Journal of Behavioral Sciences, 8*(4), 303–330.

Szapocznik, J., Santisteban, D., Rio, A., Perez-Vidal, A., & Kurtines, W. M. (1986a). Family effectiveness training (FET) for Hispanic families. In H. P. Lefley & P. B. Pedersen (Eds.). *Cross-cultural training for mental health professionals.* Springfield, IL: Charles C. Thomas.

Szapocznik, J., Santisteban, D., Rio, A., Perez-Vidal, A., & Kurtines, W. M. (1986b). Bicultural effectiveness training (BET): An experiemental test of an intervention modality for families experiencing intergenerational/intercultural conflict. *Hispanic Journal of Behavioral Sciences, 8*(4), 303–330.

Szapocznik, J., Santisteban, D., Rio, A., Perez-Vidal, A., & Kurtines, W. M. (1989). Family effectiveness training: An intervention to prevent drug abuse and problem behaviors in Hispanic adolescents. *Hispanic Journal of Behavioral Sciences, 11*(1), 4–27.

Takanishi, R. (1993). The opportunities of adolescence: Research, interventions, and policy: Introduction to the special issue. *American Psychologist, 48*(2), 85–87.

Tan, A. (1989). *The Joy Luck club.* New York: Ballantine.

Tatum, B. D. (1992). Talking about race, learning about racism: The application of racial identity development theory in the classroom. *Harvard Educational Review, 62*(1), 1–24.

The world almanac and book of facts (1991). New York: World Almanac/Pharos.

Thomas, C. W. (1985). A view from counseling of adult Afro American males. *Journal of Nonwhite Concerns in Personnel and Guidance, 13*(2), 95–99.

Tobias, M. (1990). Validators: A key role in empowering the chronically mentally ill. *Social Work, 35*(4), 357–359.

Troiden, R. R. (1989). The formation of homosexual identities. *Journal of Homosexuality, 17*(1/2), 43–73.

Tross, S. & Hirsch, D. A. (1988). Psychological distress and neuropsychological complications of HIV infection and AIDS. *American Psychologist, 43*(11), 929–934.

Trujillo, C. M. (1986). A comparative examination of classroom interactions between professors and minority and non-minority college students. *American Educational Research Journal, 23*(4), 629–642.

Unger, R. K. (1983). Through the looking glass: No wonderland yet! (The reciprocal relationship between methodology and models of reality). *Psychology of Women Quarterly, 8*(1), 9–32.

U.S. Department of Commerce. (1987). *Money income and poverty status of families and persons in the United States: 1986,* Current Population Survey, Bureau of the Census.

U.S. Department of Commerce. (1988). *The Hispanic population in the United States: March 1988* (Advance Report), Bureau of the Census.

U.S. Department of Commerce. (1991). *Current population reports, school enrollment-social and economic characteristics of students*: October 1990, Series P-20, No. 460, and unpublished tabulations for October 1991.

U.S. Department of Education. (1993). National Center for Education Statistics. *Trends in enrollment in higher education by racial ethnic category: Fall 1980 through fall 1991*. Washington, DC: Author.

U.S. Senate Select Committee on Indian Affairs. (1985). *Indian juvenile alcoholism and eligibility for BIA schools* (Senate Hearing 99-286). Washington, DC: U.S. Government Printing Office.

Vargas, L. A., & Koss-Chioino, J. D. (Eds.). (1992). *Working with culture: Psychotherapeutic interventions with ethnic minority children and adolescents.* San Francisco: Jossey-Bass.

Vernon, A. (1991). Nontraditional approaches to counseling. In D. Capuzzi & D. R. Gross (Eds.). *Introduction to counseling: Perspectives for the 1990s.* Boston: Allyn and Bacon.

Violence of American youth. (1988, November 7). *Newsweek*, p. 36.

Wahl, H. W. (1991). Dependence in the elderly from an interactional point of view: Verbal and observational data. *Psychology and Ageing, 6*(2), 238–246.

Walker, A. (1983). *In search of our mothers' gardens: Womanist prose.* San Diego: Harcourt Brace Jovanovich.

Walker, A. (1989). *The temple of my familiar.* New York: Harcourt Brace Jovanovich.

Walz, G. R. (January, 1992). Enhancing self-esteem. *Guidepost, 34*(8), insert.

Walz, G. R., & Bleuer, J. (in press). *Ten initiatives for building high self-esteem.* Ann Arbor, MI: Human Development Services, Inc. (P.O. Box 1403, Ann Arbor, MI 48106).

Wartenberg, T. E. (1988). The concept of power in feminist theory. *Praxis International, 8*(3), 301–316.

Wassermann, S. (1985). Even teachers get the blues: Helping teachers to help kids. *Childhood Education, 62*, 3–7.

Waters, E. B., & Goodman, J. (1990). *Empowering older adults: Practical strategies for counselors.* San Fransisco: Jossey-Bass, Inc.

Webster's new collegiate dictionary (1980). Springfield, MA: G. & C. Merriam Company.

Weiner, F. (1986). *No apologies: A guide to living with a disability.* New York: St. Martin's Press.

Weis, K., & Borges, S. S. (1977). Victimology and rape: The case of the legitimate victims. In D. R. Nass (Ed.). *The rape victim* (pp. 35–75). Dubuque: Kendall-Hunt.

What schools can do to help disadvantaged children. (1987). *Education Digest, 53*(2), 14–18.

Whitaker, L. C. (1989). Myths and heroes: Visions of the future. *Journal of College Student Psychotherapy, 4*(2), 13–33.

Whitbourne, S. K., & Hulicka, I. M. (1990). Ageism in undergraduate psychology texts. *American Psychologist, 45*(10), 1127–1136.

White, P. D. (1989). Reaching at-risk students: One principal's solution. *Thrust, 19*(1), 45–46.

White, T. J., & Sedlacek, W. E. (1987). White student attitudes toward Blacks and Hispanics: Programming implications. *Journal of Multicultural Counseling and Development, 15*(4), 171–183.

Wiegman, O., Kuttschreuter, M., & Baarda, B. (1992). A longitudinal study of the effects of television viewing on aggressive and prosocial behaviors. *British Journal of Social Psychology, 31*(2), 147–164.

Williams, W. C., & Lair, G. S. (1988). Geroconsultation: A proposed decision-making model. *Journal of Counseling and Development, 67*(3), 198–201.

Witt, T. (1993, Spring). Child "sexploitation" has become modern day slave trade. *Global Perspectives*, 4–5.

Wolf, T. J. (1992). Bisexuality: A counseling perspective. In S. H. Dworkin & F. J. Gutiérrez (Eds.). *Counseling gay men and lesbians: Journey to the end of the rainbow* (pp. 175–190). Alexandria, VA: American Association for Counseling and Development.

Wolpe, J. (1958). *Psychotherapy by reciprocal inhibition.* Stanford: Stanford University Press.

Wood, L. A., & Ryan, E. B. (1991). Talk to elders: Social structure, attitudes and forms of address. *Ageing and Society, 11*(2), 167–188.

Worell, J., & Remer, P. (1992). *Feminist perspectives in therapy: An empowerment model for women.* Chinchester, U.K.: John Wiley & Sons.

Wright, B. (1983). *Physical disability: A psychosocial approach* (2nd ed.). New York: Harper & Row.

Wyatt, J. (1992). Letter to the editor. *Monitor, 23*(12), 4.

Wynd, C. A. (1990). Analysis of a power theory for health promotion activities. *Applied Nursing Research, 3*(3), 118–127.

Yee, A. H. (1983). Ethnicity and race: Psychological perspectives. *Educational Psychologist, 18*(1), 14–24.

Youngstrom, M. (1992). Inner-city youth tell of life in a 'war zone.' *Monitor, 23*(3), 36.

Youngstrum, N. (1991). Campus life polluted for many by hate acts. *Monitor, 22*(12), 38.

Zelnick, M., & Shah, F. K. (1983). First intercourse among young Americans. *Family Planning Perspectives, 15*(2), 64–70.

Zimmerman, M. A. (1991). Toward a theory of learned hopefulness: A structural model analysis of participation and empowerment. *Journal of Research in Personality, 24*, 71–86.

Zimmerman, M. A., & Rappaport, J. (1988). Citizen participation, perceived control, and psycholgical empowerment. *American Journal of Community Psychology, 16*(5), 725–750.

INDEX